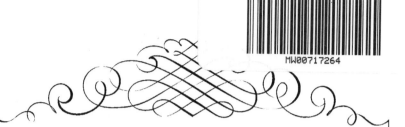

ISBN 978-1-330-18378-6
PIBN 10046895

1 MONTH OF
FREE
READING

at

www.ForgottenBooks.com

By purchasing this book you are eligible for one month membership to ForgottenBooks.com, giving you unlimited access to our entire collection of over 700,000 titles via our web site and mobile apps.

To claim your free month visit:

www.forgottenbooks.com/free46895

From the Unconscious
to the Conscious

BY

Dr. GUSTAVE GELEY

Director of the *Institut Meta-
psychique International*

Translated from the French by
S. De BRATH, M.I.C.E.

With a Foreword by
J. D. BERESFORD

HARPER & BROTHERS PUBLISHERS
NEW YORK AND LONDON

FROM THE UNCONSCIOUS TO THE CONSCIOUS

Printed in the United States of America
C–W

TO

SIGNOR PROFESSOR ROCCO SANTOLIQUIDO,

ITALIAN COUNCILLOR OF STATE, DEPUTY,

GRAND OFFICER OF THE LEGION OF HONOUR,

I DEDICATE THIS BOOK

WITH RESPECT, GRATITUDE AND AFFECTION

G. GELEY

INTRODUCTION

To many people, the nineteenth century seems to be the age of a great consummation. In the course of that century, the material sciences were freed from the shackles that had held them, and the work of the great pioneers, Newton, Franklin, Kepler, Lamarck, and the rest was developed with an amazing rapidity and resource. And to those who came to maturity in the last decades of this remarkable period, the material sciences still appear to be the consummation of mankind's intellectual opportunity. Just as our forefathers opposed and sneered at the coming of Science, so these representatives of the great materialistic age resent and combat the greater promises of our own time. For them Charles Darwin is still the splendid discoverer of man's origin and they dread the coming of the finer and more inclusive theory of Being which will turn Darwin's *Descent of Man* and *The Origin of Species* into interesting relics of an old and superseded mode of thought.

For as the earlier reactionaries were powerless to oppose the 'march of science' so will these conservative scientists of our own day be borne down under the mass of the accumulating evidence. Darwin's theory that natural selection coupled with the influences of environment were the sole instruments by which the process of physical and intellectual evolution were achieved, has failed to explain the facts. For more than twenty years now, a newer school of thought has been throwing doubt on these so-called classic factors of evolution; and, in my opinion, the work of Dr Geley not only confirms these doubts beyond all dispute, but also—and this is, indeed, the greater achievement—gives us a new and larger theory of the origin and constitution of life.

Of the content of the present work, however, I do not propose to speak in detail, but I will say that I have found in it the evidences of a new classic. I believe that, in fifty years' time, Dr Geley's *From the Unconscious to the Conscious* will be looked upon as bearing the same kind of relation to the discoveries of the twentieth century that Darwin's *Origin of Species* bore to the nineteenth. This may sound rather an extravagant claim to make, but if Geley's theory is, as I believe, a true one, it must inevitably revolutionise our knowledge both of biology and psychology, and may, at the same time, lay the foundations of a world-wide religion.

And we must remember that Dr Geley comes before us backed by the authority of the practical scientist and scholar. His medical works have already brought him a measure of fame, both in the study of local anæsthetics and of the new method of treating such specifically eruptive diseases as smallpox, erysipelas, and scarlatina. He is not a 'spiritualist,' he refuses to identify himself with any particular school of thought, but an original researcher. He was chosen by scientific men of the highest standing and repute, such as Professor Charles Richet and Camille Flammarion, to be the Director of the International Metapsychical Institute in Paris. In short, Dr Geley is not some impetuous theorist rushing into print with a premature hypothesis, but a patient, unprejudiced investigator, whose sole aim is the search for truth.

J. D. BERESFORD.

TRANSLATOR'S NOTE

In the opening chapter of the *Origin of Species* Darwin states that the 'variability,' on which selection and adaptation have to work, 'is governed by many *unknown* laws.'

In translating a book which fills this gap in the Evolutionary Theory by assigning a psychic cause as the origin of Variation (thus traversing the arguments of later biologists who refer that origin to chance or to the pressure of the environment); a book which modifies the conclusions of many schools of thought, both new and old; which replaces Bergson's famous *élan vital* by a concrete energy, and defines that energy as an influence forming all the varieties of cellular tissue out of one primordial substance, and moulding those tissues into organic form under the impulsion of a Directing Idea, the translator has a most responsible task.

One duty, and one only, lies upon him—to be faithful to the author's meaning. No attempt at literary finish can palliate or excuse the slightest departure from that duty in a work which, however scientific in essence, is necessarily somewhat controversial in form. When to this duty there are added the obligations which the honour of personal friendship involves, faithfulness in rendering the idea becomes doubly imperative. To this all other considerations must give place.

The Italian adage, 'Traduttori—traditori,' is one which the translator must ever bear in mind if he would not be a traitor also. He has therefore kept a number of words which, though used by classical English writers on philosophy, may seem more or less uncouth and foreign to those who are unfamiliar with such authors. It is quite inevitable that a book which presents an entirely new application and extension of psychology should compel the use of a terminology which some may find obscure.

'Psychism,' 'Dynamo-psychism,' 'Representation,' 'Transformism,' are words of this kind, and are all used to express ideas which, even when not absolutely new, are strange to the unaccustomed ear.

'Psychism' is a word which is, or should be, well-known; meaning the animating psychic energy which is the subject-matter of psychology.

'Dynamo-psychism' is considered cumbrous, but what other word is there that expresses a psychic energy acting as forming and motive power? It is of the very essence of the theory put forward.

'Representation' in ordinary use, means the delineation of an actuality existing elsewhere: the philosophical sense is the same, but the actuality is in the Unseen; the representation is in, and by, Matter, Energy, or Idea. It is used by Sir Wm. Hamilton (*Logic*), by G. H. Lewes, by Herbert Spencer, and by J. Ward (*Encycl. Brit.*) in this way.

'Transformism,' *i.e.* the doctrine of transformability of individuals or species, is used by Huxley. (*Crayfish.*)

'Palingenesis' is used in its correct meaning (πάλιν = again + γένεσις = production), a new or second birth: the equivalent 'reincarnation' has been spoiled by those who ignore the profound distinction between the Person and the Self, and has been intentionally avoided by the author.

'Modality' is used as it is by Caird, in the logical sense of modes hypothetically necessary on the presupposition of something else. The list might be extended: but in every case where a word seems to carry an unusual meaning, reference has been made to standard authors for its justification.

S. DE BRATH.

WEYBRIDGE, *February*, 1920.

PREFACE

THIS work is the logical sequel to my study of *The Subconscious Being*. Its intention is to include both collective and individual evolution in a larger and more complete synthesis. Its form is governed by the same procedure : to express the ideas with the utmost simplicity, the greatest clarity and conciseness that may be possible; to avoid lengthy analyses and developments; and above all to put aside easy digressions of an imaginative or poetical character.

My primary aim was to make the work a synthesis, and this synthesis should be considered as a whole, without reference to details which have been omitted or intentionally set aside. In fact, an exhaustive study of any single one of the questions treated would be a life work, but this is for those who devote themselves to analysis, and I leave it to them; my purpose is different, it aims at the ideal quest of a wide philosophical generalisation, based on facts.

Obviously such a philosophy, in the actual state of human knowledge and consciousness, can claim to be no more than an endeavour, a sketch, or as it might be called, a general plan, in which only main outlines and a few details are clearly drawn.

Necessarily incomplete, this philosophy cannot claim to be entirely original. Most of the solutions proposed are naturally to be found here and there, more or less sharply defined and more or less varied, in other naturalistic or metaphysical systems.

The general idea of this work is that which has

inspired most of the great metaphysical systems, and finds its clearest and most concrete presentment in the works of Schopenhauer. Its premises are the same; but the developments and the conclusions are totally different; my endeavour has been to bridge the chasm that Schopenhauer leaves between the Unconscious and the Conscious. Thence follows an entirely different interpretation of the evolution of the individual and of the universe. This interpretation, instead of leading to pessimism, leads, I will not say to optimism (the term being loose and questionable), but to the abiding ideal of Humanity, an ideal which is built on its highest, calmest, and most lasting hopes of justice, of joy, and of individual persistence.

But the real originality of the idealist philosophy here outlined, the only originality that is claimed, is that *it is scientific.* Unrestricted by dogmatic or mystical forms, and resting on no *a priori* or intuitional formulæ, it is based on positive demonstration. It is on the ground of *scientific* philosophy, and on this ground alone, that this work should be studied or discussed.

To build up my demonstration I have endeavoured to take account of all known facts whether in the natural sciences, in general biology, or in admitted data relating to the physiological and psychological constitution of the individual man. In the choice of the main explanatory hypotheses I have sought those which present the double character of being logical deductions from facts, and adaptable to all the facts of a group. My constant aim has been to reach wider and more comprehensive generalisations, until there should issue, if possible, a hypothesis sufficiently wide and general to present a single interpretation of the evolution of the individual and of the universe.

This general method is scarcely open to criticism. But I have been led, little by little, by the subject-matter, to adopt at first tentatively, and then systematically, a method of treatment, secondary indeed but still important, concerning which it is necessary to enter into some detail.

In considering the different biological and psychological sciences, and in studying the inductions, deductions, and received hypotheses founded on their data and accepted by most contemporary men of science, I was struck by serious and obvious errors due to a tendency to forget of the general method of treatment above referred to.

There is no single one of the main academic hypotheses on evolution, on the physical or psychological constitution of the individual, or on life and consciousness, which is capable of adaptation to *all* the facts of evolution, of physiology or of psychology; nor, *a fortiori*, is there one which can embrace general and individual evolution in a synthetic whole.

Further, most of these hypotheses are, as I shall demonstrate, certainly in opposition to at least some well-established facts.

In seeking the first origin and cause of these errors in generalisation I have been led to discover them pre-eminently in the choice of the primary facts on which the framework of contemporary scientific philosophy is based.

In all sciences, and especially in biology and psychology, facts selected with a synthetic conclusion in view, may lead to antagonistic method, and consequently to concepts which may be divergent or even opposed. Two principal methods may be outlined, each resulting from the selection of primary facts.

The first of these methods starts from the principle that science should always proceed from the simple to the complex. This method, therefore, takes as its point of departure the most elementary facts, endeavours to understand them, then passes on to rather more complex facts of the same order, applying to them the explanatory formula derived from an exhaustive study of the simpler, and so onwards from the base to the summit.

The second starts from the principle that for any given order of facts there can be no true explanation which is not capable of application to *all* the facts of that order. This method seeks first for an explanation capable of covering the most complex phenomena; and this being easily extended *a 'fortiori*, to the simpler and lower ones, will necessarily be conformable to all the available data.

This method thus proceeds from the summit to the base.

It frequently happens, we must concede, that the second method ends in an impossibility. It will do so whenever the data of fact are insufficient. It must then be admitted to be inapplicable, and should be held in reserve, disregarding minor points in which it may be satisfactory, such details being necessarily inadequate as a basis of reasoning since they refer to only one aspect of the problem.

Of these two methods, the former being primarily analytic, pertains to pure science. The second, primarily synthetic, pertains to pure philosophy.

Now when questions arise which pertain both to philosophy and to science, it is necessary to consider which of these two methods should be adopted.

Once a general truth has been established it matters little whether the explanation of different phenomena leading to a known conclusion starts from the base or the summit; the line of synthesis being known, it is not possible to stray. But when the task before us is to ascertain truth and to establish a synthesis, it becomes necessary to choose and to consider with care which method is likely to prove the more sure and fruitful of results. The first method is the one almost exclusively employed as the foundation for current theories. Its use follows on an unquestioned dogma of contemporary science. Before deciding which method to employ, let us now look somewhat closely at some of the established results to which this method has actually led.

In a philosophic study of the phenomena of life, if we proceed from the apex to the base, from man to the superior animals, and from them to inferior types, we are constrained to admit that Consciousness is that which is most important in all life, because it is that which is most important in man. We are then led to discover that consciousness, with all that it implies, extends, with a narrowing field, down to the least evolved animals, in which it exists merely in outline.

If, on the contrary, we proceed from the base to the summit, the conclusion that we draw from the phenomena of life is an opposite one. It is the conclusion that Le Dantec, among others, has endeavoured to bring out.[1]

The chemical reactions of their environment suffice to determine the vital phenomena of animals very low down in the scale. The ' ascending ' method therefore permits of the affirmation that in all the phenomena of life, even those of the superior animals, it is useless to seek for anything but the result of chemical reactions. Even the specific form of an animal is for Le Dantec, as we shall see, merely a function of these reactions.

The plastidia show rigid chemical determinism, and there is no reason to attribute to them either will or liberty of action. It would follow that bio-chemical determinism is the same in the entire animal series; and will or liberty, even in man, is but illusion.

The notion of an animal consciousness is superfluous for the plastidia; if therefore it exists for superior animals it can be only an *epiphenomenon* [2] resulting

[1] Le Dantec: *Déterminisme Biologique.*
[2] A sequential or a secondary phenomenon.

from the chemical reactions which are the essential phenomena.

In fine, as according to all evidence, animals as low in the scale as the sponges and the corals, are but a mere complex of elementary lives, the inference follows that even a very complex and highly evolved animal apparently highly centralised, is but an analogous complex, existing and maintaining itself by affinity or molecular cohesion, without the aid of a superior and independent dynamism.

Such is the reasoning and such are the conclusions of the 'ascending' method. Are these conclusions true or false?

The reasoning is rigorous and flawless. If the conclusions are false, it can only be that the method is bad.

We shall see by all that follows in the present work, that in spite of the rigour of the reasoning, the results of the method are such as cannot be accepted, and are often absurd.

It is easy to establish this without going outside the domain of biology. As an example of an induction at once absurd and inevitable from the ascending method, take sensibility.

We know by experience that we possess sensibility. We infer that sensibility pertains to humanity. Taking this apex as our point of departure, we judge that superior animals also possess this sensibility because their manifestations of pain or pleasure resemble our own.

If we descend the animal scale, the manifestations are less defined, and, in the lower animals, are of doubtful interpretation.

'The signs of pain,' says Richet,[1] 'do not suffice for the affirmation that there is pain. When the foot of a decapitated frog is pinched, the animal struggles

[1] Richet : *Psychologie Générale.*

with all the external signs of pain, just as if it were suffering. When an earthworm is cut in two both pieces move convulsively. Are we to say that both are suffering, or what appears to me much more rational, rather to think that the traumatism[1] has set up a violent reflex action ? '

Therefore if we attribute sensibility to animals low in the scale, it is by a descending induction. Our reasoning goes from the summit to the base.

Let us proceed inversely : if, setting aside our own personal experience, we consider the very inferior animals, we shall be logically obliged to deny them sensibility, since all their reactions can be explained by reflexes. Sensibility to pleasure or pain is for them an unnecessary hypothesis, and conformably to the principle of methodology known as economy of hypothesis, it should be put aside.

But then, why admit this sensibility in the highest animals ? Here also everything can be explained by reflexes. As Richet observes, the yelp of a beaten dog, may, strictly speaking, be only a reflex movement ! And this reasoning is not absurd, since it is Cartesian. Nevertheless, pushed to the negation of human sensibility it becomes untenable. It impels us to place man, as did Descartes, outside animal life; which is evidently a gross and dangerous mistake.

Thus the method which consists in starting from the base in order to explain one of the essential vital principles is convicted of flagrant error. It is therefore under suspicion for all the rest. No doubt it will be objected that the contrary method may also lead us astray: as, for instance, says Le Dantec,[2] 'the famous observation of Carter, in which an amœba *lay in wait* for a young Acineta about to detach itself from the

---

[1] Traumatism—the state of being wounded.

[2] Le Dantec : *Le Déterminisme Biologique.*

maternal body. The Acineta is a protozoon armed in
its adult state with venomous tentacles particularly
dangerous to the amœba; but these tentacles are not
found on the young Acineta, and the amœba observed
by Carter *knew* that the young one about to leave
the maternal body would be eatable during the early
days of its existence.'

The error is comical: but every one must see that
it is entirely insignificant from the philosophic point
of view, and disappears automatically before the new
knowledge relating to instinct. This error, bearing
only on a point of detail, does not in any way attaint the
descending induction which allows a relative consciousness to all animal life. Even if the extension of the
induction to the lower animals were arbitrary, it would
have no importance: there is no serious drawback in
attributing to them, even arbitrarily, rudimentary consciousness and sensibility.

On the other hand, the errors of the ascending
method are flagrant, since they would go so far as to deny
that consciousness and sensibility to superior animals!
The justice of Auguste Comte's remark is evident: ' As
soon as we are dealing with the characteristics of animal
life, we ought to take Man as our starting point, and
see how his characteristics lower in the scale little by
little, rather than start from the sponge and seek how
they develop. The animal life of man helps us to
understand that of the sponge, but the converse is not
true.'

Passing from biology to psychology, let us consider,
for instance, the phenomena attributed to subconsciousness which will have so large a place in the present work.
There, more than anywhere else, the contrast between
the two methods will be manifest.

In a study which appeared in the *Annales des Sciences
Psychiques* I recommended the synthetic method as
applicable to the philosophy of the phenomena of

subconsciousness. I endeavoured to show that only the study of the more complex phenomena would admit of a generalisation; while a study, however profound, of the elementary phenomena would always remain incapable of leading to any clear view of the whole. I concluded that from the specially philosophic standpoint, the study and comprehension of the higher phenomena alone can be of capital importance.[1]

This statement of methodology has brought on me some lively attacks, especially from M. Boirac.[2]

M. Boirac affirms, as Le Dantec does with regard to biological phenomena, that one should study and interpret from the base to the summit, first dealing with elementary phenomena and then with those more and more complex.

In support of his idea he adduces the following analogy: to seek to understand the higher subconscious phenomena before understanding the elementary ones is as illogical as to seek to understand the phenomenon of globular lightning before grasping elementary electrical principles.

To this I might reply that it is one thing to study electrical phenomena and even to apply them practically, and quite another to understand the essential nature of electricity. Our understanding of electricity, that is our philosophical comprehension of it, rests, and will continue to rest, on provisional hypotheses until we have understood its most complex manifestations.

Further, nothing is more easy than to oppose one analogy to another! Here is one which I borrow from J. Loeb :—

[1] It is expressly to be noticed, however, that in all matters concerning the subconscious, the elementary and the complex phenomena are equally unexplained. Whichever we take as our point of departure, we proceed from the unknown to the unknown. The Cartesian principle therefore cannot be advanced against our method.

[2] Boirac: *Annales des Sciences Psychiques,*' and *L'Avenir des Études Psychiques.*

'Physicists are lucky never to have known the method of sections and dyes. What would have been the result if by chance a steam engine had fallen into the hands of a histological physicist? What thousands of sections horizontal and vertical, stained in various ways, how many diagrams and figures might have been made, without arriving at an indubitable conclusion that the machine is a heat engine and is used to transform heat into motion!' (Quoted by Dastre.)

This comparison places the characteristics of the two methods in a strong light.

The method of restricted analyses and profound study of details is extremely useful in scientific research, but is without philosophical value. The method of general synthesis is the only one suitable to scientific philosophy for it alone can bring out what is really important in a given order of facts. The boiler and the motor mechanism are the truly important parts in the steam-engine. When this mechanism has been understood there will be no difficulty in understanding the part played in the accessory details, the wheels and the brakes. But it would be folly to seek to understand the locomotive by a study, however complete, of a detached bolt or the spoke of a wheel!

Psychologists who rest in the systematic study of small facts are obviously like to the 'histological physicists': both end in similar impotence.

I conclude: From the philosophical point of view, (the one to which I confine myself) and in a given order of facts, only the comprehension of the higher facts is important, for it includes, *a fortiori*, that of all others. Consequently the descending method only, starting from those higher facts, is the fruitful one.

Moreover, we judge the tree by its fruit: it is, as we shall see, by that method alone that all the phenomena of life and consciousness, all collective and individual evolution, and even the meaning of the universe, can be understood.

By the analytical and ascending method, on the contrary, we reach nothing but the serious errors in generalisation which have vitiated all contemporary philosophy, if, indeed, we do not lose ourselves in an unmeaning verbalism.

In seeking to draw general conclusions from elementary phenomena we are driven to deny sensibility to animals and to reduce consciousness to an epiphenomenon. By taking minor hypnotoid or hysteriform manifestations as our starting point in the study of psychological facts, we end by reducing the whole of subconscious psychology, even the highest, to automatism or suggestibility.

Worse still, by blind fidelity to a barren method, some very fine minds are doomed to impotence, and waste their time and trouble in inventing or changing mere labels; and failing to capture the general idea they fall back on the invention of 'Pythiatism' or 'Metagnomy '[1] . . .

The method here chosen offers two essential criteria as guides—one critical, the other practical.

The critical criterion will permit us to consider as false and to reject without further examination, every explanation or hypothesis which in a connected order of facts, is adapted to a part only of these facts, and not to all, especially to the more complex.

The practical criterion will prescribe the systematic and immediate study of the highest and most complex in any given order of connected facts.

Whether the matter in hand be universal evolution and naturalistic theories, physiological or psychological individuality, or even questions of high philosophy, we

[1]Pythiatism: pertaining to the Pythian Apollo. Metagnomy: (from Gr. γνώμη, thought)=beyond thought.

shall therefore begin by first attacking the more complex facts, these being really the only important ones; putting aside for the moment the mere trivialities of elementary and simple facts, which, in the sequel, will explain themselves.

Instead of plodding through this dust of elementary facts which by beclouding our ascent, retard it, we shall advance to the heights, from whence, after a wide view over the whole accessible area, we may descend at leisure to explore local particulars.

The present work falls naturally into two principal parts :—

Book I. is a critical study of the classical theories relating to evolution, to physiological individuality, to psychological individuality, and to the principal evolutionary philosophies, and at the same time it is a forecast of the essential inductions of Book II.

Book II. is the actual statement of our scientific philosophy.

CONTENTS

BOOK I

THE UNIVERSE AND THE INDIVIDUAL ACCORDING
TO THE CLASSICAL SCIENTIFIC AND PHILO-
SOPHICAL THEORIES—A CRITICAL STUDY

PART 1

Classical Naturalistic Theories of Evolution

Contents

Contents

Contents

Contents

PART III

Philosophical Theories of Evolution

Contents

BOOK II

FROM THE UNCONSCIOUS TO THE CONSCIOUS

PART I

Individual Evolution—The Transition from Unconsciousness to Consciousness in the Individual

Contents

PART II

*The Evolution of the Universe—Transition from the
Unconscious to the Conscious in the Universe*

Contents

PART III

The Consequences: Optimism or Pessimism?

BOOK I

THE UNIVERSE AND THE INDIVIDUAL

ACCORDING TO THE CLASSICAL SCIENTIFIC AND PHILOSOPHICAL THEORIES

(A CRITICAL STUDY)

PART I

CLASSICAL NATURALISTIC THEORIES OF EVOLUTION

FOREWORD

ALTHOUGH evolution, considered as a whole, constitutes to-day the most firmly established of all the great scientific hypotheses, it nevertheless presents some serious difficulties in its systematisation and its philosophy.

The principle of evolutionary theory, based as it is on leading facts of the natural sciences, defies any honest attempt at refutation.

Nevertheless, there are, in the doctrine of transformability as taught up to the present, weak points and serious *lacunæ*, on which its enemies base their hopes. No longer daring to attack it from the front, they hope to turn its flank.

It would be therefore, not only puerile, but also dangerous from a philosophic point of view, to deny or to dissimulate these weak points and defects. It is well on the contrary to seek for their origin and their explanation by placing them in full light.

The objections to the evolutionary theory put forward in this work are not, I repeat, objections to the principle. They do not aim at the fact of evolution. They are, however, serious because they displace the two pillars on which transformability has been erected, that is to say, the classical notions of ultimate cause and manner of effect.

The mechanism of evolution is now found to need revision. This mechanism, as is well known, arose from two great hypotheses—those of Darwin and Lamarck.

The Darwinian hypothesis assigned an essential function to natural selection, that is, the survival of the fittest in the struggle for life; the fittest being those

which distinguish themselves from their congeners by
some physical or psychological advantage relative to
the vital necessities of the environment, this advantage
having appeared by chance.

The Lamarckian hypothesis assigned a primary
function to the influence of the environment, to the use
or disuse of organs; making the environment (at need)
even the origin of new functions and new organs.

These two classical causes, perfectly reconcilable
or even complementary, necessarily implied the notion
of slow, imperceptible, and innumerable modifications
leading to the progressive formation of diverse species
from one or more primitive forms up to man.

To these two general hypotheses, there have been
added in our day, countless secondary theories intended
either to establish special laws, such as those of heredity,
or to combat the ceaselessly renewed and multiplied
objections which a rigorous analysis of facts has brought
against the classical concept of transformism.

Among these theories, some connect with Darwin,
some with Lamarck, others eclectically with both
systems. Some carry purely mechanical explanations;
others rise to dynamical concepts; a few even trench
on the domain of metaphysics.[1]

On all of them the same general judgment may be
passed: they show prodigious ingenuity and an even
more prodigious impotence.

I shall not discuss these theories nor their claims
to explain the difficulties of transformism.[2]

The innumerable arguments which have been invoked in various connections for or against transformism,
for or against the classic naturalism, relating as they

---

[1] Cf specially Delage and Goldsmith: *Les Théories de l'Évolution*
(published by Flammarion), and Deperret, *Les Transformations du Monde
Animal*

[2] Transformism This term is advisedly used by Huxley to express
the general fact, as distinguished from particular concrete transformations
or abstract transformability.—[Translator's note.]

do to secondary matters, do not carry conviction or lead to a conclusion.

Conformably to the method explained above, I shall neglect these arguments on details and only consider immediately and directly the essential and primordial difficulties, which are the only real difficulties, of transformism. The secondary imperfections of the naturalistic edifice matter little; the essential is to ascertain whether the body of this edifice, its framework and keystones, are strong or weak.

There are five capital difficulties in classical transformism, viz.:—

1. The failure of the classical factors to explain the origin of species.
2. The failure of the classical factors to explain the origin of instincts.
3. The failure of the classical factors to explain the abrupt and creative transformations of new species.
4. The failure of the classical factors to explain the immediate and definitive 'crystallisation' of the essential characteristics of new species or new instincts—the fact that these characteristics, in their main outlines, are very rapidly acquired and once acquired, remain immutable.
5. The failure of the classical factors to resolve the general philosophic difficulty with regard to evolution, which makes the complex proceed from the simple and the greater from the less.

Let us now study these five essential difficulties.

CHAPTER I

THE CLASSICAL FACTORS ARE POWERLESS TO EXPLAIN THE ORIGIN OF SPECIES

It is not difficult to show that neither the Darwinian nor the Lamarckian hypothesis enables us to understand *the origin* of characteristics that constitute a new species.

Let us take the Darwinian hypothesis first.

Natural selection, considered as an essential factor of transformism, has grave obstacles to overcome, obstacles of principle and obstacles of fact. It is unnecessary to discuss them all, for one alone, the gravest, suffices to demonstrate the impotence of the system. It is this:—

In order that any given modification occurring in the characteristics of a species or an individual, should give to that species or to that individual an appreciable advantage in the struggle for life, it is evident that *this modification must be sufficiently marked to be utilisable.*

Now an embryonic organ, a modification merely adumbrated, appearing by chance in a being or a group of beings, can be of no practical use and give them no advantage.[1]

The bird comes from the reptile. Now an embryonic wing, appearing by chance, one knows neither how nor why, in the ancestral reptile, could not give that reptile the capacity or the advantage of flight, and would give it no superiority over other reptiles unprovided with the unusable rudiment. It is therefore impossible to attribute to natural selection the transition from reptile to bird.

The batrachian comes from the fish. There is no

[1] It is needless on the other hand to emphasise further how alien to science and philosophy alike it is to make chance the principal factor of evolution.

doubt of this, since we see this evolution renew itself in the life of the tadpole by a series of changes, perfecting the heart, causing lungs to appear, and developing legs.

But rudiments of legs and lungs would give no advantage to a fish which might possess them. In order to have an advantage over its congeners, it is indispensable that its heart, lungs, and organs of locomotion should be already sufficiently developed to allow it to live out of the water; as the tadpole does, once its evolution is complete, but not till then.

The embryonic transformations of insects are more striking still. There is such an abyss between the anatomy and the physiology of the larva and that of the perfect insect, that it is evidently impossible to find in natural selection the explanation of its ancestral evolution.[1]

Alive to the validity of this objection, certain neo-Darwinians have not hesitated to call in the Lamarckian theory of the influence of the environment and to refer such modifications as are creative of new species to the joint influence of adaptation and selection.

This theory, known as organic selection, has been formulated by Baldwin and Osborn in America, and by Lloyd Morgan in England. It may be summed up as follows:—

If the variation appearing by chance should coincide or agree with an identical variation due to the environing conditions, this variation will be reinforced by the double influence. Thenceforward it may be sufficiently marked to allow selection to come in.

Delage and Goldsmith raise the objection, that 'if the inborn variation is at first too slightly marked

---

[1] The larva of the insect does not exactly represent the primitive insect, for the larva has undergone important changes following on adaptations necessitated by its modes of existence. But even if we ignore these secondary modifications, there is still undeniably a vast abyss between what the primitive insect was and the evolved insect is.

to give any advantage, and if in the definitive constitution of the animal, ontogenetic[1] adaptation plays the greatest part, this adaptation will be produced both in the individuals possessing the inborn variation in question and in those devoid of it.

Would then the premium due to general variation suffice to ensure survival of the one at the expense of the other? Most probably not, for, were it otherwise, that variation alone would have sufficed.'

To this theory a still more definite objection may be made: even admitting that the original variation might be reinforced and doubled, or even tripled, it will none the less be a *very-small variation*. It will therefore never explain the appearance of certain forms of life, such as the bird form. An embryo wing, even exuberant in type, would none the less be unusable, giving no superiority to the ancestral reptile.

Indeed this theory of organic selection adds nothing to the Lamarckian doctrine which we will now examine.

According to this doctrine it is adaptation to new conditions that brings about the formation of new species. The origin of the creative modification is not due to chance, but to need. The ultimate development of new and characteristic organs comes by the repeated use of these organs, and their atrophy by disuse.

Thus a series of adaptations produces a corresponding series of minor variations, at first very small, but cumulative till they produce major transformations.

The Lamarckian theory has been adopted by the great majority of contemporary naturalists, who endeavour to reduce all transformism to the influence of the environment.

The systems of Cope[2] and Packard[3] in America,

---

[1] Ontogenetic. Gr. τὰ ὄντα, existing things; γένεσις, generation; individual development as distinguished from genealogical development.
[2] Cope: *The Primary Factor of Organic Evolution*
[3] Packard: *Lamarck, the Founder of Evolution; His Life and Work.*

of Giard and Le Dantec in France, are Lamarckian systems.

Packard has summed up the causes of variation as seen by him as follows.

> Neo-Lamarckism acknowledges and unites the factors of the school of Saint Hilaire and those of Lamarck as containing the most fundamental causes of variation; it adds to these geographical isolation, or segregation (Wagner and Gulick), the effects of weight, of currents of air and water, the mode of life, fixed, sedentary, or *per contra*, active; the results of tension and of contact (Payder, Cope, and Osborn), the principle of a change of function as bringing about the appearance of new structures, (Dohrn), the effects of parasitism, commensalism[1] and symbiosis,[2] in short, of the biological environment, as well as natural and sexual selection and hybridism. In fine, all conceivable primary factors.

Cope has made a special endeavour to explain the appearance of variations by the action of these primary factors. He refers variations to two essential causes. The first is the direct effect of the environment, and to all the factors above enumerated Cope gives the general name of *physiogenesis*. The second is the influence of the use or disuse of organs, the physiological reactions produced in the animal in response to exciting causes in the environment. Cope calls this *kinetogenesis*.

This second cause would be of the first importance, and Cope brings this out by his study of palæontology. He adduces innumerable examples in support of his thesis. One of the best known is the formation of the foot by adaptation to speed, in plantigrade, and more especially digitograde, quadrupeds, with the characteristic

[1] Identity of food.　　　[2] Living together.

progressive reduction in the number of the digits in the latter. The horse, for example, by its adaptation to speed, has but one digit, the median, much hypertrophied and terminated by a thick layer of horn, and two rudimentary metacarpals accessible only by dissection; but the reduction in the number and size of the lateral digits is seen in the evolutionary series of its ancestors.

The formation of the articulations of the foot and hand of mammals is equally typical. He observes as follows:

> The articulation of the foot, which is very strong, presents two processes of the astragalus, the leading bone of the foot, which project into two corresponding sockets of the tibia, and a process of this latter fitting into a socket of the astragalus. This structure does not (as yet) exist either in the inferior vertebrates, such as reptiles, or in the ancestral mammals of each of the great living branches; it has been formed little by little, by reason of a certain mode of movement and a certain attitude of the animal.
>
> The external walls of these bones being formed of stronger material than their central parts, the sequence of development would seem to be as follows: the astragalus is narrower than the tibia which rests upon it, therefore the peripheral parts of the former bone, being in contact not with equally resisting parts of the latter but with portions relatively softer, these, under this pressure, have suffered a certain absorption of their substance, and two depressions corresponding to the two edges of the astragalus have been formed. This is precisely what would be produced in more or less plastic, inert substances under continuous pressure.
>
> The central depression in the upper edge of the astragalus arises from a similar cause. Here the inferior extremity of the tibia, having a relatively

slight resisting power, rests on a similarly weak portion of the astragalus and is liable to continual shocks. The consequence of such shocks must cause the malleable parts of the bones to take the form corresponding to the direction in which the weight acts; a protuberance above and a depression below will be formed. This is exactly what has resulted in the tibia and the astragalus. From the tertiary period up to our own day we can follow the formation of this articulation: first, as in the *Periptychus rhabdodon* of Mexico, a flat astragalus; then a slight concavity more and more accentuated into an actual socket (*Poebrotherium labiatum* of Colorado), and finally a protuberance penetrating into a concavity of the tibia completes the articulation appears in the *Prothippus sejunctus*, the ancestor of the present horse. (Quoted by Delage and Goldsmith.)

Cope, however, does not confine himself to mechanical concepts. He admits in evolution a kind of ' energy of growth ' not well defined, which he calls ' bathmism,' [1] an energy which would appear to be transmitted by the germinal cells, and would constitute that true vital dynamism which alone can enable us to understand how ' function makes the organ.'

Dantec, on the other hand, who also maintains the Lamarckian doctrine, adheres to pure mechanism. He bases evolution on what he calls ' functional assimilation.' According to this system, living matter, instead of being used up and destroyed by functioning, as was taught

[1] From the Greek βαθμος = a step or threshold. 'It is here left open whether there is any form of force which may be especially designated as 'vital.' Many of the animal functions are known to be physical and chemical, and if there is any one which appears to be less explicable by reference to these forces than the others, it is that of nutrition Probably in this instance, force has been so metamorphosed through the influence of the originative or conscious force in evolution, that it is a distinct species in the category of forces. Assuming it to be such, I have given it the name of *Bathmism*.'—E. D. Cope, *Meth. of Creation*, p. 26 — [Translator's note.]

by physiologists of the school of Cl. Bernard, develops by functioning. That which is worn and expended is merely reserve material, such as fat, the sugar of the tissues, etc.; but the living matter itself, such as muscle, increases by use.

He maintains that it is in virtue of this 'functional assimilation' that adaptation to environment and consecutive progress take place.

However this may be, it is evident that the Lamarckian doctrine is infinitely more satisfying than the Darwinian.

But is it completely so ? By no means.

It can account for the appearance of a number of secondary organic details and more or less important modifications, such as the atrophy of the eye of the mole, the hypertrophy of the median digit in the Equidæ, or the special structure of the articulations of the foot; but, as a general theory, it is assuredly false, because it is powerless to explain the more important facts.

It does not explain the major transformations which have been considered in our criticism of the Darwinian hypothesis.

Confronted with these, Lamarckianism is as powerless as Darwinism, because these transformations imply radical, and so to speak immediate, changes, and not an accumulation of small and slow modifications.

The transition from an aquatic to a terrestrial mode of life, and from a terrestrial to an aerial, can by no means be regarded as results of adaptation.

The ancestral species, adapted to very special surroundings, had no need to change them, and had they felt the need, would have been unable to meet it. How could the reptilian ancestor of the bird adapt itself to surroundings which were not its own and could only become its own after it had passed from the reptilian to the bird form ? Before possessing usable (not embryonic) wings, it could not have an aerial life to which to adapt itself.

15

The same line of reasoning applies, of course, to the transition from the fish to the batrachian.

But it is in the evolution of the insect that the impossibility of transformation by adaptation is yet more obvious. There is no connection between the biology of the larva, which represents, to some degree at any rate, the primitive state of the ancestral insect, and the biology of the perfect insect form. One cannot even conceive by what mysterious series of adaptations an insect, accustomed to larval life, underground or in water, could succeed in gradually creating for itself wings for an aerial life, closed to it and doubtless unknown.

When, further, one considers that this mysterious series of adaptations would have had to take place, not once, by a kind of ' natural miracle,' but as many times as there are genera of winged insects, it becomes as hopeless to deduce the appearance of these species from Lamarckian as from Darwinian factors.

This point is in fact self-evident. Plate himself perfectly understood the impossibility of explaining these major transformations by ' adaptation,' when he wrote that ' by the very fact that an animal belongs to a certain group, the possibilities of variation are restrained, and in many cases, restrained within very narrow limits.'

Therefore Lamarckianism and Darwinism are alike incapable of giving a general explanation applicable to all cases, of the appearance of new species. If the majority of biologists who hold to transformism do not yet admit this, there are, nevertheless, those who do, and endeavour to find elsewhere a superior factor in evolution which may get over the difficulties inherent in the classical evolutionary theories.

Some neo-Lamarckians, such as Pauly, attribute to the constituent elements of the organism, to the organism itself, to plants, and to minerals, a kind of profound consciousness which might originate all modifications and all adaptations. At all steps of the evolutionary

16

scale they see a continuous and intentional effort towards adaptation.

Nägeli is still more precise: according to him the organism includes two kinds of plasm: the nutritive, common to all species and not differentiated; and the specific, or idio-plasm.

This idio-plasm would contain not only the *micellian fasciculi* which characterise it, but also an internal evolutionary tendency with all the capacities and potentialities for transformation and perfectibility. This potentiality must have existed in the first living forms from the very beginnings of life. External factors henceforth would only facilitate adaptation; but would of themselves be incapable of initiating evolution. They would but aid and favour evolution, and bring it under their special rhythm.

These concepts of Nägeli's are extremely interesting. They eventuate in the conclusion that evolution has come about, not by the influence of the environment, but conformably to it.

Adaptation appears in all cases as a consequence, sometimes as a determining factor, but never as a sufficient and essential cause.

An impartial study of the modifications which originate species leads necessarily to this conclusion. But such a concept is absolutely contrary to classical naturalism.

CHAPTER II

FAILURE OF THE CLASSICAL FACTORS TO EXPLAIN THE ORIGIN OF INSTINCTS

It is well known that the instincts of animals are as innumerable as they are marvellous. They have in common the characteristic that they allow the creature to act spontaneously, without reasoned thought, without hesitation or groping, and to attain the desired end with a certainty with which neither reason, nor training, nor impulse, can compare.

Thanks to instinct, an animal of any given species always acts conformably to the genius of its kind, sometimes in a very complex manner, for attack, defence, subsistence, reproduction, and so forth. The essential instinct is identical in all the individuals of the same species, and seems as refractory to variation as the species itself. For each species it constitutes a psychical characteristic as well defined as the physical.

Now the origin of instincts is no more explicable by natural selection or by the influence of the environment than the formation of species. This can be best observed in the insect. Fabre has done imperishable work in this direction, and it is to his writings that we must refer in order to understand the characteristic variety, complexity, and sureness of these instincts, as well as the impossibility of explaining them by the classical notions.

A few examples will suffice. Take, for instance, the Sitaris, quoted by Bergson as one of the most remarkable.

' The Sitaris deposits its eggs at the entrance of the holes which a certain species of bee, the Anthophora, digs in the earth. The larva of the Sitaris, after a long wait, seeks the male anthophora as he leaves the gallery, fastens on him and remains attached until his nuptial flight; it then profits by the occasion to pass from the male to the female and waits until the latter lays her eggs. It then fastens on the egg, which will support it in the honey, devours the egg in a few days, and resting on the empty shell, undergoes its first transformation.

'Now organised to float on the honey, it becomes first a grub, and then a perfect insect. Everything happens as if the larva of the Sitaris when hatched knew that the male anthophora will emerge first from the hole, that the nuptial flight will give an opportunity of passing to the female, that this latter will convey it to a reserve of honey fit for its nourishment when transformed, and that previous to that metamorphosis it will have fed on the egg, so that the empty shell may float with it on the surface of the honey, and incidentally that it will suppress the rival which would have come from the egg. And similarly everything comes to pass as if the Sitaris knew that its larva would know all these things.'

Another classical example is that of the hunting hymenoptera. The larva of these insects requires a motionless and living prey; motionless, because any defensive movements might imperil the delicate egg and afterwards the tiny grub developing in one part of the caterpillar; and living, because this grub cannot subsist on dead matter.

To realise this double necessity for its larva, the hymenopteron must paralyse the victim without killing it. If the insect acted from reason this operation would need extraordinary knowledge and skill. It would first have to proportion the dose of poison so as to administer just enough to paralyse without killing; and further, still more important, it should have a knowledge of the anatomy and physiology of the caterpillar and an infallible

19

sureness of action to strike at once on the right spot by surprise, for the prey is often formidably armed and stronger than the aggressor.

The poisoned sting must therefore be directed with certainty on the motor nervous centres, and there only. One, two, or several stabs are needed, according to the number or concentration of the nerve-ganglions. This function, so unerringly exercised by the insect, has not been learned. When the hymenopteron tears its cocoon and emerges from underground, its parents and predecessors have been long dead, and the insect itself will perish without seeing its progeny or its successors. The instinct cannot therefore be transmitted by example nor by training. It is innate.

How can the origin of this instinct be explained by any of the classical factors of evolution?

Instinct, we are told, is but a habit acquired little by little and transmitted by heredity.

Fabre laid himself out to demonstrate the impossibility of this concept.

Some sand-wasp in the long distant past, would have reached, by chance, the nerve-centres of a grub, benefiting by the act partly herself by avoiding a struggle not devoid of danger, and partly for her larva, provided with fresh game, alive but harmless. She must then have endowed her race, by heredity, with the propensity to repeat these advantageous tactics. The maternal gift would not have favoured all her descendant's equally . . . then would have followed the struggle for life . . . the weaker would have succumbed, the strong would have prospered, and from age to age, selection in conjunction with life would have transformed the fugitive impression of the first act into the deep, ineffaceable instinct at which we marvel in the hymenoptera of to-day.

That selection (Darwinian hypothesis) or re-peated exercise (Lamarckian hypothesis), may have reinforced and perfected these instincts is possible or even probable. But according to Fabre, neither the one nor the other can explain the origin of the instinct itself.

Neither chance nor need can explain how the sting of the primitive insect found at once, without trials, the nerve-ganglion, and was able to paralyse without killing. Actually 'there was no reason for a choice: the stabs had to be given on the upper surface, on the lower surface, on the side, from the front, from behind, at random, according to the chances of a struggle . . . and how many points are there on the skin and interior of a gray cater-pillar? Rigorous mathematics would reply: An infinity.' Nevertheless the sting must strike once and infallibly: 'the art of provisioning the larva requires a master, and cannot admit apprenticeship. The wasp must excel from the first or make no attempt . . . no middle term, no half-success will suffice.' Either the caterpillar is operated upon exactly, or the death of the aggressor and therefore of her descendants ensues. But this is not all: 'Let the desired end be attained; only half the work is done. A second egg is required to complete the future pair and give progeny. Therefore, at a few days' or hours' interval, a second stab must be given as luckily placed as the first. This is to repeat the impossibility and raise it to the second power!'

It is true that these conclusions by Fabre have recently been impugned as too absolute. Researches by Marchal, by Peckham, by Perez, and by most con-temporary naturalists, seem to demonstrate that the primary instincts, in some of their details at least, are variable and perfectible.

But the primordial difficulty—the origin of the primary instinct—still remains in its entirety. Even if it be possible to attribute the appearance of secondary instincts or the various modes of primary ones to the operation of the classical factors, the *origin* of these primary instincts is as difficult to discover as the origin of species.

The instinct to use the poisoned sting puts the same problem as the origin of the sting itself. Neither the organ nor the instinct can play a useful part as agents of adaptation or selection till sufficiently developed and perfected. Therefore, as for species, so for instincts, neither adaptation nor selection can be an essential or creative factor.

CHAPTER III

FAILURE OF THE CLASSICAL FACTORS TO EXPLAIN ABRUPT TRANSFORMATIONS, CREATIVE OF NEW SPECIES.

LAMARCKISM, like Darwinism, lays down the thesis of very small, slow, and innumerable modifications as necessary to the progressive genesis of species.

This concept, which has been accepted as a dogma, would seem above controversy. When, recently, De Vries made known his observations on what he called ' mutations,' *i.e.* the abrupt appearance of new vegetable species from the ancestral species, without any intermediate transitional forms, he threw all those interested in philosophical naturalism into confusion and disorder.

For several years a curious spectacle was presented. The fact of mutation supplied the doctrine of transformability with the only proof that was lacking —experimental verification. Nevertheless it was seen, on the one hand, that transformists endeavoured to minimise the importance of the new facts and the scope of the new theory; and on the other, naïve adversaries adopted it with enthusiasm, both imagining that the ruin of the classical teaching would involve the ruin of the evolutionary idea also!

Le Dantec, in his book, *La Crise du Transformisme*,[1] thus expresses himself.

' A new theory based on verified experiments has seen the light a few years since, and has made numerous converts in the domain of the natural sciences. But this theory of mutations or abrupt variations is the negation of Lamarckism; I might

[1] Published by Félix Alcan (Paris).

23

almost say that it is the negation of transformism itself.'

He adds, ' In fact, from a philosophical point of view, transformism is the system which explains the *progressive* and *spontaneous* appearance of marvellously co-ordinated living mechanisms, such as those of Man and the higher animals.'

It will be seen in the sequel that the *spontaneous* appearance of living beings is a philosophical impossibility. The *progressive* appearance of such beings is in no way traversed by the theory of mutations.

It is only the hypothetical machinery, the supposed genesis of progressive transformations, which is in formal opposition to the new facts.

Le Dantec, and the naturalists of his school who identify transformism with its classical factors, are in some measure logical when they seek to limit as much as possible the area of mutations. But the evolutionary idea itself has nothing to fear from the new discoveries; rather the contrary, as I shall endeavour to prove.

Moreover, Le Dantec is almost alone in his opinion when he affirms that mutations affect secondary, and mainly ornamental, characteristics only, ' leaving the hereditary patrimony intact.'

Since the experiments by De Vries, very many new observations have been published, and the palmary importance of mutation is no longer denied, or indeed deniable.[1]

The only question that remains is to ascertain whether mutation is, in fact, the rule, or an exception. De Vries states clearly that abrupt transformation is the rule, for animals as for plants; and he may well be right. In fact if the whole history of transformations on the evolutionary scale is closely examined, it will be found

[1] Cf. Blaringhern, *Les Transformations Brusques des Êtres Vivants.*— (Publ. Flammarion, Paris.)

that the theory of mutations is strikingly confirmed. By its light, and with closer study, truths which have been ignored or unconsciously slurred over become immediately obvious.

These truths had, however, been already stated by great naturalists such as Geoffroy Saint-Hilaire; but they made no way, and the thesis of slow transformations found no one to contradict it until the work of De Vries appeared.

Starting from his theory of mutations, Cope resumed the study of fossil forms, more especially of the batrachians and mammals of America, and he found no difficulty in demonstrating the probability of their progressive variation by abrupt mutations.

It is, moreover, easy, on the data of the palæontological records which are ' the archives of creation,' to verify that the appearance of most of the main species, always seems to be abrupt.

Batrachians, reptiles, birds, and mammals suddenly appear in the geologic strata. Once there, they seem very rapidly to acquire the characteristics which they will subsequently retain without any essential modification as long as the species remains in existence.

No doubt, palæontology presents transitional forms. But these are rare, and (a more serious matter) they seem to be intermediary rather than transitional.

For example, let us take the archeopteryx, the most remarkable of these intermediate species. We see a bird-reptile, having affinities with each. But its species is determinate and clearly specialised. The archeopteryx has the constitution of the reptile, but it has also well-developed wings, capable of flight, bird's wings.

A reptile with embryonic wings, or wings indicated at the beginning of their development, has never been found.

What is true for the archeopteryx is equally true for all known intermediate forms; they are all well marked, special, and very distinct types, allowing of the use of the organs characteristic of each species.

Whilst palæontology presents many rudimentary organs, residues of those which are useless and discarded, it never shows organs outlined but as yet unusable.

It seems, therefore, that abrupt transformations may well be the rule in evolution.

But it is evident that the abrupt appearances of new species can be explained neither by natural selection nor by the influence of the environment. Le Dantec recognises this when he exclaims, 'a mutation produced under my eyes is a lock to which I have no key!'[1]

[1] *La Crise du Transformisme.*

CHAPTER IV

FAILURE OF THE CLASSICAL FACTORS TO EXPLAIN THE IMMEDIATE AND DEFINITIVE 'CRYSTALLISATION' OF THE ESSENTIAL CHARACTERISTICS OF NEW SPECIES AND NEW INSTINCTS

IT appears then, that whether we consider physical characteristics or instincts, both seem to be immutable. They may develop or atrophy, and may vary within narrow limits, but these changes are always changes of detail, never of essentials. This truth had been clearly brought out long before by the researches of naturalists: De Vries brought to it the support of direct experiment. He reduced it to the following law: ' New species become stable immediately.' This involves a new and serious objection to classical transformism.

If new species appear abruptly and immediately become stable, the theory of innumerable and slow transformations under selective or adaptive influences is definitely ruined as a general and essential theory.

The evolutionary question is no longer one of a vast accumulation of infinitesimal changes bringing about the formation of new species; but of considerable and abrupt changes revealing themselves by the rapid appearance of species that become permanent as soon as they have appeared.

This is an immense revolution in naturalistic philosophy. The four difficulties which have just been reviewed are of the naturalistic order. Before passing to the fifth, which is of a totally different kind, and of a metaphysical nature, I will beg the reader who may not have been convinced by the preceding demonstration of the impotence of the classical factors, to turn his thoughts to the precise and unanswerable evidence which Nature seems to have specially put forward to guard us from error. This is the testimony of the Insect.

CHAPTER V

THE TESTIMONY OF THE INSECT

To consider the insect attentively is to be convinced of the emptiness of ancient and modern theories on the creation or the evolution of species.

The insect, appearing in the first ages of terrestrial life, and showing in all cases the essential stability of its species once they have appeared, bears strong testimony against the concept of continuous transformations by innumerable slow variations.

The chasm which separates the perfect insect from its larva—an abyss in which the Darwinian and Lamarckian theories are hopelessly lost—is testimony against its evolution by the classical factors of selection and adaptation. The disconcerting and marvellous spectacle of its primary instincts, which those factors are powerless to explain, is another argument against them.

The radical, and (so to speak) spontaneous transformations in a closed chrysalis almost isolated from the action of external agencies, is opposed to the concept of evolution by such agencies.

The transformations and metamorphoses, and the progressive or regressive changes of its larval existence are equally opposed to the concept of a continuous and uninterrupted evolution by functional assimilation.

Yet more opposed to these is the amazing phenomenon of histolysis [1] in the chrysalis, by which most of its organs are reduced to an amorphous emulsion, preparatory to the coming transformation.

[1] Histolysis.—Gr. ἱστός = tissue, λύσις = solution; the solution of tissue.

This stupefying testimony, teaching us that neither the radical changes in the larva, nor the mysterious histolysis, compromise in any way the future morphology of the perfect insect, upsets all our concepts on the building up of the organism and of the transformations of species.[1]   By its whole biology the insect presents the symbol of what evolution really is, and as we shall see later, it proves that the essential cause of evolution should be sought neither in the influence of the environment, nor in the reactions of organic matter to that environment; but in a dynamism[2] independent of that organic matter directing it and superior to it.

It shows us evolution taking place primarily by an internal impulse entirely distinct from surrounding influences, by a primordial effort, unerring but still mysterious and absolutely inexplicable by classical naturalism.

Not only so: this incomparable testimony, while it is the negation of contemporaneous naturalistic theories, contradicts also the antiquated concept of Providential creation.

From the psychological point of view, the leading characteristic of the insect is that it possesses pure instinct almost without a trace of intelligence. Further, we find that this pure instinct, which has remained such for ages, is marked by a refined and cruel ferocity without counterpart in the rest of the animal world, but nevertheless perfectly innocent.

This ferocity then, if there were a responsible Creator, would be the pure, the immaculate work of

---

[1] Analogous to the testimony of the insect is that of certain species of molluscs and crustaceans. Before arriving at the adult form, animals of these species undergo extraordinary modifications, by very diverse adaptations. Nevertheless the future development of these animals continues in despite of their metamorphoses, as if governed by an unalterable and immanent directive principle.

[2] Dynamism = concrete means of power: holding the same relation to dynamics as 'mechanism' to mechanics.—[Translator's note.]

CHAPTER VI

FAILURE OF THE CLASSICAL FACTORS TO RESOLVE THE
GENERAL PHILOSOPHICAL DIFFICULTY RELATING TO
EVOLUTION, HOW THE COMPLEX CAN PROCEED FROM
THE SIMPLE, AND THE GREATER FROM THE LESS

THIS difficulty has been entirely neglected or evaded
by classical transformism. It is nevertheless a formidable
one.

The *spontaneous* appearance of forms superior to
the originals is a pure impossibility, alike from the
scientific and from the philosophic point of view.

There is no escape from the dilemma: either there
is no evolution, or it implies a potential immanence in
the evolving universe.

Evolution being demonstrated, we are compelled to
admit that all the progressive and complex transformations that have been realised existed potentially in the
primitive elementary forms or form.

This in no way means that evolution, as it has actually
come to pass, existed in germ in such and such a primitive form in like manner as the living creature exists
in germ in the egg from which it will be hatched.

Such pre-established finality seems very highly
improbable. The meaning is that the primitive form
contained all potentialities, those which have, and those
which as yet have not been realised; in the past, the
present, and the future.

In this philosophical concept what function is
assigned to the classical evolutionary factors?

Simply that they are secondary and accessory.

They have played an obvious part; they have

imposed a particular rhythm on evolution, and have favoured it, but they have not produced it.

One might, strictly speaking, imagine evolution proceeding without the intervention of selection or adaptation; but we cannot conceive it as proceeding by them alone.

This is the main conclusion to which we are irresistibly led.

Thus, classical naturalism, travelling by a very long road, which it has vainly explored in every direction, finds itself willingly or unwillingly, brought back to seek the first cause which it has sought to avoid. Its avowed inability to find the essential factors of evolution allows of no more fresh starts on the same road.

Fiske said that transformism had restored to the world as much ' teleology '[1] as it had taken away. This is not happily expressed, for it implies the kind of finality which would fix arbitrarily and in advance the trend of evolution.

But what is indubitable, and results clearly from a thorough study of transformism, is the conclusion, that evolutionary science cannot dispense with philosophy.

[1] Teleology = the doctrine of adaptation to purpose.

PART II

THE CLASSICAL PSYCHO-PHYSIOLOGICAL
CONCEPT OF THE INDIVIDUAL

most
Important
"Unity of the
Self "   11/1/21

FOREWORD

In the foregoing chapters the insufficiency of the classical concept of evolution as a whole has been clearly brought out. We shall now endeavour to show the insufficiency of the classical concept of the individual.

This concept rests on two principal notions: Unicism,[1] and the negation of the unity of the Self.

Unicism rejects the ancient spiritualist, animist, and vitalist theories which advanced the claim that there are in the individual dynamic or psychic principles different in essence from the organism.

It bases its conclusion on the chemical and morphological unity of living forms; on the absence of any positive discontinuity between living and inert matter; on the laws of biological energy, as clear and precise as those of physical energy and in agreement with them.

The negation of the unity of the Self is similarly based on the negation of the spiritualist, animist, and vitalist principles, which, in the old psycho-physiological concepts separated human from animal life, and that from the mineral. These notions being put aside, the conclusion is that the Self is but the synthesis or the complex of the elements constituting the organism.

Fundamental to a living being, says Dastre,[2] we find ' the activity proper to each cell—elementary or cellular life; above that, the forms of activity resulting from the association of cells, the collective life, the sum, or rather the complex, of the partial lives of its elements.'

But these two notions—naturalistic unicism and negation of the unity of the Self—are only connected by a philosophical misunderstanding or by a mere error

[1] Unicism = the doctrine of the uniformity of all matter.
[2] Dastre: *La Vie et la Mort.*

of reasoning. The monistic philosophy does not necessarily imply the conception of the Self as a mere cellular
complex, it even (as we shall see) agrees better with the
opposite concept of its central unity.

If, abandoning for the moment all metaphysical
ideas on the constitution of the individual, we keep
strictly to the data of fact, we are confronted with a
leading verity: there are in the individual different
modalities[1] of energy, and these modalities, even though
theoretically conceivable as proceeding from a single
energy, are not equivalent.

There are in the living being 'material energy,'
'dynamic energy,' as it may be termed, and 'psychological energy'; and these modalities of energy appear
to us to be both distinct in themselves and graded with
respect to each other. Such are the data of fact.

Starting from these verified facts we can, without
losing our way among metaphysical notions, conceive of
the living being in two different ways.

The first sees the individual only as a complex of
partial and elementary individualities. In this concept,
the apparent grades observable in a living being, are
simple functions of orientation and relative position.
This is the classical concept.

The second sees the individual as a complex yet
more complex, in which the elements form autonomous
and distinct *cadres*—a graded hierarchy. These *cadres*
or hierarchic series are not, let us repeat, necessarily
different in essence; but they have different activities
and capacities, or if the expression is preferred, are at
different evolutionary levels.

We may thus conceive of a dynamic and psychological
complex above the material and organic complex,
organising and centralising it; which psychological
complex might itself be capable of rational sub-division

---

[1] Modalities = modes in the logical sense, distinguishing between
various modes.

up to the discovery of the central entity, the real Self, one and indivisible.

These two modes of regarding the individual remain the same, under whatever mode, monist or pluralist, we may regard things at large.

The former concept has in its favour, simplicity and the methodological principle of economy of causation.

Against it there is the diversity between physiological and psychological facts, and the insurmountable difficulty of subordinating the latter to the former; and, more especially, its flagrant insufficiency in explaining, not merely psychic activity, but even vital activity.

Methodical analysis of the classical concepts of physiological and psychological individuality will bring this out.

CHAPTER I

THE concept of the physical Self as a mere complex of cells comes into collision with serious difficulties. We may classify these like those of the evolutionary theories. They are: difficulties relating to the general concept of polyzoism;[1] those relating to the specific form of the individual, to the building, the maintenance and the repair of the organism; those relating to embryonic and post-embryonic metamorphoses; and those relating to the so-called supernormal physiology.

I.—DIFFICULTIES RELATING TO THE POLYZOIS[1] CONCEPT.

The description given by Dastre[2] of physical individuality is as follows.

'We imagine the complex living being, whether plant or animal, with its form that distinguishes it from all others, as a populous city, distinguished by a thousand traits from a neighbouring city. Its elements are independent and autonomous by the same title as the anatomical elements of the organism. Each has in itself the springs of life, which it neither borrows from its neighbours nor draws from the community. All these inhabitants have a definite life, and even breathe and are nourished after the same manner, possessing all the same general human faculties; but each has, over and above, his own trade, industry, aptitudes, and talents by which he contributes to the social life, and in his turn depends

---

[1] Polyzoism = a constitution similar to a colony of living cells or animalcules.
[2] Dastre: *La Vie et la Mort.*

upon it. The statesman, the mason, the baker, the butcher, the manufacturer, the artist, all perform different tasks and supply different products, more numerous and varied as the social state is more perfect. The living being, whether plant or animal is a city of this kind.'

The grave objections to this theory are immediately apparent.

The picture set before us as that of a living being is that of an animal colony pure and simple. Possibly correct for some forms which have only the outward show of individualisation, for inferior animals of the type of zoophytes, it cannot be considered true for animals sharply marked off from other orders of life.

In the city described by Dastre the most essential feature is missing: a centralised direction, which alone is able, first to unite, and then to maintain, to order, and to direct the State for the common welfare.

2.—DIFFICULTIES RELATING TO THE SPECIFIC FORM OF THE INDIVIDUAL, TO THE BUILDING, THE MAINTENANCE, AND THE REPAIR OF THE ORGANISM.

The classical concept leaves unexplained all that relates to the life, the formation, the development, and the maintenance of the organism. To it, physiology is an entire mystery. That this mysteriousness is not immediately apparent, is due to a well-known illusion of the human mind, which is always prone to think that it understands a thing merely because it is familiar. The philosophical mind naturally reacts against this tendency; the many are irresistibly carried away by it. 'The more unintelligent a man is,' Schopenhauer writes, 'the less mysterious existence seems to him. Everything seems to him to carry in itself the explanation of its How and Why.'

Now nothing is more familiar in its main outlines than the functioning of our own organism, and nothing seems simpler to the vulgar mind; but in reality nothing is more mysterious.

What life is in itself involves a mystery as yet impenetrable. The vital mechanism, and the activity of the great organic functions, are equally unexplained. This activity, which lies outside the conscious will of the Self, is elaborated and completed unconsciously, exactly as we shall see is the case in so-called supernormal physiology. Normal function is just as 'occult' as that which is called supernormal.

Even the constitution of the organism and all that pertains to it, birth, growth, embryonic development, maintenance of the personality throughout life, organic repair (which in certain animals goes as far as the reproduction of lost members and even of viscera), all these are so many insoluble enigmas if the classical concept of individuality be accepted.

Let us try, by the light of this concept, to understand the building up and the functioning of the anatomico-physiological individuality, leaving purely philosophical and even psychological questions on one side. Let us look only at the physical being, the physiological individual, considered as a cellular complex. Whence and how does the complex of cells that makes up a living being draw its specific form? How does it keep that form throughout its life? How is its physical personality formed, maintained, and repaired?

It is not admissible, let us remark, to invoke an organising dynamism, for that is rejected by classical physiology. We cannot even resort to the 'directing idea' of Claude Bernard, which is held to be antiquated. How, then, does the cellular complex, by the mere fact of the association of its constituent elements, acquire this vital and individualising power?

Whence? How? Why? Once more, so many

mysteries! Dastre characterises as 'unfathomable' the mystery by which in embryonic development 'the ovum-cell, drawing to itself external material, succeeds in building up the marvellous structure which is the body of an animal, the body of a man, even of a particular man.' Nevertheless explanations have been sought and found. They are disconcertingly feeble. Le Dantec, for instance, declares that the form of a creature, and its whole constitution, necessarily depend on its chemical composition, on the relation established between the specific form and this chemical composition. He writes in all seriousness : 'The form of a greyhound is simply the condition of equilibrium of the greyhound chemical substance.'

'This,' remarks Dastre 'is saying a great deal too much, if it means that the body of the dog is " a substance " which behaves after the fashion of homogeneous isotropical masses like melted sulphur or dissolved salt: it is better, but means much less, if it signifies in the mind of the physiologist that the body of the greyhound is the condition of equilibrium of a heterogeneous, non-isotropic, material system under infinitely numerous chemical and physical conditions. The idea of attributing form —and therefore organisation—only to chemical com-position, has not had its birth from the mind of chemists, nor from that of physiologists.'

In reality the supposed explanation by Le Dantec is nothing but a verbal explanation, which substitutes one difficulty for another. Instead of the question: How is the specific form realised ? we are led, if we admit Le Dantec's hypothesis, to ask: How is the condition of chemical equilibrium which is the basis of the specific form, realised and maintained ? The mystery is just as great as before. But even taken as it stands, the hypothesis cannot be sustained, for it can give no account, as we shall see later on, of the changes undergone by the organism during embryonic development.

As the classical concept of the Self cannot account for the building up of the organism and its specific form, so also it cannot explain how this organism maintains and repairs itself during life.

Nothing is more curious than the efforts of naturalists and physiologists to explain individual permanence in despite of perpetual cellular renewal.

Claude Bernard sought to demonstrate that vital functions are necessarily accompanied by organic destruction and regeneration.

'When there is movement,' he says,[1] 'in a man or an animal, a part of the active substance of the muscle is destroyed or burned; when sensation and will are manifested, the nerves are used up; when thought is exercised, the brain is consumed in some measure. It may be said that the same matter is never used twice during life. When an act is accomplished, that portion of living matter which has served to produce it exists no longer. If the phenomenon is repeated, it is by the aid of new matter. . . . In a word, physico-chemical destruction is everywhere conjoined with functional activity, and we may regard as a physiological axiom the proposition: Every manifestation of action in a living being is necessarily connected with organic destruction.'

But this axiom is impugned by contemporary physiologists. In opposition to Claude Bernard, their efforts tend to establish, that really living substance, protoplasm, is much less destroyed during life than was imagined. Cellular renovation, according to them, is very slight. (Chauveau, Pflüger.)

Certain physiologists (Marinesco) have not hesitated to ascribe indefinite duration to the cerebral cells.

Finally, Le Dantec, going further still, declares that

[1] Claude Bernard : *Les Phénomènes de la Vie.*

44

not only is living matter not destroyed by use, but that it increases.

It would seem that nothing should be easier than to decide experimentally the problem of cellular destruction, by quantitative analysis of the nitrogenous waste in the urine. In fact it is very difficult to distinguish between the part that comes from the albuminoids in food, and that which comes from waste of the organism; and the best conducted researches such as those of Igo Kaup still give uncertain results.

But in default of proof from the laboratory, reasoning suffices to prove the perpetual destruction and restoration of cellular protoplasm.

At the outset and, *a priori*, without need of demonstration, it seems that such a tiny element as the living cell should necessarily have short life; much shorter in any case, than that of the organism to which it belongs. It would therefore be renewed *x* times during the life of that organism.

Further, the imperious necessity for ingestion by the living being of nitrogenous elements in considerable quantity can be explained only by the needs of cellular regeneration. Otherwise we should be driven to the absurd supposition that the nitrogen is ingested to be immediately eliminated, and is not an indispensable nutriment, while the contrary is well established.

Therefore, even if further research should prove that the living cell remains intact, as a framework, throughout life, that would by no means imply that it remains intact as to its constituent molecules.

The problem of molecular renewal replaces that of cellular renewal, and the question remains neither more nor less mysterious. Thus the ' directive idea ' necessarily presides over the maintenance of the personality as it presides at its building up.

The difficulties which we have rapidly reviewed are already considerable; but they are as nothing compared with those that we shall now examine. The problems of embryonic and post-embryonic metamorphoses, and the problem of so-called supernormal physiology, if we take the trouble to look at them conjointly, enable us to affirm that the classical concept of physical individuality is erroneous, and that the living being is quite other than a cellular complex.

We shall probe to the quick the fundamental defect of the ascending method which strives to adapt an explanation to simple or relatively simple facts, while evading the inherent difficulties of complex or relatively complex facts.

If we look at physiology as a whole and synthetically, without putting aside these primordial difficulties; and, *a fortiori*, if we give weight to them, then the concept that results is undeniably and evidently quite opposed to that which some have sought to deduce from mediocre, narrow, and tentative analytical researches.

3.—THE PROBLEM OF EMBRYONIC AND POST-EMBRYONIC METAMORPHOSES.

It is well known that embryonic and post-embryonic development, far from being uniform, proceeds by a series of metamorphoses. These sometimes retrace the previous evolutionary changes of the species, and sometimes reflect the divergent adaptations realised during larval life. Metamorphoses are common to all animals, but are specially remarkable among those which have a prolonged larval life after leaving the egg, such as batrachians, molluscs, and annelids. By these changes the development of the animal assumes successive forms, very different from one another, before reaching the definitive adult shape. These facts are a complete negation of the classical theories on the building up of the organism.

46

From the Unconscious to the Conscious

Let us return to Le Dantec's explanation of specific form. Are we to admit that the conditions of chemical equilibrium, which is its supposed basis, continually change during the development of an animal, and change in a given sense following a pre-determined direction leading to the adult form? So be it; but this is once more to have recourse to the 'directing idea,' in other words, to restore to physiology all the finality which it claimed to discard.

The tadpole has all the organs, the constitution, and the mode of life of a fish. Suddenly, without change of environment or mode of life, its conditions of chemical equilibrium are about to alter. They will be modified in such a manner, according to Le Dantec, that legs will appear, that lungs will replace gills, that the heart with two cavities will become one with three cavities; in short, that the fish will become a frog!

Consider the medusa. Its successive larval forms are so different from each other that they were long taken for distinct animals.

How is the genesis of these successive forms to be explained by modifications in the chemical equilibrium?

In these metamorphoses of embryonic life there is a double problem. First the problem of the metamorphoses themselves. How do they come about? How do they recall either the transitional forms of the evolutionary ancestry, or the details of divergent larval adaptations? Where, and how, is the ineffaceable imprint of these ancestral forms and adaptations preserved?

Then there is the problem of the individual expansion. How is it that these changes do not interfere with its reaching the definite adult form? How is it that this form is always attained, certainly and without fail? If we see nothing in the individual but a cellular complex, the double problem cannot be solved.

47

The mystery becomes clearer only if it be admitted that above the metamorphoses, above the organic and physiological modifications and the revolutions in the chemical equilibrium of life, there exists the directive dominant of a superior dynamism.

4.—THE HISTOLYSIS OF THE INSECT

It is in the post-embryonic development of certain insects that the evidence of this dominant appears in the most striking manner. As is well known, certain insects undergo their last and greatest transformation in the chrysalis. They are then subject to an extremely curious change—histolysis.

In the protective envelope of the chrysalis, which shuts off the animal from light and from external perturbing influences, a strange elaboration takes place, singularly like that which will presently be described under the head of the so-called supernormal physiology. *The body of the insect is dematerialised.* It is disintegrated, and melts into a kind of uniform pap, a simple amorphous substance in which the majority of organic and specific distinctions disappear. There is the bare fact in all its import.

Doubtless the question of histolysis is far from being fully elucidated. Since its discovery by Weissmann in 1864, naturalists have not been able to come to entire agreement on the extent of the dissolution nor on its mechanism. It is, however, well established, ' that when the larva becomes immobile and is transformed into a pupa, most of its tissues disappear by histolysis. The tissues thus destroyed are the hypodermic cells of the first four segments, the breathing tubes, the muscles, the fatty body and the peripheral nerves. Of these there remain no visible cellular elements. At the same time the cells of the middle intestine assemble in a central mass, making a sort of magma.'[1]

Then a new generation of tissue takes place, partly from the magma resulting from the histolysis, partly from the proliferation of special corpuscles called image-bearing discs. The newly-formed portions of the organism thus seem to have no direct filiation with the destroyed parts of the larval organism.

Whether we like it or not, the evidence of such facts upsets all the classical biologic concepts—chemical equilibrium as conditioning specific form, cellular affinity, functional assimilation, the animal as a cellular complex, all become so many vain formulæ and nonsense!

Either we must be content to bow before the mystery and declare it impenetrable, or we must have the courage to avow that classical physiology has lost its way.

In order to understand all these—the mystery of specific form, embryonic and post-embryonic development, the constitution and maintenance of the personality, organic repair, and all the other general problems of biology—it is necessary and sufficient to accept a notion, which is certainly not new, but is placed in a new light, the notion of a dynamism superior to the organism and conditioning it.

This is not the ' directive idea ' of Claude Bernard, which is a kind of abstraction, an incomprehensible metaphysico-biological entity. This is a concrete idea —that of a directing and centralising dynamism, dominating both intrinsic and extrinsic contingencies, the chemical reactions of the organic medium, and the influences of the external environment.

We shall find the existence of this dynamism affirmed in like manner, not more certainly, but more evidentially, in the so-called supernormal physiology. There indeed

[1] Félix Henneguy : *Les Insectes.*

49

the manifestations of the physiological dynamism pass outside the limits of the organism, are separate from it and act outside it. Yet more, it can partially disintegrate the organism and with its substance, can reconstitute new organic forms exterior to it, or, to use the correct philosophical formula, can make new representations.[1]

[1] *Vide* Translator's Note, p. viii.

CHAPTER II

THE PROBLEM OF SUPERNORMAL PHYSIOLOGY

No one nowadays is ignorant of what is meant by the so-called supernormal physiology. It is manifested in persons of special gifts and constitutions, called mediums, by dynamic and material effects inexplicable by the regular play of their organs and transcending the field of organic action.

The most important and complex phenomena of this so-called supernormal physiology are those called materialisation and dematerialisation. Conformably to our method, these are the only ones which we shall first endeavour to understand, in order, later, to apply the solution of the problem to other less important facts of the same order, such as the movements of objects without contact.

I.—MATERIALISATIONS

I have no intention of making here a historical or critical study of materialisations, a study which the reader will find in the special works named below.[1] I shall only bring my personal contribution to the analysis and synthesis of this phenomenon, which is of primary

---

[1] Works to consult: Aksakoff: *Animisme et Spiritisme;* J. Bisson: *Les Phénomènes dits de Matérialisation;* Crookes: *Researches in the Phenomena of Spiritualism;* Delanne: *Les Apparitions Matérialistes;* D'Esperance: *Au Pays de l'Ombre;* Flammarion: *Les Forces Naturelles Inconnues;* Maxwell: *Psychic Phenomena;* Richet: *Etudes sur les Matérialisations de la Villa Carmen;* Dr Schrenck-Notzing: *Matérialisations Phénomènes;* De Rochas: *Œuvres Complètes.*

importance since more certainly than any other it reverses the very foundations of physiology.

The sequence of materialisation may be summed up as under :—

From the body of the medium there exudes, or is exteriorised, a substance at first amorphous or polymorphous. This substance takes on diverse forms, usually representations of more or less complex organs.

We may therefore consider in turn:—

1. The substance which is the substratum of the materialisations;
2. Its organised representations.

This substance may be exteriorised in a gaseous or vaporous form, or again as a liquid or a solid.

The vaporous form is the more frequent and the best known. Near the medium there is outlined or amassed a kind of visible vapour, a sort of fog, often connected with the body of the medium by a thin link of the same substance. In different parts of this fog there then appears what resembles a condensation, which M. Le Cour has ingeniously compared to the supposed formation of nebulæ. These areas of condensation finally take the appearance of organs, whose development is very rapidly completed.

This substance of materialisation is more amenable to examination under its liquid or solid forms. Its change into organs is then sometimes slower. It remains longer in the amorphous state, and allows of a more precise notion of the genesis of the phenomenon.

It has been observed under this form, from several mediums, especially from the famous medium Eglinton.[1] But it is from the medium Eva that this solid substance is generated with astonishing completeness. The reader should refer to the books of Mme Bisson and of Dr Schrenck-Notzing for the description of the innumerable forms that it takes.

[1] Delanne : *Les Apparitions Matérialisées*, vol. ii. pp. 642 *et seq.*

From the Unconscious to the Conscious

Having trained and educated Eva, Mme Bisson has been able during long years of research to study at her leisure this phenomenon whose scientific import has long remained unrealised. Her book is therefore a mine of documentary evidence generously offered to scientific and philosophic minds.

The work of Dr Schrenck-Notzing is a methodical and complete account of his studies on the same medium; it is drawn up with skill, it is clear, exact, and provided with references; it contains also the record of similar experiments with another medium having the same faculties as Eva.

Thanks to the complaisance and goodwill of Mme Bisson, I had the honour and privilege of studying Eva with her for a year and a half, at bi-weekly séances, held at first in her house, and afterwards, for three consecutive months, exclusively in my own laboratory.[1]

After my study of Eva, I was able to verify analogous though elementary phenomena in new subjects from whom I endeavoured to induce materialisations.

I shall now give a synthetic *résumé* of my experiments and records; and it is my own testimony only that I give in this book, a testimony in complete accord with that of a very large number of men of science, chiefly physicians, who are to-day completely convinced of the authenticity of this phenomenon, although for the most part starting from absolute scepticism.

I have been able to see, to touch, and to photograph the materialisations of which I am about to write.

I have frequently followed the event from its beginning to its end; for it was formed, developed, and disappeared under my own eyes. However unexpected, strange or impossible such a manifestation may

[1] The results were the subject of a conference at the Collège de France, published under the title, *La Physiologie dite Superanormale*. This will be found, illustrated by 24 photogravures in the *Bulletin de l'Institut Physiologique* of January-June, 1918, published at No. 143 Boulevard Saint-Michel, Paris. Now reproduced in the Appendix, p. 328.

F

appear, I have no right to put forward the slightest doubt as to its reality. With Eva, the mode of operation necessary to obtain materialisations is very simple: the medium, after having been seated in the dark cabinet, is put into the hypnotic state, slightly, but enough to involve forgetfulness of the normal personality. This dark cabinet has no other purpose than to protect the sleeping medium from disturbing influences, and specially from the action of light. It is thus possible to keep the séance-room sufficiently well lit for perfect observation.

The phenomena appear (when they do appear) after a variable interval, sometimes very brief, sometimes an hour or more. They always begin by painful sensations in the medium; she sighs and moans from time to time much like a woman in childbirth. These moans reach their height just when the manifestation begins, they lessen or cease when the forms are complete.

There first appear luminous liquid patches from the size of a pea to that of a crown-piece, scattered here and there over her black smock, principally on the left side.

This constitutes a premonitory phenomenon, appearing sometimes three-quarters of an hour to an hour before the other phenomena. Sometimes it is omitted, and sometimes it appears without being followed by anything more. The substance exudes specially from the natural orifices and the extremities, from the top of the head, from the nipples, and the ends of the fingers.

The most frequent and most easily observed origin is from the mouth; the substance is then seen to proceed from the interior surface of the cheeks, the roof of the palate, and the gums.

The substance has variable aspects; sometimes, and most characteristically, it appears as a plastic paste, a true protoplasmic mass; sometimes as a number of fine threads; sometimes as strings of different thickness in narrow and rigid lines; sometimes as a wide band;

sometimes as a fine tissue of ill-defined and irregular shape. The most curious form of all is that of a wide-spread membrane with swellings, and fringes, whose general appearance is remarkably like that of the epiploön (caul). In fine, the substance is essentially amorphous, or rather, polymorphous.

The quantity of the substance exteriorised is very variable; sometimes there is extremely little, sometimes it is abundant, with all intermediate degrees. In certain cases it covers the medium completely, like a cloak. It may show three different colours: white, black, or gray. The white seems the more frequent form, perhaps because it is the easiest to observe. The three colours are sometimes seen simultaneously. The visibility of this substance is also very variable. Its visibility may wax and wane slowly and repeatedly. To the touch it gives very different sensations, usually having some relation to the form of the moment; it seems soft and somewhat elastic while spreading; hard, knotty, or fibrous when it forms cords.

Sometimes it feels like a spider's web touching the hand of the observer. The threads of the substance are both stiff and elastic. It is mobile. Sometimes it is slowly evolved, rises and falls, and moves over the medium's shoulders, her breast, or her lap with a crawling, reptilian movement; sometimes its motion is abrupt and rapid, it appears and disappears like a flash.

It is extremely sensitive, and its sensitiveness is closely connected with that of hyperæsthetised medium; and touch reacts painfully on the latter. If the touch should be at all rough or prolonged the medium shows pain which she compares to a touch on raw flesh.

The substance is sensitive even to light-rays; a light, especially if sudden and unexpected, produces a painful start in the medium. However, nothing is more variable than the light-effects; in some cases the substance can stand even full daylight. The magnesium flashlight causes a violent start in the medium, but it is borne, and allows of instantaneous photographs.

In the effects of light on the substance, and its repercussion on the medium, it is difficult to distinguish between real pain and mere reflex; both, whether pain or reflex, impede investigation. For this reason the phenomena have as yet not been cinematographed. To its sensitiveness the substance seems to add a kind of instinct not unlike that of the self-protection of the invertebrates; it would seem to have all the distrust of a defenceless creature, or one whose sole defence is to re-enter the parent organism. It shrinks from all contacts and is always ready to avoid them and to be re-absorbed.

It has an immediate and irresistible tendency towards organisation; not remaining long in its first state. It often happens that this organisation is so rapid as not to permit of the primordial substance being seen. At other times the amorphous substance may be observed with more or less complete representations immersed in its mass; for instance, a finger may be seen hanging in the midst of fringes of the substance; even heads and faces are sometimes seen enwrapped by it.

I now come to the representations; they are of the most diverse character. Sometimes they are indeterminate, inorganic forms; but more often they are organic, of varying complexity and completeness.

Different observers—Crookes and Richet among others—have, as is well known, described complete materialisations, not of phantoms in the proper sense of the word, but of beings having for the moment all the vital particulars of living beings; whose hearts beat, whose lungs breathe, and whose bodily appearance is perfect.

I have not, alas, observed phenomena so complete, but, on the other hand, I have very frequently seen

56

complete representations of an organ, such as a face, a hand, or a finger.

In the more complete cases the materialised organ has all the appearance and biologic functions of a living organ. I have seen admirably modelled fingers, with their nails; I have seen complete hands with bones and joints; I have seen a living head, whose bones I could feel under a thick mass of hair. I have seen well-formed living and human faces!

On many occasions these representations have been formed from beginning to end under my own eyes. I have, for instance, seen the substance issue from the hands of the medium and link them together; then, the medium separating her hands, the substance has lengthened, forming thick cords, has spread, and formed fringes like epiploic fringes. Lastly, in the midst of these fringes, there has appeared by progressive representation, perfectly organised fingers, a hand, or a face. In other cases I have witnessed an analogous organisation in substance issuing from the mouth.

Here is one example taken from my notebook: 'From the mouth of Eva there descends to her knees a cord of white substance of the thickness of two fingers; this ribbon takes under our eyes varying forms, that of a large perforated membrane, with swellings and vacant spaces; it gathers itself together, retracts, swells, and narrows again. Here and there from the mass appear temporary protrusions, and these for a few seconds assume the form of fingers, the outline of hands, and then re-enter the mass. Finally the cord retracts on itself, lengthens to the knees, its end rises, detaches itself from the medium, and moves towards me. I then see the extremity thicken like a swelling, and this terminal swelling expands into a perfectly modelled hand. I touch it; it gives a normal sensation; I feel the bones, and the fingers with their nails. Then the hand contracts, diminishes, and disappears in the end of the cord. The cord makes a few movements, retracts, and returns into the medium's mouth.'

It is possible to observe the vaporous form of the substance at the same time as its solid form; it emerges from the body of the medium invisible and impalpable, no doubt through the meshes of the clothing, and condenses on the surface of this latter, appearing as a small cloud which develops into a white spot on the black smock, at the level of the shoulders, the breast, or the knees. The spot grows, spreads, and takes on the outlines or the reliefs of a hand or a face.

Whatever may be the mode of its formation the materialisation does not always remain in contact with the medium; it may sometimes be observed quite detached: the following example is typical in this respect:—

'A head appears suddenly, about three-fourths of a yard from Eva's head, above, and to her right. It is the head of a man, of normal size, well formed and in the usual relief. The top of the head and the forehead are completely materialised. The forehead is large and high, the hair short and abundant, brown or black. Below the brows the contours shade off; only the top of the head and the forehead are clearly seen.

'The head disappears for a moment behind the curtain, then reappears as before; but the face, incompletely materialised, is masked by a band of white substance. I put my hand forward and pass my fingers through the tufted hair and feel the bone of the cranium . . . an instant later everything has vanished.' The forms have, it will be observed, a certain independence, and this independence is both physiological and anatomical.

The materialised organs are not inert, but biologically alive. A well-formed hand, for instance, has the functional capacities of a normal hand. I have several times been intentionally touched by a hand or grasped by its fingers.

The most remarkable materialisations which I have myself observed are those produced by Eva in my laboratory, during three consecutive months of the winter of 1917-1918. In the bi-weekly séances in collaboration with Madame Bisson, the Medical Inspector General,—M. Calmette, M. Jules Courtier, and M. Le Cour, we obtained a series of records of the greatest interest. We saw, touched, and photographed representations of heads and faces formed from the original substance. These were formed under our eyes, the curtains being half-drawn. Sometimes they proceeded from a cord of solid substance issuing from the medium, sometimes they were progressively developed in a fog of vaporous substance condensed in front of her, or at her side. For reproductions of some of these photographs see the Appendix, p. 328.

In the former case, when the materialisation was fully formed, traces more or less marked of the original cord of substance could be seen.

The materialised forms, photographs of which were given in my study on so-called Supernormal Physiology and are reproduced at the end of this volume, were remarkable from several points of view.

1. They were always three-dimensional. During the séances I could convince myself of this by sight, and on several occasions by touch. Moreover, the relief is evident in the stereoscopic pictures taken.

2. The different faces in this series presented some similarities together with great differences:—
   Differences in the features;
   Differences in the size of the forms, some less than natural size, but of dimensions variable from one séance to another, and in the course of the same séance;

Differences in the perfection of the features, these being sometimes quite regular, in other cases defective;

Differences in the degree of materialisation, which was sometimes complete; sometimes incomplete, with rudiments of substance; sometimes merely indicated.

I wish to call attention to the interesting nature, from every point of view, of these rudiments of substance. The importance of rudiments in ' metapsychical embryology ' is comparable with their importance in normal embryology. They give evidence as to the origin and the genesis of the formations.

The better materialised the forms were, the more power of self-direction (*autonomie*) they seemed to have. They evolved round Eva, sometimes at some distance from her. One of these faces appeared first at the opening of the curtain, of natural size, very beautiful and with a remarkably life-like appearance.

At another séance, through the curtain of the cabinet, I could feel with my hands the contact of a human body which caused the curtain to undulate. (Eva was stretched out in the arm-chair, in full sight, and her hands were held.)

It is needless to say that the usual precautions were rigorously observed during the séances in my laboratory. On coming into the room where the séances were held, and to which I alone had previous access, the medium was completely undressed in my presence, and dressed in a tight garment, sewn up the back and at the wrists; the hair, and the cavity of the mouth were examined by me and my collaborators before and after the séances. Eva was walked backwards to the wicker chair in the dark cabinet; her hands were always held in full sight outside the curtains; and the room was always quite well lit during the whole time. I do not merely say, ' There was no trickery '; I say ' There was no possibility of trickery.'[1] Further, and I cannot repeat it too often, nearly always the materialisations took place under my own eyes, and I have observed their genesis and their whole development.

Well constituted organic forms having all the appearance of life, are often replaced by incomplete formations. The relief is often wanting and the forms are flat. There are some that are partly flat and partly in relief, I have seen in certain cases, a hand or a face appear flat, and then, under my eyes assume the three dimensions, entirely or partially. The incomplete forms are sometimes smaller than natural size, being occasionally miniatures.

Instead of being apparent by an alteration in height, breadth, or thickness, the incompleteness of the formations is often manifest by deficiencies: the materialisations are of natural size, but show gaps in their structure.

Dr Schrenck-Notzing, by taking simultaneous stereoscopic photographs from the front, the side, and the back, has seen that usually only the first reveal a complete materialisation; the dorsal region being in the condition of a mass of amorphous substance.

I have personally remarked the same thing.

It is not improbable that the loose veils, turbans, and similar drapery with which ‘phantoms’ so often appear, mask defects or gaps in the newly-formed organism.

There are all possible gradations between the complete and the incomplete organic forms, and they develop under the eyes of the observers.

Along with these complete and incomplete forms it is necessary to mention another strange category which

---

[1] I am, moreover, glad to testify that Eva has always shown, in my presence, absolute experimental honesty. The intelligent and self-sacrificing resignation with which she submitted to all control and the truly painful tests of her mediumship, deserve the real and sincere gratitude of all men of science worthy of the name.

covers imitations of organs. They are true *simulacra.*
There are *simulacra* of fingers, having the general form
but without warmth, flexibility, or joints; *simulacra* of
faces like masks, or as if cut out of paper; tufts of hair
adhering to undefined formations, etc.

These *simulacra*, whose reality is undeniable (a
point which is of great importance) have disconcerted
and perplexed many observers. ' One would think,'
said M. de Fontenay, ' that some kind of malicious sprite
was mocking the observers.'

But really these *simulacra* may be easily explained.
They are the products of a force whose metapsychic
output is weak and whose means of execution are weaker
still. It does what it can. It rarely succeeds, precisely
because its activity, directed outside the normal lines,
has no longer the certainty which the normal biologic
impulse gives to physiological activity.

The fact that normal physiology also has its *simulacra*
enables us to understand this better. Besides well-
developed organic formations and complete fœtal growths
there are miscarriages, monstrosities, and aberrant forms.
Nothing is more curious in this respect than the dermoid
cysts in which are found hair, teeth, viscera, and even
more or less complete fœtal forms. Like normal
physiology, the so-called supernormal has its complete
and aborted forms, its monstrosities, and its dermoid
cysts. The parallelism is complete.

The disappearance of materialised forms is at least
as curious as their appearance. This disappearance is
sometimes instantaneous, or nearly so. In less than a
second the form whose presence was evident to sight
and touch, has disappeared. In other cases the disappearance is gradual; the return to the original
substance and its reabsorption into the body of the
medium can be observed by the same stages as its
production. In other cases again the disappearance
takes place, not by a return to the original substance,

but by progressive diminution of its perceptible characteristics, the visibility slowly lessens, the contours are
blurred, effaced, and vanish.

During the whole time that the materialisation lasts
it is in obvious physiological and psychological relation
with the medium. The physiological connection may
sometimes be perceived as a thin cord of the substance
linking the form to the medium, a link which may be
compared to the umbilical cord that unites the embryo
to the mother. Even when this cord is not seen the
physiological relation is close. Every impression received
by the ectoplasm [1] reacts on the medium, and *vice versa*;
the extreme reflex sensitiveness of the forms is closely
connected with that of the medium. Everything goes
to prove that the ectoplasm is, in a word, the medium
herself, partially exteriorised. I am speaking, of course,
only from the physiological point of view and not at
present of the purely psychological side of the matter.

Such are the facts. It remains to interpret them, if
possible. Of course, no claim can be advanced to define
in a few words and off-hand what Life is! It is sufficient
at the outset to state the terms of the problem clearly.

2.—THE UNITY OF ORGANIC SUBSTANCE

The first term of that problem relates to the actual
constitution of living matter. The study of supernormal
physiology from this point of view confirms the results
of profound research in normal physiology; both tend
to establish the concept of the unity of organic substance.
In the foregoing experiments we have seen first of all,
exteriorised from the medium's body, a single unique
substance, from which were derived different ideoplastic [2] forms. This unique substance we have seen

[1] Gr. ἐκτός, outside; πλάσμα, a thing formed; the exteriorised substance.
[2] Ideoplastic = moulded by an idea.

many times organise and transform itself under our eyes. We have seen a hand emerge from a mass of the substance; we have seen a white mass become a face; we have seen in a few moments the representation of a head give place to that of a hand; we have been able, by the concordant evidence of sight and touch, to perceive the passage of the inorganic amorphous substance into a formal organic representation having for the moment all the attributes of life—in flesh and bone, to use a popular expression. We have seen these representations disappear, melt into the original substance and be re-absorbed into the body of the medium. Therefore, in supernormal physiology there are not diverse substances, bony, muscular, visceral, or nervous, as the substrata of different organic formations; there is simply one substance, unique and basic, as the substratum of organic life.

It is precisely the same in normal physiology; though this is less apparent. It is nevertheless evident in certain cases. The same phenomenon takes place, as has already been said, in the closed chrysalis of the insect as in the dark cabinet at the séance. Histolysis reduces the greater part of its organs and its different parts into a single substance which will materialise into the organs and different parts of the adult form. The same phenomenon belongs to both physiologies; the parallel is legitimate and complete.

Only ordinary semblances can be set in opposition to this concept of the unity of organic matter. First the commonplace physiology of daily experience; this superficial semblance proves nothing, and observation shows that it is illusory. Physico-chemical appearances are just as misleading.

Analyses of the exteriorised substance are, of course, not to be had. The moral impossibility of amputating from the medium's ectoplasm a portion which might grievously injure or kill her, will always prevent this.

We therefore are ignorant of the exact chemical composition of this substance. Is it decomposable into the various simple substances which we find in the living body—carbon, oxygen, hydrogen, iron, nitrogen, phosphorus? Does it imply an absolute unitary atom? We do not know, and it matters little. What we do know is that it shows biologic unity.

In fine: everything in biology takes place as if the physical being were formed of a single primordial substance; organic forms are mere representations.

Therefore, the first term of the biological problem is the essential unity of organic substance.

3.—THE EVIDENCE OF A SUPERIOR DYNAMISM

The second term is implied by the necessity of admitting a superior, organising, centralising, and directing dynamism.

The necessity of this notion follows from the whole of our physiological knowledge.

It has already been said that only this notion explains the mechanism of life, the specific form, the maintenance of the personality, and its organic repair. This notion of a superior dynamism is forced upon us by a study of embryonic and post-embryonic development, and especially by a consideration of animal metamorphoses. Finally, it has been definitely and absolutely demonstrated by the dematerialisations and rematerialisations of the insect in its chrysalis and of the medium in her dark cabinet.

In the two latter cases no further doubt or discussion is possible: the facts prove that the constituent molecules of the organic complex have no absolute specificity; that their relative specificity proceeds entirely from the dynamic or ideal mould which conditions them, and

makes from them visceral, muscular, or nervous substance, etc., and gives to them definite form, position,
and functions.

In a word, everything takes place in normal and
supernormal physiology as if the organic complex were
built up, organised, directed, and maintained by a
superior dynamism. This is the second term of the
biologic problem.

4.—THE CONDITIONING OF THE DYNAMISM BY THE IDEA.

There is a third term, the most important of any:
the directing dynamism itself obeys a directing idea.
This directing idea is found in all biological creations,
whether in the normal constitution of an organism or in
the abnormal, and more or less complex, materialisation.
It reveals a well-defined goal. The directing idea does
not always reach this goal; the result of its activity is
often imperfect. As may be seen both in normal and
supernormal physiology, it sometimes produces fully
developed forms, sometimes abortions or monstrosities,
sometimes even *simulacra*; but whether it attains completeness or not, the directing idea is always manifest.
This is so evident that the right word, applicable to the
phenomena of materialisation, has been found instinc-
tively. That word is 'ideoplasticity,' to which has been
added 'teleplasticity' to describe the same phenomenon
when occurring at a distance from the decentralised or
dematerialised organism.

What is the full meaning of this word? It means
the modelling of living matter by an idea. The notion
of ideoplasticity forced upon us by the facts is of con-
spicuous importance; the idea is no longer a product
of matter. On the contrary, it is the idea that moulds
matter and gives form and attributes to it.

In other words, matter—the unique substance—is resolved by final analysis into a superior dynamism which conditions it, and this dynamism is itself dependent on the idea.

This is nothing less than the complete reversal of materialist philosophy. As Flammarion says in his admirable book, *Les Forces Naturelles Inconnues,* these manifestations 'confirm what we know from other sources: that the purely mechanical concept of nature is insufficient; and there is more in the universe than matter. It is not matter that governs the world, but a dynamic and psychic element.' This is so, the ideoplastic materialisations demonstrate that the living being can no longer be considered as a mere cellular complex. It appears primarily as a dynamo-psychism, and the cellular complex which is its body appears as the ideoplastic product of this dynamo-psychism. Thus the formations materialised in mediumistic séances arise from the same biological process as normal birth. They are neither more nor less miraculous or supernormal; they are equally so. The same ideoplastic miracle makes the hands, the face, the viscera, the tissues, and the entire organism of the fœtus at the expense of the maternal body, or the hands, the face, or the entire organs of a materialisation.

This singular analogy between normal and so-called supernormal physiology extends even to details; the ectoplasm is linked to the medium by a channel of nourishment, a true umbilical cord, comparable to that which joins the embryo to the maternal body. In certain cases the materialised forms appear in an ovoid of the substance. The following instance taken from my notebook is characteristic. 'On the lap of the medium there appears a white spot which very rapidly forms an irregular rounded mass like a ball of snow or cotton wool. Under our eyes the mass partly opens, divides into two parts, united by a band of substance; in one of them appears the admirably modelled features of a woman. The eyes especially have an intensely living expression. At the end of a few moments, the phenomenon fades, diminishes in visibility, and disappears.' I have also seen, on several occasions, a hand presented wrapped in a membrane closely resembling the placental membrance. The impression produced, both as to sight and touch, was precisely that of a hand presentation in childbirth, when the amnion is unbroken.

Another analogy with childbirth is that of pain. The moans and movements of the entranced medium remind one strangely of a woman in travail.

The proposed assimilation of normal to supernormal physiology is therefore legitimate, for it results from the examination of facts. It raises, however, some serious objections, which we shall briefly examine.

In the first place, it may be objected, that if normal and supernormal physiology both result from the same biologic process, whence comes their apparent diversity? Why is the one regular, and the other exceptional, cut off from the usual accessories of time, space, generative conditions, etc.? We reply that normal physiology is the product of organic activity such as evolution has made it. The creative and directing idea normally works in a given sense, that of the evolution of the species, and conforms to the manner of that evolution. Supernormal physiology, on the other hand, is the product of ideoplastic activity directed in a divergent manner by an abnormal effort of the directing idea.

To explain this activity, divergent from the usual conditions, there is no need to invoke a miraculous or supernormal agency. Science and philosophy are logically harmonised by an explanation at once more simple and more satisfying. These abnormal ideoplastic possibilities, these apparently mysterious powers over Matter, simply prove that the laws which preside over the material world have not the absolute and inflexible rigour which they were thought to have; they are only relative. Their action may be temporarily or accidentally modified or suspended.

5.—THE SECONDARY MODALITIES OF SUPERNORMAL PHYSIOLOGY

These notions as to the sequence and the facts of materialisation being established, it will be easy, conformably with our method, to understand the less complex facts of so-called supernormal physiology, which are so inexplicable when considered apart from other facts.

The phenomena of telekinesis (movement of objects without contact) are explicable by the action of the vital dynamism exteriorised and obeying a subconscious impulse.

The experiments by Ochorowicz[1] have clearly established the genesis of this phenomenon. They show the meaning, from this point of view, of the elementary forms of materialisation, the threads of substance and rigid rods, sometimes visible, sometimes invisible, proceeding from the fingers of the medium and serving as a substratum to the exteriorised dynamism. The facts of telekinesis, though less complex, are of no less importance than those of materialisation. I do not think it necessary to describe them, but simply refer the reader to special works on the subject.[2]

---

[1] *Annales des Sciences Psychiques.*

[2] See especially the luminous report of M. Courtier on the experiments made by the Psychological Institute with the medium Eusapia Palladino in 1905, 1906, 1907, on the premises of the Institute, by MM. D'Arsonval, Gilbert Ballet, M. et Mme Curie, Bergson, Ch. Richet, and de Gramont. Here, for instance, are the accounts given by M. Courtier of two of these experiments :—

1. 'At the fourth séance of 1905, a table weighing 15 lb with a weight of 22 lb. placed on it, was twice completely raised for several seconds. This was also done at the sixth séance, when the feet of the table near the subject were encased in a sheath. . . .

'At the moment of the raising of the table, M. D'Arsonval and M. Ballet were completely controlling the hands and knees of Eusapia, and

The phenomena of stigmatisation and affections of the skin effected by suggestion or auto-suggestion, are but elementary ideoplastic effects much more simple than materialisations, though of the same order.

Miraculous healing, so called, is a result of the same ideoplasticity directed by suggestion or auto-suggestion in a sense favourable to organic repair, and concentrating for this purpose all the energies of the vital dynamism. It is to be remarked that this subconscious and recuperative ideoplastic force is much more active in the lower animals than in man; no doubt because with him cerebral activity engrosses the greater part of his vital activity. There is no miracle in ascribing to the human organism some part of the dynamic and ideoplastic action which is the rule in the lower grades of the animal scale.

The phenomena of mimetism so frequent in animal forms and so mysterious in their mechanism, may also be

no contact was made with the legs of the table. . . . We must also remember the complete levitations of tables at the end of séances when every one was standing up, under conditions of control of which precise and circumstantial stenographic notes were taken.

'The tables were then raised to greater heights than during the séances, as much as 80 centimetres to a metre from the floor, the hands and feet of the subject being rigorously controlled.

2. Movements of the small table towards and away from the medium. 'This table advances and retreats . . . when it advances towards her it might be imagined that in spite of stringent precautions against fraud, she uses a thread fine enough to be invisible and draws the table by this means. . . . But how can its retreat be explained? Let us suppose that one of those present should take Eusapia's place and act by ordinary means. Only one procedure can be imagined—to hold a rigid rod and push and pull the table by its means. But a rigid rod, however thin, could not escape the sight of closely attentive observers. There could be no question of retreat obtained by passing the thread over a pulley or some projection from the wall, which would involve preparation. The recording apparatus was, of course, entirely motionless; and on the other hand any supposition of collective hallucination must be set aside, as the Marey's cylinder recorded the displacements of the table. Further, it is to be observed that this is no question of attractions and repulsions like those of a magnet, always quick and in a fixed direction. The table is moved relatively slowly, and its path is curved and irregular. It avoids obstacles to reach a final position '

I have cited these observations of the skilled experimenters of the Psychological Institute, not for their special value, which is inconsiderable in view of the great variety and complexity of the phenomena of telekinesis; but only in order to give one undeniable and irrefutable instance.

explained by subconscious ideoplasticity. Instinct would direct the ideoplasticity in a given direction and the effects would be fixed by selection and adaptation.[1]

The table below shows in a striking manner the contrast between the new and the classical concepts.

6—THE PHYSIOLOGICAL CONCEPT OF THE INDIVIDUAL

Summary.

Classical Concepts.

The organism is a mere cellular complex. The vital dynamism is but the resultant synthesis of biologic sequence and physiological functions.

Primordial vital fact:
        mysterious.
Specific form: mysterious.
Formation of the organism: mysterious.
Maintenance of the organism: vague and insufficient hypotheses.
Repair of the organism: vague and insufficient hypotheses.
Embryonic development: mysterious.
Post-embryonic development: mysterious.
Metamorphoses:
        mysterious.
Histolysis of the Insect: mysterious.

New Concept.

The organic complex, its physiological functions, and all the vital process, are conditioned by a superior dynamism.

All these phenomena are easily explicable by the action of a superior dynamism, generating, directing, centralising, preserving, and repairing the organism. The concrete notion of this dynamism must be substituted for the abstract notion of a directive idea.

[1] See, in this connection, *Les Miracles de la Volonté*, by E. Duchatel and Warcollier.

Sensorial manifestations outside the organs of sense: mysterious.	All these phenomena are explicable by the action of the vital dynamism act-
Motor manifestations outside the muscular system: mysterious.	ing outside the organism. This dynamism conditions the organism in place of
Ideoplastic manifestations: mysterious.	being conditioned by it. It can therefore separate
Materialisations: mysterious.	itself from it, and even partially disorganise and reorganise it in diverse forms and representations.

It is clear that the mystery in which physiology was enveloped is in some measure dispelled; the triple concept of the unity of substance, the organising dynamism, and the conditioning of this latter by the Idea, enables us to make a decided step towards truth.

But how much still remains unknown!

What are the origin, the end, and the exact nature of this dynamo-psychism which organises, centralises and directs the cellular complex? How does this mysterious dynamo-psychism exist potentially in the fertilised ovum, in the cutting, or in the bud, whence a new creature will grow? What, in a word, is its exact relation to all vital process? We have spoken of ideo-plastic power. But what exactly is this power? The directing idea, and the ideoplastic capacities which normal and supernormal physiology reveal, do not depend on the consciousness in which we are accustomed to sum up and localise our 'Self.' They arise from the depths of a mysterious and impenetrable unconscious-ness.

The conscious directing will of our being has no action on the great organic functions, and does not come into play for the ideoplastic materialisations. These, produced at the expense of the substance of the organism, seem, nevertheless, often if not always, to be directed and formed outside that organism by entities distinct from it.

Will it then be said that to speak of ideoplasticity, the modelling of matter by the Idea, and of an organising dynamo-psychism is only to push the mystery further back, not to solve it? Will it be said that the enigma is not less insoluble for being put back one step? Insoluble! By no means!

The truth is, once more, that starting from the elementary but essential data which have emerged from our demonstration, the biological problem becomes terribly complex.

It is not related to physiology alone, but to psychology, to all the natural sciences, and to philosophy.

In a word, we are dealing no longer with Life alone, but with the whole constitution and evolution of the universe and the individual.

Before closing the reference to physiology we must enter upon a new and larger application of the synthetic method. We must interrogate first psychology, and then philosophy; the partial answers which we now feel the want of, will be given by the general answer to the great enigma, which is the aim of the present work.

CHAPTER III

THE bankruptcy of the classical concept of physiological individuality has now been demonstrated. We shall next show that the classical psychological concept is equally defective.

It is based on two principal notions:—

1. The notion of the Self as a synthesis of states of consciousness.
2. The notion of the close dependence of all that constitutes a thinking being on the functions of the nervous centres.

These two essential propositions will now be successively examined.

I.—THE SELF CONSIDERED AS A SYNTHESIS OF STATES OF CONSCIOUSNESS

In succession to the physiological concept quoted from M. Dastre (Ch. I.), let us consider the psychological concept which we borrow from M. Ribot.[1]

' *The organism, and the brain which is its supreme representation, are the real personality*, containing in itself the remnants of what we have been and the possibilities of what we shall be. The individual character in its entirety is inscribed there, its active and passive aptitudes, its sympathies and anti-pathies, its genius, its wisdom, or its foolishness, its virtues and its vices, its torpor or its activity. That

[1] Ribot: *Les Maladies de la Personnalité.* (Italics are Dr Geley's.)

74

part which emerges into consciousness is slight in comparison with that which, though always acting, remains buried. *The conscious is always but a small part of the psychic personality.*

'The unity of the Self is not therefore that single entity claimed by spiritualists, manifest in many phenomena, *but the co-ordination of a number of states perpetually renewed*, having as their only link the vague sensations of our bodies. This unity does not proceed from above downwards, but from below upwards; it is not an initial but a terminal point. . . .'

'The Self is a co-ordination. It oscillates between two extreme points at each of which it ceases to exist—perfect unity or absolute lack of co-ordination.

'The last word in all this is; that the consensus of consciousness being subordinate to the consensus of the organism, the problem of the unity of the Self is, in its simplest form, a biological problem. It is for biology to explain, if it can, the genesis of organisms and the solidarity of their parts. The psychological interpretation can but follow.'

Le Dantec comes to the same conclusions.[1] Individual consciousness, according to him, is but the sum of consciousness of all the neurons, so that 'our Self will be determined by the number, nature, dispositions, and reciprocal connections among the elements of our nervous system.'

It appears then that for the contemporaneous classical psycho-physiology the conscious Self has no essential unity; it is a mere co-ordination of states, just as the organism to which it is linked is a mere co-ordination of cells.

The objections which arise to this are the same as those which hold with regard to the physiological concept of the individual; they take no account of the need for

[1] Le Dantec: *Le Déterminisme Biologique et la Personnalité Conscient; L'Individualité; Théorie nouvelle de la Vie.*

75

a directing and centralising principle, creating the Self and maintaining its permanence.

Le Dantec thus explains the permanence of the Self.

> 'Individual consciousness,' he says, 'is not invariable; it is slowly and continuously modified along with the incessant changes produced in our organism by the functional assimilation which accompanies all our acts; it is this which constitutes the variation of our personality; but in accordance with the laws of assimilation and the specific coherence of plastic substances, there will be continuity in time between these successive personalities; and it is for this reason that the psychological Self accompanies the physiological individual through all its unceasing modifications from birth to death.'

By a reaction against the old vitalist or spiritualist hypotheses, this concept of the Self as an elementary synthesis is accepted by the vast majority of contemporary psycho-physiologists, all their efforts being directed to force it into agreement with the usual consciousness of personal unity. Hoeffding,[1] Paulhan,[2] Wundt,[3] and many others have rivalled each other in this impossible task. To get over the difficulty they sometimes have recourse to psycho-metaphysical entities. Claude Bernard in physiology invoked the 'Directing Idea.' Wundt, in psychology, attributes the unifying function to what he calls 'apperception.'

These subtleties have not advanced the matter a single step. 'Whatever point of view we take,' says Boutroux, 'multiplicity does not contain a reason for unity.'[4]

[1] Hoeffding: *Esquisse d'une Psychologie Fondée sur l'Expérience.*
[2] Paulhan: *L'Activité Mentale.*
[3] Wundt: *Physiologische Psychologie.*
[4] Boutroux: *De la Contingence des Lois de la Nature.*

This is obvious, and the time has come to draw the logical inference from this aphorism. To do this it is necessary to get rid of all abstractions, preconceived ideas, and vain disputes over names.

The question is very simple and admits of no equivocal answer: Is the Self merely a synthesis of elements, or is it not?

Is this synthesis the sum of the consciousness of neurons closely and exclusively linked to the functioning of the nervous centres, or is it not? Yes, or No?

This is what we have to examine by the light of all psychological facts.

2.—THE SELF AS A PRODUCT OF THE FUNCTION OF THE NERVE-CENTRES

The classical concept is based on the old notion of psycho-physiological parallelism, in support of which the following arguments are adduced.

The development of conscious intelligence accompanies the development of the organism, and its later progressive diminution is parallel with senile decay.

Psychological activity is proportional to the activity of the nervous centres.

Psychological activity disappears in the repose of those centres in sleep or in syncope.

Psychological activity implies the normal function of the nervous centres; lesions of these centres, infection, or serious intoxication affecting the brain, disturb, restrain, or suppress psychic action altogether.

This psychic action is closely conditioned by the extent of the organic powers and is inseparable from them. The materials which the intellect uses come from the senses: ' *Nihil est in intellectu quod non prius fuerit in sensu.*' Therefore the range of the senses limits the range of conscious intelligence.

Finally, all psychological faculties arise from clear and definable cerebral localities. The destruction of one of these centres extinguishes the corresponding faculty.

Such is the classical teaching so long considered unquestionable, and generally unquestioned. Nevertheless serious difficulties have recently arisen and forced themselves on our attention.

3.—FACTS OF NORMAL PSYCHOLOGY AT ISSUE WITH THE
THESIS OF PARALLELISM

In the first place the parallelism, analysed by the light of new facts does not seem so close as was thought; the attempts at cerebral localisation which promised so well, have been checked if not ended. The work of Pierre Marie, and the thesis of Moutier have proved that the best established localisation, that of speech in the third frontal on the left side is not rigidly correct. Speech, like all other functions, requires that several centres should work together.

Certain pathological cases have proved that the excision of large portions of the brain in the very parts which were thought essential, may be followed by no grave psychic disturbance, and no restriction of personality.

Here is an abstract of the principal cases, quoted from the *Annales des Sciences Psychiques* of Jan., 1917.[1]

' M. Edmond Perrier brought before the French Academy of Sciences at the session of December 22nd, 1913, the case observed by Dr R. Robinson; of a man who lived a year, nearly without pain, and without any mental disturbance, with a brain reduced to pulp by a huge purulent abscess. In July, 1914,

[1] Summary by M. de Vesme.

78

From the Unconscious to the Conscious

Dr Hallopeau reported to the Surgical Society an operation at the Necker Hospital, the patient being a young girl who had fallen out of a carriage on the Metropolitan Railway. After trephining, it was observed that a considerable portion of cerebral substance had been reduced literally to pulp. The wound was cleansed, drained, and closed, and the patient completely recovered.'

The following report of the session of the Academy of Sciences at Paris, March 24th, 1917, appeared in the Paris newspapers:—

'*Partial removal of the brain.*—Following on previous communications on this operation, which runs counter to ideas generally received, Dr A. Guépin of Paris communicates a fresh study on this question. He mentions that his first patient, the soldier Louis R——, to-day a gardener near Paris, in spite of the loss of a very large part of his left cerebral hemisphere (cortex, white substance, central nuclei, etc.), continues to develop intellectually as a normal subject, in despite of the lesions and the removal of convolutions considered as the seat of essential functions. From this typical case, and nine analogous cases by the same operator, known to the Academy, Dr Guépin says that it may now safely be concluded:—

(1). That the partial amputation of the brain in man is possible, relatively easy, and saves certain wounded men whom received theory would regard as condemned to certain death, or to incurable infirmities.

'(2). That these patients seem not in any way to feel the loss of such a cerebral region.

'This study is referred to Dr Laveran for a separate report.'

This question is obviously of such importance in

the present connection and from the general human point of view, that we think it useful to translate and reproduce here, part of an address by Dr Augustin Iturricha, President of the Anthropological Society of Sucre (Chuquisaca, Bolivia), at a session of that society:—

' Here, moreover, are facts still more surprising from the clinic of Dr Nicholas Ortiz, which Dr Domingo Guzman has had the kindness to communicate to me. The authenticity of the observations cannot be doubted, they proceed from two authorities of high standing in our scientific world.

' The first case refers to a boy of 12 to 14 years of age, who died in full use of his intellectual faculties although the encephalic mass was completely detached from the bulb, in a condition which amounted to real decapitation. What must have been the stupefaction of the operators at the autopsy, when, on opening the cranial cavity, they found the meninges heavily charged with blood, and a large abscess involving nearly the whole cerebellum, part of the brain and the protuberance. Nevertheless the patient, shortly before, was known to have been actively thinking. They must necessarily have wondered how this could possibly have come about. The boy complained of violent headache, his temperature was not below 39°C. (102.2°F.); the only marked symptoms being dilatation of the pupils, intolerance of light, and great cutaneous hyperesthesia. Diagnosed as meningo-encephalitis.

' The second case is not less unusual. It is that of a native aged 45 years, suffering from cerebral contusion at the level of Broca's convolution, with fracture of the left temporal and parietal bones. Examination of the patient revealed rise of temperature, aphasia, and hemiplegia of the right side. The director and physicians of the clinic undertook an interesting experiment in re-education of speech; they succeeded in getting him to pronounce consciously and intelligibly eight to ten words. Unfortunately the experiment could not be continued, the patient after twenty days showed a great rise in temperature, acute cephalalgia, and died thirty hours later. The autopsy revealed a large abscess occupying nearly the whole left cerebral hemisphere. In this case also we must ask, How did this man manage to think? What organ was used for thought after the destruction of the region which, according to physiologists, is the seat of intelligence?

' A third case, coming from the same clinic, is that of a young agricultural labourer, 18 years of age. The *post mortem* revealed three communicating abscesses, each as large as a tangerine orange, occupying the posterior portion of both cerebral hemispheres, and part of the cerebellum. In spite of these the patient thought as do other men, so much so that one day he asked for leave to settle his private affairs. He died on re-entering the hospital.'

Psycho-physiological parallelism is therefore entirely relative. This is not all. Many other objections arise counter to the classical concept, without going outside commonplace and ordinary psychology. M. Dwelshauvers has summed up clearly the chief of these objections in his book, *L'Inconscient*.

In the first place the localisations are simply and solely anatomical.

' To start the cerebral cells of the localised centres into action, presupposes a preliminary excitation, and this excitation arises from a psycho-physiological act which cannot be localised.

' There are no psycho-physiological localisations; localisation is purely fantastic.

' And if it is impossible to localise the least sensation, it is much more so to assign determinate areas in the cerebral cortex to what used to be termed " faculties "; abstraction, will, sensation, imagination, and memory.'

Therefore the materialist hypotheses which made thought a secretion of the brain, and would assign centres to mental faculties, are erroneous.

' There are no special nervous centres, one presiding over abstraction, another over the emotions, another over memory, another over imagination. This cerebral mythology is given up; our spiritual activity does not obey local divinities erected by credulous scientists in the different corners of their cerebral schemes.'

Further, it seems really impossible ' to explain mental by cerebral activity, and to reduce the former to the latter.' In fact, ' each time that the thinking being is not limited to repetition, but acquires some new thing, he transcends the mechanism resident in him . . . the effort goes beyond the acquirement; he combines what has already been acquired with the new impressions; and this implies an increase of activity on his part. The cerebral mechanism lags behind the intelligence. . . . In this activity, which is really progressive and characteristic of human effort, there is a synthesis perpetually renewed which is not a repetition of what has already been acquired. This effort, which is proper to mental life, is to be observed among animals also, when, being placed in unusual conditions, they modify their habits and adapt themselves to the altered circumstances. . . .'

From the Unconscious to the Conscious

'Therefore, there is no strict parallelism between the biological and the psychological sequence; the latter transcends the former.' [1]

There is a final and important argument.

> 'Education, from first sensations up to the grouping of ideas, consists (as to its anatomical and physiological conditions) in the association of numerous elements, none of which is in itself, properly speaking, psychological, but which are, in fact, exceedingly complex movements. In reference to them psychological activity appears indeed as a synthesis, *but this synthesis is different from the elements of which it is composed, it is other than those elements.'* [1]

The arguments we have now reviewed displace the old absolute psycho-physiological parallelism. They displace it even without going outside current commonplace psychology, which is to-day known to be only a part, and the less important part, of individual psychism. We have kept our summary of the difficulties of the classical theory within the limits of its own method, by keeping to the analysis of elementary facts. We shall now see what results are given by the opposite method adopted in this work; we shall consider first the highest and most complex qualities of the psychological being, namely, its subconscious psychism.

[1] My italics, G. G.

CHAPTER IV

SUBCONSCIOUS PSYCHOLOGY

I.—CRYPTOPSYCHISM

It has been said that 'the subconscious is *the* problem of psychology, rather than a psychological problem.'

This is profoundly true; every investigation, every theory, every philosophical concept which does not allow to the Unconscious its legitimate part (which is the weightier part), is at once falsified in its essence and in its teaching. Facts immediately rise up against it and nullify it.

It is only in our own day that subconscious psychology has forced itself on scientific criticism. Entirely disregarded till the nineteenth century, it was then considered only as the anomalous outcome of disease or accident; it now asserts its increasing importance, and henceforward all researches and all new discoveries form parts of its domain and extend its reach.

We are compelled to allow to the Unconscious a primary function in instinct, in inborn character, in latent psychism, and in genius. In every modern work that appears, subconscious psychism takes a larger and larger place and is seen to be infinitely complex and varied. Its functions are shown to be clearly preponderant in all the departments of intellectual and affectional life.

The well-known work of Dr Chabaneix, *Le Subconscient chez les Artistes, les Savants, et les Ecrivains,* gives a certain number of striking examples. Indeed examples are innumerable; it may be said that there is

84

no artist, man of science, or writer of any distinction, however little disposed to self-analysis, who is not aware by personal experience of the unequalled importance of the subconscious.[1]

This subconscious influence is sometimes imperative and supreme; it is then called 'inspiration.'

/ Under its influence the artist or the inventor produces his work (sometimes a masterpiece) at one stroke, without pondering over it or reasoning about it; it often transcends his design without effort on his part. The subconscious inspiration is sometimes experienced in sleep in the form of lucid and connected dreams./

More frequently the Conscious and the Unconscious would seem to collaborate. The work is initiated by an act of the will, and completed partly by considered effort and partly by spontaneous and involuntary inspiration. This collaboration sometimes ends in results quite different from those at first intended. It is very rare that any great artist or writer draws up the plan of his work and follows it faithfully, from beginning to end, composing regularly and without interruption, as a mason builds a house.

A great artist works irregularly; the plan as first conceived undergoes great and sometimes complete alteration. The outlines do not follow one from another regularly from the beginning to completion; they vary according to the inspiration of the moment. In fact the artist is not master of his inspiration; it is sometimes absent; and if he persists, he will on that day produce only moderate work which he will afterwards reject.

If he is wise enough not to persist, he will find himself able on some other day to complete the work as if by enchantment, for the subconscious activity has proceeded during repose; especially during sleep.

---

[1] I think it needless to cite well-known examples Besides the work of Dr Chabaneix, M. Dwelshauvers' *L'Inconscient* may be referred to; and generally, other works on the same subject.

From the Unconscious to the Conscious

An artist is quite aware whether he is inspired or not. If he is, the work proceeds easily, almost without check, to his complete satisfaction or even exultation. If he is not, he experiences fatigue not only of mind, but of body also; he makes constant false starts, and his wearisome and painful efforts are accompanied with a sense of powerlessness and discouragement. Inspiration does not come from effort; on the contrary, it comes often when least expected, and especially when the mind is at ease; not during the times of connected work.

There are writers and artists who always keep a notebook handy in order to note down whatever the caprice of inspiration may whisper, some verses to a poet; a philosophic point to a thinker; the solution of some problem vainly attempted, to a man of science; a happy phrase to a literary man, etc., etc. Thus they keep on the watch for the beneficent action of inspiration; in the study, or during a walk; alone or in a crowd; in bed, or in the train which takes them on a journey; in the carriage on the way to business; in the midst of some social reunion; in the course of some commonplace conversation to which they are barely listening and answering by monosyllables; sometimes in conscious dreams.

In the most remarkable cases of subconscious collaboration, it seems that the work consciously begun is elaborated little by little in the subconsciousness, with a definite plan, with all its divisions and details, till it reaches completion. But these divisions and details come only by degrees and not in a regular order and sequence. It is only when the work is far advanced that the plan and the arrangement of its parts appear. The action resembles putting together a kind of subconscious puzzle, and the artist or the writer (and it is more especially to writers that we refer) has to make an effort to allocate correctly the pages or the phrases which have been subconsciously inspired.

86

When the work is finished it is found to be quite different from the plan sketched out; but it may give an impression of beauty and order above the writer's own powers; it seems to be partly strange to him and he may even admire it as if it were not his own.

There are all possible degrees and modes in this collaboration of the conscious and the unconscious. Certain artists and writers, usually (but not always) of moderate ability, do not perceive this. They quite sincerely think that all they produce is the result of their own endeavours. Others perceive it more or less and use it without questioning its origin. Others again, understand it so well that they restrain effort, and are quite aware whether or not they are making progress or are straying into byways.

Inspiration, however, except in very rare cases, does not dispense from effort. It simply fertilises effort and reduces it to a minimum. Effort, however, cannot dispense with inspiration, and it is in the collaboration of both that the highest and best work is produced. Without rationalised effort and conscious control, even the inspiration of genius is liable to stray. Disordered and uncontrolled inspiration may result in fine work disfigured by want of proportion, by want of order, by redundance, errors, and mistakes.

Just as a virgin forest presents magnificent foliage against the sky, and dark impenetrable thickets stifled by parasitic vegetation, so in a powerful work the beauty of genius may disappear under clumsy errors and aberrations resulting from creative inspiration unrestrained by sane and healthy consciousness.

Side by side with inspiration must be placed Intuition, also subconscious and all-powerful, on the one condition that it is under due control by reasoned judgment.

The data of intuition lie beyond facts, experiences, and reflection, and surpass them all. Intuition is the very essence of subconsciousness. Outlined only in the animal, where it appears as instinct, it acquires in man the higher aspect of genius.

The subconscious reveals itself not by inspiration and intuition alone, but also by frequent intrusions of emotional, æsthetic, or religious thought. Unexpected decisions, abrupt changes of opinion, many unreasoned feelings, originate largely in subconsciousness or from subconscious collaboration.

Who can say if even some ideas which seem to us the result of reason, may not be the flowering of an invisible and subconscious growth?

Finally, all the foundations of our being, that which is the principal part of the Self, innate capacities, good or bad dispositions, character—all that makes the essential difference between one mind and another—all that is not the results of personal effort, of education, or of surrounding examples, are modes of subconsciousness.

Effort, education, and surrounding examples may develop that which is inborn and essential, they cannot create it. The subconsciousness whose activity constitutes that cryptopsychism whose far-reaching effects we have reviewed, is the innate and essential groundwork of our being.

2.—CRYPTOMNESIA

CRYPTOMNESIA—the subconscious memory—follows naturally on cryptopsychism.

In point of fact, the subconscious not only contains that which is psychically essential in the Self; it also preserves and conceals all that the Self seems to have acquired by conscious psychic action in the course of existence.

It does not forget; it keeps all, integrally.

Cryptomnesia may be observed both in normal and

in abnormal psychology; but it is naturally more prominent in the latter.

Flournoy[1] is perhaps the psychologist who of all others has studied cryptomnesia most thoroughly. The fact of the re-emergence of forgotten memories which the mind wrongly takes to be new and unpublished matter, is, he says, much more frequent than is supposed.

'Plain men, as well as great geniuses, are subject to these lapses of memory, bearing not on its actual content, since that very content reappears with distressing and treacherous accuracy, but on the local and temporary associations which would, if remembered, have caused its recognition as matter already seen, and would have prevented the user from decking himself in borrowed plumes. Helen Keller—the famous blind deaf-mute—who, at eleven years old, composed her story of the Frost-king, found herself most unjustly and cruelly accused of plagiarism because this story presented a marked likeness to a story which had been read to her three years before. Nietzsche's *Zarathustra* has been discovered to contain little details coming, unknown to him, from a work of Kerner's which he had studied when 12 to 15 years old. But it is among persons most disposed to mental dissociation and duplicate personality that cryptomnesia reaches a climax.'

A classical example of cryptomnesia in normal psychology is the instantaneous recollection of latent impressions at a time of violent psychological disturbance, such as may be produced by the sudden danger of accidental death. Cases have been cited in which all the events of a lifetime, all its acts and thoughts, even those which were insignificant and quite forgotten, are said to have passed through the mind.

[1] Flournoy : *Esprits et Mediums.*

Cryptomnesia may also appear in dreams.

The classical case of Delbœuf[1] is quite characteristic in this respect: in a complicated dream he saw, among other things, a plant with its botanical name, *Asplenium ruta muraria.* Now Delbœuf was totally ignorant of this name, or thought he was. After long search he found that two years before he had turned over the leaves of a botanical album and there had seen both the plant and the name, of which he had not thought again.

In hypnosis and connected states cryptomnesia sometimes is strikingly manifested. If the subject is carried back, spontaneously or by suggestion to a remote period of his life, all the forgotten impressions reappear and the psychism manifested is precisely that which he had at that age. The experiments of Janet, and, subsequently, those of de Rochas, on the regression of memory have brought this out clearly.

Sometimes the subject, in this state of regression to a former age, shows knowledge totally forgotten, such as a language learned in childhood. Pitres[2] cites the case of a patient, Albertine M., who thus used the *patois* of Saintonge, which she had only spoken in childhood. During this regressional delirium, says Pitres, 'she expressed herself in *patois*, and if we begged her to speak in French she invariably answered, always in *patois*, that she did not know the talk of the townspeople.'

Take, also, the famous case of one of Flournoy's subjects, who, in a state of mediumistic somnambulism, spoke in Sanskrit, a tongue of which he was completely ignorant, and had never learned. Flournoy, in spite of all his investigations, could never discover the origin of this phenomenon.[3]

It is in mediumship that cryptomnesia shows a climax. It may be the unsuspected source of quite stupefying messages.

[1] Quoted by M Dwelshauvers.
[2] Pitres: *L'Hystérie et l'Hypnotisme.*
[3] Flournoy: *Des Indes à la Planète Mars.*

90

M. Flournoy cites a number of facts which he attributes entirely to cryptomnesia,—mediums giving biographical details of persons unknown to them but which they may have unconsciously known from a forgotten glance at a newspaper which contained those details; mediums speaking fragments of a language of which they are ignorant simply because these phrases have fallen under their eyes on some forgotten occasion, etc., etc.

'In fine,' Flournoy concludes, 'by whatever mode the mnemonic content has been received, whether by reading, conversation, etc., it emerges in sensorial automatisms (visions, voices, etc.), in motor automatisms (raps or automatic writing), or in total automatisms (trances, controls, or somnambulistic personifications). This diversity, of course, is further complicated by the embroidery which the fancy of the medium adds to fragments properly referred to cryptomnesia.'

Among the examples given by Flournoy there are some of the most remarkable kind. Some are here quoted.

Case of Eliza Wood.—Mrs Wood, widowed in the previous week, received a visit from a friend, Mme Darel (the well-known authoress of Geneva), who possessed remarkable mediumistic faculties. Mme Darel brought to her, on behalf of the defunct, the following message, obtained at her table: 'Tell her to remember Easter Monday.' It was a striking allusion to an event known only to Mr and Mrs Wood, referring to a walk kept secret from their families, prior to their engagement, which had left an ineffaceable memory. This striking proof of identity convinced Mrs Wood, who soon had a second, still more valid, at the séances which she attended at Mme Darel's house. Mr Wood had died not long after their wedding trip, his widow thought he had left no will, and the search which she made was fruitless, till the day when she and Mme Darel were at the table, which, on the part of the defunct, rapped out: 'You will find something from me under a saucer in the drawer of the washstand.' She found there a sheet of paper constituting the document in question. She then remembered that when they were just starting on their journey, her husband had made her wait a moment while he returned on some pretext to their bedroom, evidently to write and hide his will there.'

'Now,' says M. Flournoy, 'there is nothing to prove that Mme Darel or one of her people, out for a walk on Easter Monday (which is a holiday) in the environs of Geneva, had not met the pair, or seen them from a distance, and this forgotten impression may have been the source of the message which so impressed the young widow; similarly the second message regarding the hidden will may well have been due to reminiscences and subconscious inferences of Mrs Wood's.'

Case of the Curé Burnet.—Flournoy's subject produced one day a message claiming to be from one Burnet, who had died a century previously, the curé of a commune in the department Haute Savoie. The researches of the professor showed the absolute identity of the writing and the signature to the message with that of the deceased clergyman.

How can this be explained? The medium, M. Flournoy supposes, had once, in childhood, passed through the commune where the curé had lived. He had (on Flournoy's hypothesis) seen on some document, such, for example, as an old marriage contract, the writing and the signature of the curé. He had not, however, the slightest recollection of this journey. It was therefore a question of some impression received without conscious knowledge forgotten, but yet intact, which, in the hypnotic state, had awaked this strange and perfect reminiscence.

Along with these remarkable examples which spiritualists attribute, not to cryptomnesia but to post-mortem manifestations, Flournoy gives many others, which, equally mysterious in appearance, certainly proceed from pure cryptomnesia; mediums giving from supposed defunct persons proofs of identity found on inquiry to be erroneous, but conformable to records which had appeared in such and such a newspaper which had evidently fallen under the eyes of the medium at some moment or other without arousing conscious attention.

However little philosophical thought one may bring to the study of subconscious psychology, what strikes one most forcibly is that it does not fall under any known physiological law. The same question inevitably recurs to the mind of the inquirer—why, and how, is it that the portion of the psychism which constitutes the more important part of the Self, remains cryptoid? Why, and how, does it come to pass that the consciousness and the will of the living being, without which there would be no Self, let go the major part of that Self? Whether the matter is cryptopsychic or cryptomnesic, the mystery is equally profound. It is physiologically impossible to understand how the conscious memory, under the control and the direction of the person, should be weak, untrustworthy, and decrepit, while the subconscious memory, only accessible incidentally or in abnormal or supernormal states, should seem both extensive and unfailing.

Nevertheless this is what everything tends to prove.

Yet more, the weakness and impotence of the normal memory is sometimes such that the subconscious knowledge or powers which escape from the direction of the Self appear totally strange to the individual and constitute a secondary consciousness.

In the bewildering complexity of the subconscious, there arise not only duplicate, but even multiple, personalities.

3.—ALTERATIONS OF PERSONALITY

The chief problems which are presented by the appearance of secondary personalities, are two, both equally difficult.

1. The problem of the psychological differences from the normal personality, differences not only of manner and will, but of general character, inclinations, faculties, and knowledge; differences occasionally so radical that they imply complete opposition and even hostility between the normal and the secondary personality.

2. The problem of the supernormal powers which are frequently linked with the manifestation of secondary personalities.

Now although there are numerous works on multiple personality, which have brought to light the frequency, the importance, and the many forms of these manifestations, they have done nothing towards the elucidation of these two problems.

They have only succeeded in showing the abyss that exists between the commonplace personalities of hypnotic suggestion, devoid of originality of any kind, and the psychic changes arising from pathological or traumatic causes on the one hand, and the autonomous and complete personalities which sometimes seem to occupy the whole psychic field of the subject, on the other.

They have, above all, shown the complete inability of the classical psycho-physiology to explain the supernormal faculties at all.

CHAPTER V

SUPERNORMAL psychology is a world whose exploration is hardly begun. Without entering here on an analytical description which the reader will find in special works, it is expedient to examine its principal aspects as a whole.

1.—SUPERNORMAL PHYSIOLOGY IS CONDITIONED BY SUPERNORMAL PSYCHOLOGY

Imprimis, supernormal physiology is conditioned by the supernormal psychology which has already been described.

All the phenomena of exteriorisation, telekinesis, mysterious action on matter, materialisation and ideoplasticity, in no way depend on the conscious will of the subject. They are always produced subconsciously; either, as it would seem, by the external will of an entity, or by a subconscious idea, or by a subconscious personality.

I do not, for the moment, insist further on this truth which is obvious to all observers in the supernormal domain. As I have shown in my book, *L'Être Subconscient*, supernormal physiology is merely an aspect and a province of supernormal psychology. It is inseparable from it, and cannot be observed or understood apart from it.

2.—MENTO-MENTAL ACTION

In the second place, supernormal psychology includes mento-mental action, by which is to be understood those

95

effects which are produced from mind to mind without any appreciable physical intermediary, such as thought-reading, mental suggestion, or telepathy. I see nothing to add to the summary of these reactions given in *L'Être Subconscient*, here reproduced. Thought-reading seems well established in hypnotic and mediumistic states. It is the convenient, (much too convenient since much-abused), explanation of many facts. It seems, up to a certain point, to be possible in the waking state, or at least in a state of hypnosis or auto-hypnosis so slight as to pass unperceived.

Outside hypnosis and mediumship, thought-reading is rarely observable in any satisfactory manner. Cases of alleged thought-reading obtained by contact between the agent and the subject, must be excluded, for these are often the results of divination by unconscious muscular movements.

Mental suggestion.—The possibility and reality of mental suggestion have been proved in the most rigorous manner.[1]

An order suggested by the magnetiser can be transmitted by a mere effort of the will, without any external manifestation, when the patient is in the hypnotic state.

Mental suggestion may be effected at a distance, sometimes at very considerable distances, and across material obstacles.

Telepathy.[2]—Telepathy consists essentially in the fact of a strong psychic impression generally unlooked for, produced in a normal person (either asleep or awake), which is found to coincide with a real distant event.

Sometimes the psychic impression constitutes the

[1] *Vide* the standard work of Dr Ochorowics : *La Suggestion Mentale*; all required proofs will be found therein.

[2] *Phantasms of the Living*, by Messrs Gurney, Myers, and Podmore, which contains 700 cases all well described and authenticated. See also Flammarion's book : *L'Inconnu et les Problèmes Psychiques*; also the file of *Revues Psychiques*, and more especially the *Annales des Sciences Psychiques*, which contains numerous very remarkable cases of telepathy.

whole fact. Sometimes it is accompanied by a vision which appears objective and external to the percipient.

Telepathy may be spontaneous or experimental.[1]

Spontaneous telepathy may be:—

(*a*) Relative to some event in the immediate future, *e.g.* presentiments, premonitions, premonitory visions, apparitions of the dying.

(*b*) Relating to the present or the recent past. Cases of ' second sight ' or intimations of distant events to persons in the normal state; apparitions of the dead a few moments, hours, or days after decease; cases of apparitions of a living person usually then in abnormal or pathologic sleep (lethargy, febrile delirium, or nervous disturbance, etc).

Most frequently the phenomenon refers to some person united to the percipient in more or less close bonds of affection. The cases usually relate to misfortunes; rarely to happy events; very rarely to indifferent ones.

The telepathic manifestation is usually unexpected. It often occurs to persons alien to the marvellous both by tastes and occupations, and who are seldom so influenced more than once in their lives.

It occurs either in waking life, or in sleep, which it interrupts.

As to the phenomenon itself, two important characteristics should be noted:—

(*a*) The telepathic vision is generally very precise; the details relating to the event and the surrounding circumstances are quite exact.

(*b*) Neither distance nor intervening obstacles seem to have any appreciable effect.

A third characteristic (exceptional) is the following. The vision may affect several persons either at the same time or successively—it seems able to affect animals

[1] We shall not analyse experimental telepathy, which as yet covers only elementary facts.

—sometimes it leaves physical traces. Finally, the
telepathic impression may not affect sight alone, as in
the case of a seemingly objective vision, but hearing and
touch also.

3.—LUCIDITY [1]

Lastly, supernormal psychology includes all the
infinite varieties of lucidity; presentiments, sensorial
impressions beyond the range of the senses, the precise
vision of distant or past events, and even prevision of
the future.

Lucidity may be described as that subconscious
faculty which permits the acquisition of knowledge
without the assistance of the senses, and outside the
conditions which, in normal life, regulate the relation
of the Self with other selves or with the external world.

(*a*) 'Without the assistance of the senses.' The
senses do not, in fact, intervene. The subject
is asleep or anæsthetised; the events described
are beyond the sensorial range; they are often
far distant and shut off by physical barriers;
the knowledge acquired relates sometimes to
events which have not yet come to pass. The
whole evidence shows that the senses are not
in action.

Nevertheless, by a psychological habit, the subject
gives to his perceptions a sensorial semblance and refers
them to sight or hearing; even in cases when neither
sight nor hearing could possibly have been their cause.

One subject, for instance, self-hypnotised by a glass
of water or a crystal globe, claims to see therein past,
future, or distant events. He is but projecting, exteriorising, and objectifying, a sensation abnormally received.

[1] Consult specially Bozzano: *Les Phénomènes Prémonitoires*; and
Dr Osty: *Lucidité et Intuition*.

In another, the abnormal perception may cause an auditory illusion which may run to hallucination.

    (*b*) ' Outside the conditions which in normal life regulate the relation of the Self with other selves or with the external world.'

In fact these perceptions proceed neither from reasoning, nor from any of the normal modes of expressing thought, neither from language, nor writing, nor sight, nor hearing. They require neither induction nor deduction, reflection, research, nor effort.

In its more perfect instances lucidity appears like a flash which suddenly illuminates the recipient and gives him, it may be, knowledge of an unknown fact removed from all possibilities of sensorial perception, or complex knowledge which would normally require much intricate work on many points of research.[1] As lucidity shows itself to be beyond psychological conditions, whether sensorial, dynamic, or physical, so it also shows itself as being outside the conditions of time and space.

Neither space nor material obstacles exist for it, and time seems to be unknown.

The event which it reveals and the knowledge it gives, are not placed in Time at all. When, for instance, in the famous case of lucidity by Dr Gallet, he announces the election of M. Casimir Perrier to the Presidency of the Republic 'by 451 votes,' this is given in the present and not in the future; ' M. Casimir Perrier *est elu* . . .' Similarly the Sonrel prediction of the wars of 1870-71, and 1914-18, *given in* 1868, shows extremely precise and true details on both wars, but gives them in the present and not in the future. The visionary describes the disasters of 1870, Sédan, the siege of Paris, the Commune; the war of 1914, beginning by a disaster

---

[1] Psychic manifestations which suddenly bring out a calculation of probability or a result of subconscious reasoning are not to be confounded with lucidity. Such cases have only the semblance of lucidity.

and ending in complete victory . . . as if these were events he were actually witnessing.[1]

4.—SPIRITOID PHENOMENA

Under this title may be grouped all the phenomena which seem to be produced and directed by an external and autonomous intelligence acting through the physical, active, or psychic powers of a medium. I shall not enter here on the description of these, which the reader will easily find elsewhere,[2] but will content myself with a few remarks.

In the first place, a very large part of supernormal psychology puts on these spiritoid semblances. The simplest as well as the most complex phenomena, from automatisms and telekinesis, up to predictions of the future, are very often attributed by the subject to spiritist influence.

The alleged personalities frequently make affirmations agreeing in this respect with those of the medium; and often endeavour to give proofs of their identity. These proofs are sometimes very simple, sometimes very intricate, as in the cases of cross-correspondence.

Very often no other objection can be made to these spiritoid assertions except the possibility that they may all be explained by the supernormal faculties of the medium. In that case very large extensions of the faculties of crypto-psychism, cryptomnesia, second-sight, mento-mental action, lucidity, and teleplasticity must be admitted.

For all the details of supernormal subconsciousness I must refer the reader to special works, for at the present moment I am not presenting these facts descriptively,

---

[1] These astonishing cases, certainly true, were reported in detail, after minute investigation, in the *Annales des Sciences Psychiques*.

[2] For the philosophic discussion of these facts, see Book II.

or as data, but regarding them from a strictly philosophic point of view.

From this standpoint what lesson can and ought to be drawn? Surely that the subconscious everywhere outstrips and transcends the categories of sensorial and cerebral capacity; that in all essentials it is beyond all representations,[1] outside even the category of representations, that is to say, outside Space and Time. This will be brought out with all necessary clearness in a future chapter.

But before doing this it is needful to examine the attempts that have been made to reconcile the phenomena of the Unconscious with the classical concept of the Self as a synthesis of states of consciousness and as a product of cerebral activity.

---

[1] 'Representation' is used by Dr Geley in the strictly philosophical sense; "the energy of the mind in holding up to contemplation what it is determined to represent."—Sir William Hamilton, *Metaphysics*, xxiv. —[Translator's note.]

CHAPTER VI

CLASSICAL THEORIES OF THE SUBCONSCIOUS

IT would seem that the recent influx of ideas on the Subconscious should have disconcerted the classical psycho-physiology.

Nevertheless many attempts have been made to reconcile the new facts with the old theories.

Most are based on very conscientious work, but none has attained its object. We shall examine each in turn and endeavour to show wherein they are insufficient and inadmissible.

Classical theories of the subconscious may be placed in two categories: the physiological and the purely psychological.

Physiological Theories.

There are two physiological theories: the theory of Automatism and the theory of Morbidity.

I.—THE THEORY OF AUTOMATISM

For the tentative interpretation of the subconscious, the first hypothesis was that of psychological automatism, following naturally on that of physiological automatism. In each case what is observed is held to be merely a passive manifestation; and unconscious psychism, according to this, is simply a result of the automatic activity of the brain—unconscious cerebration.

To support this theory P. Janet specially studied

certain pathological conditions, such as minor epilepsy, elementary symptoms of hysteria, hypnosis, somnambulism, and mediumship.

The psychological automatism in these cases was beyond doubt, and to generalise from these data, extending automatism to the whole area of subconsciousness, was but one step. It was soon taken.

But when, leaving the lower and commonplace order of phenomena, higher subconscious manifestations had to be examined, insurmountable difficulties arose.

The physiological automatism with which psychic automatism was compared, is of two kinds—innate and acquired.

Innate automatism is shown by the activity of the main organic functions such as circulation of the blood, or digestion. This is the same from birth to death, if not quantitatively at least qualitatively. It always remains within the limits proper to these functions and initiates nothing new. Besides the fact that this automatic dynamism is, as we have seen, unexplained, it is clear that it cannot help us to understand a subconscious psychism that innovates and creates.

Acquired automatism is the result of complicated interactions,—certain modes of activity, needing at first attention and continued exercise of the will, come by habit to be performed without continuous attention, and with a minimum of effort.

This acquired automatism also remains within the limits prescribed by habit, and does not go beyond them. But the higher subconscious manifestations are usually sporadic, and in no case do they resemble habits.

This is obvious in the case of supernormal manifestations; these can never become customary. Even for the less mysterious phenomena, automatism is no explanation.

Multiple personalities brought to light in certain individuals show spontaneity and self-directing will.

They do not act according to some autonomous habit, but take an original direction. The will manifested is not only sharply defined; it also differs from that of the subject, and may be opposed or even hostile to it, as in the case of Miss Beauchamp, studied by Dr Morton Prince.[1]

In mediumship, this spontaneity, will, and autonomy of the so-called secondary personalities appear still more remarkably; they sometimes show a quite complete psychism of their own, with their own faculties of willing, knowing, and reasoning; with acquirements often very different from those of the conscious subject, such, for instance, as the knowledge of a language unknown to the latter. In the more notable cases, there would seem to be really nothing in common between the two personalities. How can the term 'automatism' be applied to these facts?

Let us now pass to subconscious productions of an artistic, philosophic, or scientific order. Only defective reasoning can attribute inspiration and genius to cerebral automatism.

Let us analyse what happens in these subconscious productions.

To take a typical case, a man of science, an artist, or a thinker undertakes a certain work. Confronted with some unexpected difficulties, he is discouraged, and stops. To his surprise, some time later, the solution which he had vainly sought comes to him without effort, and the work he had planned is easily completed.

This, it is said, is because the brain has continued to work automatically in the direction of the original impulse; but it is impossible to find in physiology an analogous example of automatic function.

When, for instance, one learns to ride a bicycle, a long series of voluntary efforts have to be repeated to reach the stage of automatic direction. If the learner

[1] Dr Morton Prince: *The Dissociation of a Personality.*

were to break off discouraged, no amount of waiting
would find him more advanced for a second attempt.
In the interval there would have been no 'latent
physiological work' allowing a cessation of the effort
necessary for learning, and standing in lieu of that
effort.

Again, when in training, a man habituates not only
his muscles, but his lungs and heart to endure the
fatigue of running; a single effort can never take the
place of methodical and continued training. When,
then, 'latent work by the brain' is alleged, that is a
mere guess contrary to all that physiology teaches; it
is a hypothesis which involves an entirely new and
purely gratuitous notion ; that the cerebral organ
works in a manner essentially different from all other
organs.

Let us now take another case :—

The artist, thinker, etc. . . . does not foresee the
work he means to do, and does not prepare it. He
produces under the influence of an 'inspiration' independent of his desire and will, sometimes contrary to
them. There is not in this case the original impulse
for the supposed automatism. Here he does not
direct the inspiration, he is directed by it. How, then,
can we speak of psychological automatism?

'The unconscious sequence here,' says M. Dwelshauvers, 'is not an automatism but a vital action.'

M. Ribot also says, 'Inspiration reveals a power
superior to the conscious individual, strange to him
though acting through him—a state which many
inventors have described by saying of their work—I
had no part in it.'

M. Dwelshauvers, in his recent study of subconscious production, has abundantly shown that above
the psychological automatism (which is but a commonplace and inferior form of the Unconscious), there is an
active latent unconsciousness which 'serves as an arsenal

for creative synthesis and aids a man in producing his most perfect mental work.'

What are we to conclude? Simply that the theory of psychological automatism is applicable only to a small number of the less important facts and cannot claim to furnish any general explanation.

P. Janet finds himself obliged to admit this, and he admits it reluctantly and ungraciously when he writes as follows.

> 'Since the time when I used this word "subconscious" in a clinical and commonplace sense, other authors have used the word in a very much higher one.'
>
> 'This word has been used to designate marvellous activities which exist, so it would seem, within ourselves without our suspecting their presence; it has been used to explain sudden enthusiasms and the divinations of genius. . . . I shall not venture to discuss theories so consoling, which may perhaps be true.'
>
> 'I shall limit myself to the observation that I am busied with quite other things. The poor sick folk that I was studying had no kind of genius; the phenomena which in them had become subconscious, were very simple matters which are part of the consciousness of other men without giving any cause for surprise. They had lost personal consciousness and the power of self-direction; they had sick personalities—that is all.'[1]

This, in fine, is all that is covered by automatic subconsciousness properly so called. The higher active subconsciousness, being entirely different in essence and nature, must be clearly distinguished from the former.

[1] P. Janet, Preface to J. Jastrow's *Subconscience*.

2.—THE THEORY OF MORBIDITY

Another general explanation which, although still less logical and more vain and arbitrary than the first, has had, and still has much currency, is the explanation by morbidity.[1]

One hesitates to avow it, but it is this poverty-stricken explanation to which the majority of psychologists to-day are not afraid to appeal. According to them everything which, from the psychological point of view, departs from the average, must proceed from disease. They would have subconscious powers to be morbid products; hypnotism, akin to neurosis; multiple personality, a pathological disintegration of the Self; supernormal phenomena, symptoms of hysteria; and as for the works of genius, they are simply results of madness.

At the base of all these morbid manifestations they always discover an essential pathological cause—'degeneration.' This factor of 'degeneration' is the more convenient in that it is elastic; it is supposed to rule both ordinary and hysteriform neuropathic cases (inferior degeneration), and the manifestations of genius (superior degeneration).

Thus everything that from the intellectual point of view is either above or below the normal, must be the result of disease.

The label 'morbid' is affixed with more or less discretion or indiscretion by different schools of psychiatry;[2] but its use is nearly general.

Dr Chabaneix speaks of auto-intoxication and over-pressure among the predisposed: ' The more an organ works,' he writes, ' the more it develops, and at the

[1] The chief psychological review in France is entitled: *Revue de Psychologie Normale et Pathologique.*

[2] Mental therapeutics; treatment of insanity.

same time, the more liable it becomes to disease. One of the diseases of the brain is automatism, or the appearance of the subconscious. And this subconsciousness, instead of being a trouble to the mind, is often a ferment of creation, when it is not itself creation.'

A curious disease, which, instead of being a cause of 'trouble' and of diminution to the individual, increases his capacities and powers!

Lombroso, for his part, boldly invokes madness.

Others define differently, they reduce talent and genius to arthritism. But the record in this respect is held up to the present by Dr Pascal Serph.[1] He takes no half-measures and has the courage of his opinions. According to him the origin of genius is looked for much too far away—genius is purely and simply the product of . . . hereditary syphilis!

' If syphilis,' Dr Serph gravely concludes, ' does the harm which medical men are unanimous in recognising and fearing for mankind, it nevertheless gives, as a set-off, by its hypertrophic action on the brain, the possibility of perfecting human action, and being thus creative of the special ideas of genius, it compensates to some extent for its ravages.'

It is scarcely possible to restrain some impatience when men of science maintain such theories, and one feels a certain disgust at having to refute ideas which deserve only contempt.

It is, however, necessary to do this.

Let us remark, in the first place, that among the various morbid factors invoked, one only—neuropathy—seems to be coincident with facts, if not supported by them.

It is true that men of great talent or genius are almost invariably neuropathic. But what is neuropathy?

Medical science does not know. Neuroses, and

[1] *Gazette Médicale de Paris,* July 12, 1916.

even madness are pure enigmas from the point of view of pathological anatomy.

We shall see that, far from explaining the mechanism of abnormal or superior psychism, neuroses receive their explanation from the deeper study of the essential nature of the subconscious.

But this is not all, even if we suppose the theories of morbidity justified, they in no way solve the problems which the manifestations of subconsciousness set before us. To say ' genius is neurosis or madness ' does not help us to understand the mechanism of the works of genius. The great thinker, artist, or man of science, brings something new to humanity; he creates. You say—he is mad ! So be it, but how is madness creative ? Until you have laid before our eyes the mechanism of the subconscious psychism, you have only put the difficulty one step back by affixing the epithet ' morbid ' to it.

To say that secondary personalities are only products of the disintegration of the Self, is not to make them comprehensible, rather the contrary. The disintegration of a psychic entity may give the key to alterations of personality, but only to those alterations which diminish the personality.

This diminution of personality is evident in certain cases of amnesia[1] following on cranial wounds, on great emotions, severe infection, epilepsy, etc.

Diminished personality appears also in the psychologic automatism described by P. Janet. But in the cases of complete and autonomous secondary personalities it is not observable. When these secondary personalities occupy the whole psychic field of the subject, when they show a very original will, and give proof of powers and knowledge different from those of the patient and sometimes much above those which he normally possesses, one can no longer invoke the disintegration of the Self

[1] Loss of memory.

as a complete explanation. It is impossible to admit that the secondary personality, the fraction of the Self, should be as extensive, or even more extensive than the total Self. The part is never equal to or greater than the whole.

Psychological disintegration must therefore be given up as a general explanation of modifications of the personality.

It is not by saying that such and such a medium is hysterical that we can understand the action at a distance of her motor faculties and her intelligence, apart from her muscles, her senses and her brain; or can acquire the key to the difficult problem of supernormal psycho-physiology involving the faculties of thought-reading, lucidity, and ideoplastic or teleplastic action.

There is this final argument against the theory of morbidity—it is contrary to the logic of facts. It is contrary to the whole teachings of physiology to declare that a diseased organ can produce results superior to those of a healthy one, especially when those results occur in a constant and semi-regular manner.

There is an untenable contradiction in declaring physical power a function of health, and the mental power of genius a function of disease.

Is it now necessary to speak of other less general theories of morbidity, restricted to one or another group of subconscious phenomena? It will suffice briefly to indicate them.

Azam explained the duplication of personality by the separate action of the two cerebral lobes; a thesis which, since the manifestation of multiple, and not merely double, personalities in the same individual, has only a historic interest.

Dr Sollier explains hysteria by disjunctions among the cerebral cells; all the symptoms of the neurosis being explained by the non-activity or the hyper-activity of certain among these neurons.

Professor Grasset thinks to explain subconscious manifestations by a disjunction between the functioning of Charcot's schematic 'polygon' and a certain centre O, localised somewhere in the gray matter of the brain.

To all these theories the same objections can be raised:—

1. They are adapted only to a few facts, leaving out of account the very thing which is most important in subconsciousness—the higher crypto-psychism, and the supernormal.

2. Even for the limited facts which they cover they are insufficient, since they assign as cause the very thing which has to be explained—the why, and how, of these disjunctions.

Leaving the physiological, we will now pass on to the psychological theories of the subconscious.

PSYCHOLOGICAL THEORIES OF THE SUBCONSCIOUS

These theories are many and of unequal value. There are some which start from vicious reasoning, they are *petitiones principii*, or verbal explanations. We will discuss them briefly.

3.—PETITIONES PRINCIPII

A *petitio principii* consists in carrying back a mysterious occurrence to another not less mysterious, but previously known and more familiar. Among supernormal phenomena for instance, telepathy and thought-reading are the most familiar and the best known, which gives them a kind of priority of privilege, so that it is sought, by any and every means, to reduce all intellectual mediumship to them; which is absurd, and only complicates the whole subject, for thought-reading and telepathy are

as contrary to known laws as are clairvoyance or transcendental mediumistic communications.

Professor Pouchet [1] writes as racily as he does
logically when he says:—

> ' To demonstrate that a brain by some kind of
> gravitation acts at a distance on another brain like
> a magnet on iron, the sun on the planets, or the
> earth on a falling body! To arrive at the discovery
> of an influence, a nervous vibration propelling itself
> without any material conductor! The amazing
> thing is that those who believe, more or less, in
> something of the sort, seem, poor fellows! not
> even to suspect the importance and the interest of
> the novelty which is involved, and what a revolution
> this would be for the social world. *Prove* that, my
> good people, and your names will stand higher than
> that of Newton; and I can assure you that the
> Berthelots and the Pasteurs will take off their hats
> to you! '

A still more familiar begging of the question consists
in explaining hypnotism by hysteria, or hysteria by
hypnotism. ' What is there astonishing in manifestations under hypnotism ? Analogous and spontaneous
occurrences are known in hysteria! Why marvel at
hysterical manifestations ? Similar manifestations can
be brought about by hypnosis.'

Then yet another step is taken in the way of begging
the question, when both hysteria and hypnotism are
referred to suggestibility or to Professor Babinsky's
' Pythiatism.'

But suggestion, a usual and convenient factor in
hypnosis or hysteria, is absolutely valueless and of no
import, as a philosophic explanation.

We have demonstrated as much in *L'Être Subconscient.*

---

[1] Quoted by M. de Rochas : *Extériorisation de la Motricité.*

M. Boirac has also established the same thing. He writes:—

> 'What conclusion can we draw from the whole discussion? To begin with, the method which consists in explaining concrete facts by abstract terms, such as "suggestion" and "suggestibility," appears to us highly unscientific; it is a relic of the old scholastic method—a recourse to occult entities, qualities, and virtues. In a certain patient I can induce at will the most unlikely hallucinations; I can paralyse his organs as I please. What can be the cause of such extraordinary effects? Nothing simpler; it is suggestion. But how is this suggestion to be explained? Whence comes its power? That is still simpler; it comes from suggestibility, a natural property of the human brain. So they think to explain facts by dressing them up in a name, just as the schoolmen thought they were explaining the sleep produced by opium by saying that opium has a dormitive virtue.'[1]

M. Boirac's reasoning may be applied to all the classical explanations of subconscious phenomena, both metapsychic and supernormal.

Equally valueless are the explanations which may be called purely verbal, which abound in the classical psychology of the Subconscious.

4.—ARTIFICIAL DISJUNCTIONS AND VERBAL EXPLANATIONS

Psychologists are prone to have recourse to artificial disjunctions among the subconscious capacities. Their efforts are directed to classifying and then labelling the

[1] Boirac: *L'Avenir des Sciences Psychiques.*

facts they have classed. They thus give themselves the illusion of understanding them.

Among the facts of subconsciousness there are some quite familiar and well known—the facts of inspiration, so these are made into a class apart, the *active sub-consciousness*, opposed to the automatic subconsciousness spoken of by P. Janet. But the classification goes neither higher nor further; this main class is sub-divided into secondary classes—unconscious invention; unconscious memory; unconscious tendencies; unconscious association of ideas; unconscious emotional states; religious unconsciousness, etc. . . . .

The main class of multiple personalities is divided into sub-classes, labelled infra-consciousness, super-consciousness, co-consciousness, etc., etc.

In the same order of ideas eminent psychologists distinguish subconscious psychism properly so called from what they term ‘ metapsychism,’ between which there are, however, only analogies, and no essential distinctions.

The normal subconsciousness and the metaphysic subconsciousness are manifested in very closely allied states :—

The state of ecstasy, of rapture, of absent-mindedness, in a poet, an artist, or a philosopher composing under the influence of inspiration, is, at bottom, identical with the secondary state of the medium. Let it not be said that the medium speaks, acts, and writes quite automatically, whilst the artist, even when his conscious will does not intervene, nevertheless knows what he is producing. This distinction does not always obtain. Many mediums know quite well what is about to be given through them; just as the artist knows bit by bit what he will produce under an inspiration of which he is neither the master nor the guide.

Rousseau covering pages of writing without reflec-tion or effort, in a state of rapture which drew tears,

Musset listening to the mysterious ' genius ' who dictated his verses, Socrates listening to his dæmon, Schopenhauer refusing to believe that his unexpected and unsought postulates were his own work, all behaved exactly like mediums.

Moreover, it is not infrequent that mediumship co-exists with manifestations of artistic inspiration. Musset, for instance, was a sensitive and almost a visionary.

It is needless to remark that cryptomnesia and cryptopsychism are the foundation both of mediumship and of normal subconscious psychism. In fact it is not always easy to distinguish one from the other. Will it be said that the distinction between subconscious psychism properly so called, lies in the appearance of the supernormal element ?

But where does the supernormal begin ? The emptiness and futility of this term ' supernormal ' has been shown in the chapter on physiology. It was there demonstrated that normal and so-called supernormal physiology are equally mysterious and involve one and the same problem. The case is the same for psychology. The subconscious, as a whole, is incomprehensible by classical psychology.

All that classical psychology has been able to do with the supernormal is to multiply the number of labels. The more numerous the labels the greater the illusion of understanding. We shall then have exteriorisation of sensation, exteriorisation of motor power, exteriorisation of intelligence, telesthesia, telepathy, telekinesis, teleoplasticity, ideoplasticity, etc., etc.

M. Boirac, finding this nomenclature still too poor, proposes to add hypnology, psychodynamics, telepsychism, hyloscopy, metagnomy, biactinism, diapsychism, etc.[1]

These classifications, indeed, answer to an innate

[1] Boirac : *La Psychologie Inconnue* and *L'Avenir des Études Psychiques.*

need of the human mind, and in one sense are legitimate. But their danger lies in the fact that they come to mean something more than classifications, they come to mean a quite illusory interpretation; they turn aside the logical endeavour to understand and reason, or put it to sleep. They have yet another danger, they mask the essential unity of psychological synthesis, and lead to the notion that the 'diverse subconscious manifestations may be susceptible of isolated and partial explanation. Thus they mislead the investigator and retard all philosophical progress.

The question of the Subconscious is passing through the stage which all important questions of scientific philosophy have passed through. Sooner or later the common link between all questions of the same order is found, and then a harmonious synthesis is constructed, which is capable of explaining, if not all the minor difficulties of detail (which will finally be resolved little by little under the direction and control of the general idea), at any rate all the major difficulties. But before reaching the synthetic phase, the human mind struggles painfully through a long analytical phase, during which it only observes facts and classifies them more or less skilfully.

Nevertheless, from the beginning of this phase it endeavours to find explanations, but these are based on a small number of facts specially studied by this or that investigator, and hastily generalised upon by him by the help of an arbitrary and forced adaptation to other groups of analogous facts.

Then one of two things happens.

Either these hasty and superficial theories are also vague and inexact, and end in an insidious and deceptive verbalism; or they are exact but cover only a small number of facts, and cannot stand the test of general application.

Theories of these two categories are already

numerous in the domain of the philosophy of the subconscious.

We have already cited the partial theories of Janet,
of Grasset, and of Sollier.

Two more may be cited, both of a general character,
but still insufficient.

5.—PROFESSOR JASTROW'S THEORY

The vague, inexact, and merely verbal type of theory
is represented by that of Professor Jastrow. The conclusion of his long study on Subconsciousness is as
follows:—[1]

'The impression left on us by this study is
that the mental life of Man does not rest on his
consciousness alone. Below consciousness there
exists a psychic organisation *anterior to it*,[2] which is
doubtless the source whence it has been derived.

'It is to be presumed that the origin of consciousness is due to the necessity of satisfying some
need which otherwise would not have been completely satisfied.

'Its birth marks the beginning of a greater
co-ordination of functions. Its duty consists primarily
in integrating experiences, and thus establishing
the unity of the mind. *Morbid dissociations*[2] only
bring into higher relief that unity which the normal
mind retains during its whole development, by
which it resists all the vicissitudes through which it
passes.

'We have explained the different psychic
phenomena by the light of evolutionist concepts.
. . . The interpretation of *the different varieties of*

---

[1] J. Jastrow: *La Subconscience* (Alcan). [2] My italics, G. G.

K

subconscious activities[1] ought to be considered as pertaining to a system founded on mental evolution. Subconsciousness should appear as a natural product of mental constitution. It should also be shown that in proportion as the complexity of the mind increases, the subconsciousness is modified so as to continue to fill the function which it holds in that mind. But all evolution implies arrest, weakening, decadence, and dissolution; and in examining the products of the dissolution of a function we often come to understand its normal development better; and it is for this reason that we have in this work studied *the alterations of the mind* with so much care.'

This theory of Dr Jastrow's, if it explains nothing, at least gives a very clear idea of the state of mind of contemporary psychologists. It appeals to differentiations which are not essential differences, to impotent and vain 'morbid factors,' and to a mere verbalism still more impotent. Finally it is absolutely and systematically inexact. It seems from time to time to have a glimpse of a part of the truth, but is incapable of rising to a free flight above the classical routine and the medley of commonplaces. It sheds absolutely no light on the nature, the origin, or the essence of subconsciousness. It in no way explains how the subconsciousness, together with a far-reaching cryptomnesia, can contain so many marvellous and powerful faculties, so much unexpected knowledge, latent, unused, unusable, and necessitating a morbid disintegration of the Self in order to be apparent!

6.—M. RIBOT'S THEORY

There is a recent theory which may be considered as the last word in the classical concept of the

[1] My italics. G. G.

subconscious; it is by M. Ribot.[1] M. Ribot finds it
quite simple: there is no unconscious Self.

'This term and the concept which it implies,
are an abuse of language, and inadmissible. The
Self, the person, is a whole, composed of constantly
varying elements, which in their perpetual "becoming" preserve a certain unity. But nothing similar
is found in this imaginary Self, no principle of unity,
but on the contrary a tendency to disperse and to go
to pieces. . . .
'To sum up, this supposed Self is a fraction,
made up of motor elements and mechanisms. When
it becomes active, it is an orchestra without a con-
ductor.
'Unconscious function does not differ from
conscious activity except by the want of order and
unity. Its structure is made up of "psychic
residues," that is to say, of "isolated or associated
elements which were once states of consciousness
. . . it is extinct consciousness, frozen and crystal-
lised as to its motor elements.'

Nevertheless, M. Ribot admits there is in the
unconscious 'some impenetrable basal matter.'

'This fact—however it may be explained—that
there is in us a buried life which appears only by
glimpses and never in its entirety, is far-reaching;
the fact is that this self-knowledge (γνῶθι σεαυτόν)
is not merely difficult, but impossible. We must
recognise our "absolute incapacity to know with
any certainty our own individuality in its entirety."'

In fine, according to M. Ribot, the conscious Self is
a co-ordination of states; and the unconscious Self is

[1] Ribot: *La Vie Inconsciente et les Mouvements.*

a residue of former states of consciousness. The activity of the former reveals a certain unity, while that of the latter is entirely anarchic and disordered. No doubt, he admits, there are obscurities, but these cannot be helped; what we do not understand in psychic individuality is only that which it is impossible to understand.

We can take note of this avowal of impotence. As to M. Ribot's actual theory, its insufficiency puts it beyond discussion. The data on which it rests take no account of what we may, with M. Dwelshauvers, call the latent active subconsciousness, nor of the supernormal. It has, therefore, no claim to be considered a general theory.

7.—CONCLUSIONS FROM THE STUDY OF CLASSICAL PSYCHO-PHYSIOLOGY

Such are the classical explanations of subconscious phenomena.

The entire and flagrant insufficiency of these explanations is obvious. The classical concept of physiological and psychological individuality appears on examination yet more limited and deficient than the classical concept of evolution.

The latter has, at all events, succeeded in bringing to light the secondary factors; and if mistaken as to their import, if it has not been able completely to explain transformism, it has, at any rate, placed its reality beyond question. The former, on the contrary, has not succeeded in solving any one of the problems which it undertakes.

Shut in by the narrow limits of polyzoism and polypsychism, which hide from it the essential reality of things, it is faced by riddles on all sides; the riddle of the formation and the maintenance of the organism, the riddle of Life, the riddle of personality, the riddle of consciousness, and the riddle of sub-consciousness.

Incapable of a synthetic outlook, its analyses have resulted in the factitious generalisations of a sterile method, which only escape from insufficiency to fall into absurdity. The classical concept of the individual carries on it the brand of lamentable impotence in what we may call the contemporary official academic psycho-physiology.

Devoid of originality, depth, and truth, this official psycho-physiology presents a striking contrast to the other sciences which form a part of the marvellous developments of our age.

Deprived of their light, it makes as it were a dark zone in which the best minds blindly grope and struggle in vain. . . . It is time that a strong wind of pure air should blow away the thick and heavy fog of petty ideas linked to petty facts.

CHAPTER VII

RATIONAL PSYCHOLOGICAL INFERENCES BASED ON THE SUBCONSCIOUS

OUR study of classical psycho-physiology has enabled us to probe to the quick the errors and illusions due to the ascending method which, starting from elementary facts, claims to interpret complex ones.

Let us now boldly use the opposite, descending method; and consider first and foremost the most complex facts of psychology ; *i.e.* the subconscious phenomena.

This method will give in the psychic domain the results it has given in the physiological; a new and brilliant light on our path, making our investigations simple, easy, and fruitful.

I.—THE SUBCONSCIOUS IS THE VERY ESSENCE OF INDIVIDUAL PSYCHOLOGY

Starting without preconceived ideas, and proceeding to the study of subconscious psychology without heed to the formulæ and dogmas of classical teaching, we experience a great surprise.

The subconscious appears as the very essence of individual psychology.

That which is most important in the individual psychism is subconscious. The foundation of the Self, its characteristic qualities, are subconscious. All the innate capacities are subconscious; likewise the higher faculties—intuition, talents, genius, artistic or creative inspiration. These faculties are cryptoid in their origin, cryptoid in their manifestations, the greater part of which escape from the will, from the normal and regular direction of the individual, and show their existence only by bringing to light intermittent and apparently spontaneous results.

This subconscious psychic activity, powerful in itself, is reinforced by a still more potent and infallible memory which leaves the feeble and limited conscious memory far behind.

By the side of the subconscious, the conscious seems but a restricted, limited, and truncated psychism; and even this psychism in its more important manifestations is conditioned by that cryptoid portion of the Self which is its foundation.

In a word, everything happens as though the conscious were but a part, and that the smaller part, of the Self; a part, moreover, entirely conditioned by the more important part which remains cryptoid in the ordinary circumstances of normal life.

Such a declaration is an insoluble mystery for the classical psychology which considers the Self to be the sum of the consciousness of its neurons. Starting from that concept it is impossible to understand either cryptopsychism or cryptomnesia, or even to attempt any but purely verbal explanations of them.

2.—THE IMPOTENCE OF CLASSICAL PSYCHOLOGY BEFORE CRYPTOPSYCHISM AND CRYPTOMNESIA

From the point of view of individualist psychology cryptopsychism appears nonsense. How can a part of the mental activity escape from the control of the individual or be accessible to him only irregularly and fortuitously? How can this involuntary and latent mental activity be superior to that which is voluntary and conscious? How can all the higher powers, not only the supernormal faculties, but also creative inspiration, genius, and all that is essential in the intellect from the psychic point of view, be for the most part inaccessible and unknown ? Why, in a word, are they subconscious and not conscious ? Once more this is impossible to understand from the data of classical psychology.

Basing his reasoning on these arguments, Myers had no difficulty in demonstrating the impossibility of making cryptopsychism a product of normal physiological evolution. There is, in fact, an absolute contradiction in establishing the existence of faculties at once very powerful and very useful, but at the same time mostly unusable in the normal life of the individual.

Let us now pass to cryptomnesia.

This, as we have seen, seems to have an immense power, a reach which seems limitless. It seems to register faithfully everything which has come under our senses, whether consciously or unknown to us, and to register indelibly.

Such a concept differs *in toto* from all the classical concepts of memory.

The ordinary memory is most precise when the fact has forcibly arrested the attention and is also recent.

If the fact registered by the memory is of little or no importance to the individual, it soon disappears for ever, unless it should chance to be retained by reason of an association with more important ideas. Similarly if the fact registered is distant in time, remembrance becomes vague, and in the end disappears, often entirely. This is a regular and normal sequence conformable to all that physiology teaches.

The impression produced on the brain is superficial and ephemeral for states of consciousness of moderate intensity, and even for more important states this impression tends to disappear in time. Le Dantec[1] thus sums up his psychological theory of memory.

[1] Le Dantec: *Le Déterminisme Biologique.*

'There are two things to consider in memory from the objective point of view :—

'1. The fact that we have not really forgotten anything which it is possible for us to recall.

'2. The operation in which this recollection consists.

'The former is a histological[1] peculiarity, the latter is the correlative of a physiological fact.

'If we execute any operation, mental or other, a certain number of times, the path traversed by the corresponding reflex will be beaten into a thoroughfare by that reflex in accordance with the law of functional assimilation. In our nervous system, therefore, there will be a certain number of histological modifications correlative to the operation in question. As long as these histological modifications persist, the histological memory of the operation will persist; it will suffice to repeat it from time to time to maintain this histological memory by functional assimilation. If a long time passes without repetition, the plastic destruction which accompanies the repose of an organ will destroy this particular path in the nervous system; there will be forgetfulness.

'When the forgetfulness is complete and absolute it is irremediable. The histological memory having vanished, no psychological memory can remain. This seems obvious, and seems to be, in fact, the sequence and the condition of the ordinary memory.'

Now cryptomnesia is entirely different; it retains not only important facts but unimportant ones, even those which have not claimed the conscious attention of the person.

Further, the registration of states of consciousness

[1] Histological, Gr. ἱστός = tissue, pertaining to the tissue (of the brain).

by the occult memory is not affected by the lapse of time. The registration seems indelible.

The range of latent memories extends from the most insignificant details, even those unconsciously registered, to the most important facts of conscious life. The remembrance, even when it seems to have wholly vanished, and is inaccessible to the normal self, can reappear in its entirety as the foreground of abnormal states, especially in somnambulism or mediumship.

Cryptomnesia records not only external experiences but internal ones also. It retains not only real impressions but also those of an imaginative order. Imagination, which plays so large a part in normal psychism, creates and realises fictitious positions, and these, as well as real facts, are registered by cryptomnesia. Similarly, of course, all the emotions and states of the soul.

In fine, everything which has occupied the psychic field, consciously or unconsciously, remains indestructibly even when it seems for ever lost. No matter whether a very long time has elapsed since the sensorial or psychic impression was made, no matter that the cerebral cells, which vibrated synchronously, have doubtless since then been many times renewed,[1] in despite of time and change the remembrance remains integrally and indelibly graven in the Subconscious.

How? Why? To classical physiology the mystery is insoluble.

The entire subconscious memory seems, therefore, to be independent of cerebral contingencies. Cases have even been quoted in which it has reappeared by flashes, in spite of the loss of normal memory through injuries to the brain. Such is the case of Mr Hanna, a very characteristic one in this respect.[2] Mr Hanna, by reason of a fall on his head, forgot entirely the whole of his

---

[1] In any case the impression made on them has been effaced and has disappeared.

[2] Sidy and Goodhart: *Multiple Personality*.

past life, all his knowledge and all his acquirements, and returned to the psychological state of a new-born babe who has everything to learn. But curiously enough, though the memory had disappeared, the capacity to learn was intact. Now during this process of re-education, M. Flournoy records, ' he had dreams and visions, incomprehensible to himself, which he described with astonishment to his relations, and in which they recognised very exact recollections of places where the patient had been before his accident.' There was, therefore, a latent memory, also clearly shown by his power of very rapid learning.

In fine, the study of cryptomnesia clearly brings out that everything happens as though the psychic state which we call a remembrance, registered by the cerebral cells,—ephemeral as they and destined soon to disappear with them,—were at the same time registered in 'a something' permanent, of which this remembrance will henceforward be an integral and permanent part.

Let us clearly retain this conclusion; its importance will appear later. It will suffice at present to establish a first inference from the facts.

There are in the living being powerful and extended but subconscious faculties which, although cryptoid and not in the main within the consciousness nor under the normal and direct control of the will, yet condition the individual psychism.

There is a subconscious memory different from the normal memory, more certain and more extensive than it and seeming almost illimitable.

These facts take us far beyond the limits of classical notions on the Self, its origin, its end, and its destinies. There is nothing in the academic knowledge which we have thought definitely established by the natural sciences, by physiology or psychology, that can account for subconscious phenomena, or which is not in flagrant opposition to them.

In a word, this truly far-reaching induction puts **a** question more far-reaching still. We are imperatively led to ask ourselves whether the whole classical psychophysiology is not a mere monument of errors ?

From this point forward it becomes a duty to reconsider all its teaching, and above all to examine by the light of facts the main dogma on which the whole structure is founded, the dogma of psycho-physiological parallelism.

It is important to investigate this parallelism wherever it is affirmed to exist, and verify whether it can be adapted to the subconscious facts.

3.—ABSENCE OF PARALLELISM BETWEEN THE SUBCON- SCIOUS ON THE ONE HAND, AND THE STATE OF DEVELOPMENT OF THE BRAIN, HEREDITY, AND SENSORIAL AND INTELLECTUAL ACQUIREMENT ON THE OTHER HAND

To begin with, we are taught that psychic development accompanies quite regularly the development of the brain, and is proportional to that development during childhood and up to maturity.

But subconscious psychism has, among its other characteristics, that of appearing, often in all its force, long before the complete development of the brain.

Without here speaking of the supernormal subconsciousness, which is more frequent in children than in adults, the precocious manifestation of genius, especially in art, is a commonplace, and it is needless to cite instances of what is so well known. This emergence of genius in advance of the complete development of the brain is one fact at issue with the theory of psycho-physiological parallelism. Another point, still more important, is that psychic development, as far as it

128

concerns the subconscious, appears to be independent of hereditary conditions, independent also of sensory acquirement, and of the effort necessary for conscious intellectual acquirement.

Whence, indeed, do the subconscious powers come? These powers, manifest as talent, genius, or inspiration, are not acquired, they are innate. Work, enthusiasm, or repeated effort, may, to some degree, develop them; it cannot create them.

How can we comprehend these innate powers? The failure of all attempts at interpretation, whether by heredity or cerebral conformation is now definite.

The examples adduced of well and clearly established psychic heredity are quite exceptional.

The best known is that of the family of John Sebastian Bach, which, between 1550 and 1846, produced twenty-nine eminent musicians. But is this entirely due to heredity? To be sure of this, the other factors—surrounding influences, education, family traditions, collective enthusiasm, and so forth, should be eliminated.

What is extraordinary is not that here and there we should find cases of seeming psychic heredity, but rather that, having regard to the frequency and triteness of physical inheritance, we meet with so few. The fact is that the function of heredity is as indistinct and secondary in psychology as it is important and predominant in physiology. Certain predispositions, especially the artistic, are sometimes hereditary, but, as is well known, high psychic faculties—talent and genius—are not traceable to ancestry oftener than they are transmitted to posterity.

The differences between physical and psychical inheritance are too distinctive to be referred to physiological causes. How can we explain why two brothers may resemble each other outwardly, and morally have nothing in common?

The very marked psychic inequalities between persons of the same parentage and of similar life and education, are in no way correlative to their physical inequalities.

Physiologists, indeed, no longer seek the cause of these psychic inequalities in the weight, size, or conformation of the brain; they invoke imperceptible and inappreciable variations in the cerebral tissue, unperceived causes, diverse influences (pathological or other) during intra-uterine life, unknown conditions of conception, genealogical combinations, etc. . . . all of them hypotheses without even the beginnings of proof.

To sum up: from the fact that it is inborn and not hereditary, the subconscious appears to be as independent of the anatomical organisation of the brain as it is of intellectual acquirements and the efforts these require.

From the fact that it often appears from infancy, it seems independent of the complete development of the brain.

Here, then, is one point established. There is no psycho-physiological parallelism between the appearance or the development of the subconscious, and the individual development of the nerve-centres.

4.—ABSENCE OF PARALLELISM BETWEEN THE SUBCONSCIOUS AND THE CEREBRAL ACTIVITY

'Psychic activity,' we are next taught, 'is proportional to the activity of the nerve-centres.'

There the reasoning is simple and clear. If there is one axiom which physiology cannot deny without stultifying itself, it is that 'the output of an organ of given power is proportional to the degree of its activity.' The analytical study of *conscious* psychism, taking the seeming psycho-physiological parallelism as its basal fact, was led to the conclusion that the Self is a function of the brain, or, at least, cannot exist apart from it.

'We can no more,' writes Haeckel, 'separate our individual soul from the brain, than the voluntary movement of the arm can be separated from the contraction of our muscles.'[1]

Now in subconscious psychism, this parallelism no longer exists. If, for the moment, we ignore the results of the automatic activity of the brain (which constitutes a kind of inferior subconsciousness), no connection can be found between the active or superior subconsciousness and the degree of cerebral activity.

On the contrary, the less active the cerebral organ, the greater the activity of the superior subconsciousness. It appears in full strength, not by a voluntary psychic effort, but in the inaction or the repose of the brain; in states of distraction, reverie, or even of natural or induced sleep.

Beaunis [2] who has studied the subconscious, not as a psychologist, but as a physiologist, remarks as follows. 'Subconscious work does not produce weariness like conscious work . . . and I would say to all those who live by the work of their brains, to those who follow science, literature, and art, "let the subconscious do the work, it never gets tired."'

After that, one wonders how a physiologist of the standing of Beaunis has failed to see the momentous inference from such a declaration. This inference is, however, inevitable—subconscious psychism is entirely and specifically distinct from voluntary effort.

Effort can do nothing to create subconscious psychism. At most it can start its activity and guide it in a given direction, that is all. Far from continued effort helping it, cessation of effort is the condition for the successful realisation of intuitive and artistic works of genius.

[1] Haeckel: *Le Monisme.*   [2] Quoted by M. Dwelshauvers.

Moreover, while intellectual effort is intermittent, and cerebral function demands long periods of repose, the capacities of the subconscious remain permanent. Not only does it not disappear in this repose of the brain, but it takes its highest flights in states of cerebral torpor, reverie, and distraction. It is in these very various states, all characterised essentially by the absence of work and effort, that inspiration reveals its full powers and spontaneity.

The dissociation of subconscious output from activity of the brain and voluntary effort cannot be over-emphasised.

In this subconscious output everything happens as if it were entirely independent of cerebral physiology.

5.—ABSENCE OF PARALLELISM BETWEEN CRYPTOMNESIA AND CEREBRAL PHYSIOLOGY

Parallelism is as absent from cryptomnesia as it is from cryptopsychism. As has already been shown at length, the registration, the retention, and the recollection of states of subconscious memory, do not depend on effort, and, strictly speaking, are independent of the conditions and contingencies of the normal cerebral memory.

Further, the subconscious memory is vastly more extended and deeper than the normal memory; and, above all, it is as indelible as the normal memory is ephemeral, like the neurons with which it is associated.

Nowhere can there be found any trace of psycho-physiological parallelism for the subconscious.

6.—ABSENCE OF CEREBRAL LOCALISATIONS FOR THE SUBCONSCIOUS

We are told that ' psychological faculties proceed from clearly defined (cerebral) localisations.'

Is it necessary to point out that it is impossible to find cerebral localisations for subconscious faculties? When the entire want of psycho-physiological parallelism in all subconscious action is borne in mind, even the search for it in this instance will seem absurd, *a priori*. Let us pass on.

7.—ABSENCE OF PARALLELISM BETWEEN THE SENSORIAL AND THE SUBCONSCIOUS POWERS

It is affirmed that 'psychical activity is narrowly conditioned by the extent of organic capacity. It is strictly inseparable from it. The material which the intelligence uses comes to it from the senses. The range of the senses therefore limits the range of psychism.'

There are as many errors as words in this, so far as the subconscious is concerned.

The origin of subconscious capacities is not sensorial, for these capacities are inborn. The range of subconscious capacities transcends in every direction the categories of the sensorial powers.

The higher inspiration, intuition, and genius, are totally independent of acquired knowledge.

8.—ABSENCE OF PARALLELISM BETWEEN ORGANIC CAPACITY AND THE SUPERNORMAL SUBCONSCIOUSNESS

Supernormal facts prove finally that the subconscious psychism outranges all the organic capacities, since it manifests itself without their aid or even altogether externally to them.

The phenomena of materialisation, described in Chapter II., show a dynamo-psychism actually separable from the organism. We have here the absolute negation of classical parallelism.

There is no psycho-anatomical parallelism, for sensorial action may appear completely outside the organs of the senses; motor actions may be exercised outside the muscles; psychic action may develop outside the brain!

There is no psycho-physiological parallelism, for all apparent sensorial, motor, or intellectual action may be suppressed or inert. The body of the subject whose sensibility is exerted at a distance, is usually during the whole time, profoundly anæsthethetised. Her muscles do sometimes make vague associated reflex movements during motor exteriorisations, but these synergetic contractions (not always present) never represent an effort corresponding to the effect. As to her nervous centres, they are in a state of annihilation varying from torpor to a special kind of trance, a kind of transitory coma, during which all functions except those of vegetative life are completely suppressed.

The more profound this functional annihilation, the more remarkable are the metapsychic manifestations. The more complete the exteriorisation and its separation from the organism, the more complex and advanced are the phenomena.

As to vision at a distance and telepathy, the most remarkable cases are those that go furthest, and in the most incredible degree, beyond the range of the senses.

As to ideoplastic materialisation, the more distinct, and the further they are separated from the medium, the more self-activity and apparent autonomy do they show.

In fine, as I have set forth in *l'Être Subconscient,* the classical demonstration in favour of psycho-physiological parallelism in the so-called normal function of the person, turns entirely against the existence of any such parallelism in the so-called supernormal functions.

This negative demonstration may be summed up in a triple formula.

1. No correlation between anatomic physiology and metapsychic manifestations.
2. Metapsychic activity is in the inverse ratio to functional activity.
3. Metapsychic activity (sensorial, dynamic, motor, intellectual, or ideoplastic) is separable from the organism.

It may be affirmed without reserve, that everything happens as if there were no psycho-physiological parallelism for the supernormal subconsciousness.

9.—THE SUBCONSCIOUS OUTRANGES THE ORGANISM AND CONDITIONS IT

The subconscious carries internal proof of this truth. Not only do its manifestations, in fact, transcend all dynamic and material contingencies, but it also conditions them.

We have seen this in psychology, for the conscious psychism is but the smaller part of the whole, and is actually conditioned by that subconscious psychism which is the very foundation of the thinking being and his essential characteristic.

This is still more evident in physiology. It has already been demonstrated that the organic substance is resolvable into a superior dynamism, which has its directive Idea in the subconscious. The subconscious directive Idea shows itself even able, in supernormal states, temporarily to disintegrate organic substance and to reorganise it in new representations. It is therefore certain that the organism, far from being generative of the Idea, as the materialist theory teaches, is, on the contrary, conditioned by the Idea. The organism appears as only an ideoplastic product of that which is essential in the being, that is, of its subconscious psychism.

But even this is not all.

This subconsciousness, which contains within itself the directive and centralising capacities of the Self in all its representations, has also the power to rise above even these representations.

The faculties of telepathy, of mento-mental action, or lucidity, are faculties which transcend representation because they transcend the dynamic or material conditions which rule representation.

In intuition, genius, and lucidity, the subconscious stands above the category of representation, that is, of time and space.

Thus the thesis which Carl du Prel maintained in works that are admirable in intuition; which Myers based on solid documentary proofs; which we have advanced on reasoning which has not been refuted, is now offered in its fullness to all thinkers and men of science who will examine it in good faith.

It may be affirmed without reserve that there is in the living being a dynamo-psychism constituting the essence of the Self, which absolutely cannot be referred to the functioning of the nervous centres. This essential dynamo-psychism is not conditioned by the organism; on the contrary everything happens as though the organism and the cerebral functions were conditioned by it.

10.—CONCLUSIONS FROM THE SYNTHETIC EXAMINATION OF PSYCHO-PHYSIOLOGY

Such are the first essential conclusions of an inclusive psycho-physiology, based on all the facts, but more especially on the higher and more complex facts, enforced by the deeper study of the subconscious, yet easily adaptable, as we shall show further on, to the simplest facts, upon which it throws full light.

Science thus offers materials of high quality, which

if collated, co-ordinated, and classified, will suffice to replace the indescribable chaos of classical psycho-physiology by a harmonious edifice upheld on two pillars.

These are, first the notion of a superior dynamism conditioning the organic complex; and second, the notion of a superior psychism independent of cerebral contingencies, and co-ordinating the multiple states of consciousness.

But before entering upon the work of synthesis, it is necessary to investigate what is offered to us by known systems of philosophy.

PART III

PHILOSOPHICAL THEORIES OF EVOLUTION

FOREWORD

THE philosophies that are founded on known facts
bearing on general and individual evolution, reach
widely different conclusions according as they recognise
a larger or smaller number of these facts, and go more or
less beyond them.

And as the physical sciences steadily progress,
philosophy has to adapt itself to new discoveries, and
must therefore undergo successive modifications, which
are sometimes very radical.

The general questions raised by evolution can be
reduced to three:—

Is there an evolution?

What is it that evolves?

How, and why, does evolution act?

Is there an evolution? This question can be considered as scientifically disposed of. Yes, there is, an
uninterrupted progress from the simple to the complex.

What is it that evolves?

This question is vastly more complicated and
difficult. Present scientific notions tend to establish the
unity of substance. They tend moreover to analyse this
single substance into atoms. They tend, to-day, to
view the atom, not as (strictly speaking) material, but
as a centre of force.

'Matter,' writes M. Gustave le Bon,[1] 'has
passed through widely differing phases. The first
carries us back to the very beginning of the universe

[1] M. Gustave le Bon: *L'Évolution de la Matière.*

141

and is beyond the reach of experiment. It is the period of chaos of ancient legend. That from which the universe was to develop was but formless clouds of ether.

'Directed and condensed by unknown forces acting for unknown ages, the ether finally organised itself into atomic forms. Matter, as it exists on our earth, or as we can observe it in celestial bodies at different evolutionary stages, is an aggregation of these atoms.

'During this period of progressive formation the atoms stored up the energy which, under the modes of electricity, heat, etc. . . . . they gradually expend as time goes on.

'In thus slowly losing their accumulated energy, they underwent diverse evolutionary change, and have put on diverse aspects.

'When they have radiated all their energy under the forms of luminous, calorific, or other vibrations, they must return, by the very fact of this radiation, to the dissociated state—to the primitive ether whence they were derived. This, therefore, represents the final nirvana to which all things must return after a more or less ephemeral existence.

'These summary glances over the origin of our universe and its end are obviously but feeble lights thrown on the darkness which enshrouds our past and veils our future. They are very insufficient explanations. Science can put forward no other, and cannot catch a glimpse of the true first reason of things, nor even reach the real cause of any single phenomenon. It must leave to philosophy and religion the task of imagining systems which can satisfy our need to know.'

We shall endeavour, in the course of this work, to show that our actual knowledge allows us to go much further than M. le Bon thinks, in seeking the meaning of evolution.

Let us first analyse the systems as yet proposed in answer to the third question: How, and why, does evolution act ?

Philosophical theories of evolution may, strictly speaking, be reduced to two—the Deistic or Providential, and the Pantheistic.

Pantheistic metaphysics are infinitely complex, since they include all systems which locate beginning and end in the universe itself. These systems, both in their development and in their conclusions, are widely different one from another, and cannot be blended into a single study.

We could not, within the limits of this work, review them all. We are constrained to make a choice, and that choice is naturally determined by the end at which we aim. We shall therefore only consider :—

1. The philosophy of Providential evolution according to dogma.
2. Contemporary pantheistic or monistic theories.
3. M. Bergson's theory of ' Creative Evolution.'
4. The philosophy of the unconscious, according to Schopenhauer and von Hartmann.

CHAPTER I

I.—TENTATIVE RECONCILIATIONS OF EVOLUTIONARY AND DOGMATIC IDEAS

AFTER having struggled long and desperately against the evolutionary idea, some partisans of theological and dogmatic philosophy, have come, little by little, willingly or unwillingly, to admit it. They are aware, in fact, that the dogma of creation is not more satisfying than materialist teaching.

As Vogel very well says,[1]—

' From a strictly rational point of view it comes to much the same to proclaim that man is the result of chance, or to affirm that his creation is due to the arbitrary act of a personal God. From the moral point of view, that a human being, after a life determined by chance, and without any sanction for his acts, should cease to be, is equivalent to his judgment by absolute and eternal decree on the basis of material acts of infinitesimally small import and duration proceeding from an equally limited freedom of action. But this equipoise of probabilities and absurdities which the materialist schools and the Western religions bring to the solution of the cosmic problem vanishes before the evolutionary theory.'

According to religious believers who have accepted evolutionism, the universe has evolved by the will and under the guidance of a supremely powerful, supremely

[1] Vogel : *La Religion de l'Évolutionnisme* (Fischlin, Brussels).

144

just, and supremely good Providence. Transformism is said to be in no way incompatible with the idea of a Divine plan and with traditional teaching disencumbered of puerile and obsolete dogmatic impedimenta.

Far from being contrary to the providential idea, they say, the evolutionary formula would remove the grave objections arising from the imperfections of the universe. These imperfections, too marked to be reconcilable with the notion of a responsible Providence and a definitive creation, are, on the contrary, easily comprehensible in a world in process of evolution. They would then appear only as necessities inherent in an inferior state, and even as the measure of the inferiority of that state at the moment.[1]

It is not without some hesitation that I discuss the cogency of this reasoning.[2] Such discussions must seem useless and wearisome alike to partisans and opponents of the idea of Providence, for all that can be said on this subject has already been said; also the question is one of those that go with unshakable convictions or beliefs.

But as soon as men claim to substitute logical arguments for an ancient act of faith apart from any criterion, it is necessary to follow them into the domain of facts, and to set forth once more the objections which inevitably rise up against their thesis.

These objections can be reduced to two leading ones :—

(a) That based on the evidence of gropings and errors in evolution.

(b) That based on the prevalence of evil in the universe.

[1] See the curious collection of Conferences of the Rev. F. Zahn, translated under the title, *L'Évolution et le Dogme*, by the Abbé Flageolet, published by Lethellieux, 10 rue Cassette, Paris.

[2] This chapter must on no account be considered apart from the rest. Those which precede it and those which follow, prove that there is no need to have recourse to the providential idea in order to recognise an ideal harmony in the universe. We shall endeavour to demonstrate that evolution tends towards the realisation of sovereign consciousness, sovereign justice, and sovereign good.

2.—THE OBJECTION BASED ON THE EVIDENT GROPINGS AND ERRORS IN EVOLUTION

An evolution proceeding on a Divine plan or constantly governed by a sovereign and perfect Providence, cannot involve gropings or errors. But these gropings and errors are innumerable. They are not the exception, they seem almost the rule.

Thousands and thousands of species have disappeared in the course of the ages. In these evolutionary forms there has been what looks like reckless squandering of vital force and energy.

Everything in evolution shows a creative force that is not sure of itself; which produces to excess in order to reach concrete results in selected forms.

These gropings are very clear in the lower phases of evolution. Germs of species, as of individuals, are produced by thousands ; a small number only succeed in growing at all; among these privileged ones only a few reach the adult state.

How can we attribute to a divine plan a wastage which appears useless and inexplicable ?

Everything happens, in fact, as if there were no appreciable plan. De Vries has shown that among vegetable species mutations arise quite independently of the vital factors; suddenly, anarchically, and in different directions, without reference to the utility of this or that new character. Selection then operates. The classical factors come into play to repress or to develop the characters that have appeared, causing the survival or the disappearance of the new species. But the interior creative impulse, in plants and no doubt in inferior animals also, is a *blind* impulse, a kind of incoherent and disorderly explosion.

In the higher animals, even if the impulse is less blind, if it corresponds with a need, or with something

146

resembling an obscure aspiration towards higher forms, it nevertheless still shows gropings and errors.

In the history of the reptiles of the Secondary epoch how can we fail to see a groping after the higher evolutionary series of mammals ? Is the whole of evolution anything but a series of such gropings ?

These gropings and errors are found in details as well as in the mass; useless organic characters which do not fit into any plan are in no way exceptional.

Delage and Goldsmith cite many instances.

' The diverse colouration of the wings of insects, of the shells of molluscs, characteristics which, to follow the expression of Eimer, are no more useful to them than the brilliant colour of gold to that metal, or its iridescent tints to the soap bubble. The exaggerated dimensions of the antlers of the fossil Irisk elk; the curved and practically unusable tusks of the mammoth; the extraordinarily developed fangs of the modern babiroussa; the eyes of certain crustaceans placed at the end of over-long pedicles ? etc. . . . It would seem as if the development once begun is carried on by a kind of inertia.'

There are even organs which are not only useless, but even injurious, such as the appendix in man.

Instincts also sometimes go astray; deceived by their instincts some game-birds, such as woodcock, always return to the same places, where they meet their death; migratory fish are unable to avoid certain dangerous zones where they perish by thousands; etc.

3.—OBJECTIONS BASED ON EVIL IN THE UNIVERSE

If the existence of errors and gropings is hardly compatible with a Divine plan, there is another consideration even less so. It is the prevalence of evil in the universe.

In fact we find evil everywhere. It seems that the extinction of the feeble dominates human and animal life. Earth, air, and water are just immense and incessant fields of war, compared to which the battles of Man seem slight and intermittent.

The most beautiful birds, and the most delicate insects are very often more ferocious than the large carnivora.

Why should there be this instinct of refined ferocity in the insect, even though it be devoid of thought or responsibility ?

There is no unavoidable necessity that animals should devour one another, since certain of the more powerful among them are entirely vegetable feeders.

Why so much sickness, epidemics, and so many cosmic catastrophes ? Why, always and everywhere, so much suffering and evil ?

The prevalence of evil is really the most serious objection that can be raised against the idea of creation by an all-wise and all-good Providence. The old irrefutable argument inevitably recurs to the mind: If there is a Creator, that Creator must have been wanting either in the knowledge, or in the will, or in the power, to prevent evil; therefore that Creator cannot be at once supremely wise, or supremely good, or supremely powerful.

The strength of this argument is manifest by the futility of the refutations which have been attempted.

It has been said that if there were no evil, the creature would be the equal of the Creator. This sophism cannot hold. Unless it were the work of a Demiurgus of but moderate power, and not of a true Providence, creation could not be based on universal suffering. It should involve the minimum, not the maximum of suffering. It has also been said that evil is the consequence of the liberty given by God to his creatures. But it is evident that great epidemics, most infirmities and diseases, great cosmic catastrophes, etc. . . . . have nothing to do with human liberty.

Finally, ' original sin ' has been alleged. This dogma does not absolve Providence from responsibility. Guyau has put this in a masterly way in his *Irreligion de l'Avenir*:—

' The great resource of Christianity and of most religions is the idea of a Fall. But this explanation of evil by a primitive failure comes to explaining evil by itself; necessarily there must, before the fall, have been some defect in the supposed freedom of the will or in the circumstances which caused it to weaken; no fault is really primal. A man who is perfect and walks under God's eye does not fall when there are no stones on the road. There can be no sin without temptation, and thus we come back to the idea that God was the first tempter; it is God himself who fails morally in a failure which He Himself has willed. To explain the primal fall— the source of all others—the sin of Lucifer, theologians have imagined a sin of the intelligence instead of a sin of the flesh; it is by pride that the angels fell from their first estate, and that sin arises in the deepest element of being. But Pride, that sin of the mind, arises in fact from short-sightedness; the highest and most complete knowledge is that which best knows its own limitations. Pride, therefore, involves to restricted knowledge, and the pride of angels can only proceed from God. Evil is desired and wrought only because of reasons for it, but there are no reasons against reason itself. If, according to the apologists of Free Will, human intelligence by its interior pride and perversity can create and arouse motives for ill-doing, it can at least only do that when its knowledge is limited, doubtful, and uncertain. There is hesitation only in matters concerning which there is no complete evidence to the understanding—one cannot err in the light and against the light. A Lucifer was therefore by his very nature impeccable. In a hypothetically perfect world the desire of evil could arise only from the opposition which an imperfect intelligence would mistakenly think existed between his own good and the general good. But if God and his work had been really perfect, the opposition between personal and general good would have been impossible. Even to the best human minds this opposition appears merely temporary and provisional; much more would it seem so to the archangel of Intelligence itself—the Light-bearer of thought. To know, is to participate in a measure in the supreme Truth—the Divine Consciousness—to have all knowledge would be to be able to reflect the very consciousness of God: how could a Satanic mentality emanate from the all-divine ?'

Moreover, the doctrine of original sin is only applicable to Humanity. Disciples of Descartes have grasped this argument so thoroughly that they have put the objection aside by declaring that animals are automata.

' If animals could think,' they said, ' they would have a soul. If this soul is mortal, that of man may easily be so. If it is immortal, it is impossible to understand how or why the animals should suffer. Have the beasts also eaten forbidden fruit ? Do they also await a Redeemer ?'

In these days when the existence of an 'animal soul' is no longer doubted, the Cartesian argument necessarily turns against the existence of any divine plan. As a last resource the dogmatists are reduced to deny man's capacity to understand the Divine plan.

Doubtless human judgment is still very weak, but to deny it the right to pronounce judgment on the painful conditions of earthly life is to disparage it unduly. That judgment has been given as follows.

Evolution cannot be the work of a supremely wise, just, good, and powerful divinity, whether that divinity had laid down its smallest details in advance, or would intervene from time to time to correct errors.

Endeavours have, however, been made to reconcile the idea of Providence with the facts. It has been said that gropings and errors might be comprehensible after the following manner: Providence, in creating the primitive universe, with a progressive impulse and all potentialities contained within it, would have set bounds to Itself. The impulse once given would proceed automatically, and its objectifications would develop freely, outside any pre-established plan, and without intervention on the part of Providence.

This is more or less what is expressed by the Rev. F. Zahn in his book, *Evolution and Dogma.*

'For the old school of natural theology God is the direct cause of all that exists. For the evolutionist He is the cause of causes—*causa causarum* —of the world and all that it contains. The old theories were that God created everything directly in the state in which it at present exists. According to Evolution, creation, or rather the development of living creatures, has been a slow and gradual process needing vast periods of time to transform the chaos into a cosmos, and to give to the visible universe the beauty and the harmony which it now shows. . . . This is the true meaning of Evolution; and so understood, Evolution, to borrow Temple's expression,[1] " teaches us that the execution of the Divine plan derives more from the primordial act of

[1] Temple : *Relations between Religion and Science.*

creation, and less from the ulterior acts of providential governance; there is thus, on the one hand, more of God's foresight, and on the other fewer interventions; and what is taken from the latter, is added to the former.'

On this theory the responsibility of the Creator for evil is diminished but not abolished, for it cannot be admitted that God in His omniscience would not have foreseen the future predominance of evil.

Deists are then led to the conclusion that evolution could not have been directed differently because evil is the condition under which evolution acts, containing in itself the germ of future good.

This involves a curious restriction of Divine omnipotence, although, by definition it cannot be conditioned by anything.

Further, it is by no means demonstrated that evil is an indispensable factor in evolution. Many contemporary naturalists think differently, basing their conclusion on the impartial examination of facts, and not on preconceived ideas.

What do these facts prove? That new variations appear and prosper most readily where the surrounding conditions demand the least effort to survive.

Kropotkine, studying the Siberian regions, remarks that life there is scanty, and that periods of hard climatic conditions are followed, not by progressive evolution but by regression in all directions.

The Russian botanist Korschinsky[1] reaches similar conclusions. New forms do not appear under adverse conditions of life, or, if they do appear, they immediately perish. Variation is most frequent when the environment is favourable, and inclement conditions, far from favouring evolution, slow it down by restraining

[1] Korschinsky; *Hétérogenèse et Évolution*, Contribution à la Théorie de l'Origine des Espèces (Mem. Acad. Petrograd, IX. 1899).

variation and eliminating new forms which have begun to develop.

Another botanist, Luther Burbank,[1] a grower in California, after much research, concludes that a rich soil and generally favourable conditions encourage frequent variations and assist them, while rigorous conditions of life arrest variation and bring about general regression.

For humanity, as for the lower forms of life, years of famine, of epidemics, and of war, give rise to an enfeebled and inferior generation.

Two things therefore are certain: (*a*) evil, when too pronounced, does not favour evolution, but impedes it. It is no longer a spur, but a curb; and (*b*) evil is not an indispensable condition of evolution, since life is more abundant and varied in regions which are favoured by conditions of climate, food, and well-being.

Another decisive consideration is, that since adaptation and the struggle for life are secondary factors, and since evolution can be conceived to take place without them, it is clear that evil can no longer be considered as the *sine qua non* of evolution.

It is plausible that evil should be inevitable in the lower phases of evolution, and should then appear as the measure of their inferiority; but it cannot be so considered in all cases, unless we imagine the worlds evolving under a primitive impulse which is both blind and unconscious. This will not fit with any hypothesis of a divine plan.

No arguments, however subtle, can hold against this evidence: 'a Creator is a Being in whom all things have their reason and their cause, and consequently supreme and final responsibility vests in Him. He thus bears the weight of all that there is of evil in the universe. In the degree that the ideas of infinite power and supreme

[1] Delage et Goldsmith : *Les Théories de l'Évolution.*

liberty are inseparable from our ideas of God, He loses all excuse, for the Absolute depends on nothing, and has no joint liability with anything; on the contrary, everything depends on Him and has its reason in Him. Therefore all culpability carries back to Him; His work, by reason of the interdependence of its effects, no longer appears to modern thought as anything but a single act; and that act is amenable to moral judgment, and by the same right we judge any other act it is permissible to judge its author; the condition of the world itself is for us the verdict on God. And as, with the increase in moral perception, the evil and immoral tendencies in the universe shock our sensibilities more and more, it seems more and more clear that to affirm a ' Creator ' of the world, is, so to speak, to bring all evil to a focus in Him, to centralise all this immorality in one being, and to justify the paradox that ' Evil is God.' To affirm a Creator is, in fact to transfer evil from the world to God as its primary source; it is to absolve Man and the universe, and to lay the onus on its author who in freedom of action created it.' [1]

4.—NEO-MANICHEISM

A last resource remains in order to absolve not only man and the universe, but God also from responsibility: it is to refuse to see in God an untrammeled Creator, and to attribute the creation of the world to a demigod or an evil dæmon; to see in the universe ' a dual principle, good and evil struggling on an equality and victorious by turns.'

However complicated, absurd, and foolish, the Manichean concept may appear to the philosophic mind, it is not dead. It would seem to be still current in the mystical sects which have inherited mediæval teaching.

[1] Guyau: *L'Irreligion de l'Avenir.*

The echo of these old traditions is heard elsewhere. It is not without profound surprise that we find Manichean ideas in minds imbued with Christian tradition. Flournoy[1] who has not hesitated to put forward such ideas, endeavours to avoid the inevitable objections to them by a subterfuge:—

' If God exists He has been from the beginning in conflict with some independent Principle whence Evil is derived. He is therefore not the Absolute, the All-powerful, the omnipotent Creator of this universe, and we revert inevitably to the ancient Manichean doctrine. I admit that I am not enough of a theologian or of a philosopher to clear up the mystery! But this, perhaps, would not be the first time that a heresy condemned by the Councils might be found to have reason on its side, and to be more conformable to the thought of Christ than received tradition. However that may be, the notion of a God, limited, no doubt, but entirely good, cease-lessly working to bring the greatest possible good out of evils which He has not created, and striving to establish His reign of Love in primeval chaos (which would be the cause and the last word on evolution); and this notion, I say, which seems to me to be the inference from the whole life of Jesus, appears infinitely more *generous* than the current concept of a vindictive God awarding death, visiting the sins of the fathers on the children, and heaping on His creatures (and by choice on the best of them) trials for which it is their duty to thank Him! '

Is there any need to discuss Manicheism or neo-Manicheism any further? Evidently not. It is sufficient to point out that both are ineffectual and complicated, and therefore contrary to all scientific or philosophical method.

[1] Flournoy : *Le Génie Religieux.*

155

Manicheism appears only as a striking proof of the impossibility of reconciling the hypothesis of a Providential creation with the problem of evil. It cannot meet the argument—that the hypothesis of a First Cause external to the universe is a useless hypothesis.

Since, in spite of ourselves, we must always come to the concept of a First Cause, itself uncaused, it is unnecessary to place this primal cause anywhere else than in the universe itself.

The notion of creation *ex nihilo* gives no solution to the inherent difficulty that attends the search for a First Cause. It only reveals that difficulty and increases it by superadding the terrible problem of evil.

CHAPTER II

MONISM

MONISM, which is an adaptation of pantheism to the natural sciences and to the evolutionist hypothesis, is a very attractive theory. On the one hand it simplifies high philosophy conformably to scientific principle and method, by reducing it to a single hypothesis; and, on the other, it is in evident agreement with the evolutionary synthesis as a whole, as applicable to the universe and the individual.

The pantheistic philosophy presents an aspect of undeniable probability, and in the sequel will be seen to be supported by the new psychological concepts.

Without going outside the natural sciences it can be stated that the mechanical, determinist, and teleological concepts which have been the subject of endless philosophical controversy are easily reconciled in the pantheistic synthesis; while apart from that synthesis they are without positive foundation and remain vain and sterile speculations. Apart from the pantheistic philosophy, all concepts of the universe which claim to be scientific, come to this:—

That 'the evolution of the universe is determined by the mechanical addition of new elements to the primitive elements, these increments giving rise to a more and more perfect and complex whole.'

Facts, however, are against this hypothesis. As M. Bergson remarks, 'a single glance at the development of an embryo shows that life does proceed by the association and addition of new elements, but by the fission and dissociation of the old.'

157

And, as we have seen, the greater cannot proceed from the less unless potentially contained in it.

Teleological ideas, unless they are founded in pantheistic ideas and start from them, necessarily end in the commonplace and childish theories, so easy to turn into ridicule, according to which all the components of the universe must have been made for each other. To dismiss this idea it is only necessary to point out, as Russel Wallace does, that every adaptation *necessarily* presents the semblance of an intentional design.

Starting from pantheism on the other hand, both the mechanical means and the teleological end are of a different kind, involving as they do a single metaphysical hypothesis. They imply the idea that our comprehension of Space and Time is relative to our understanding; and that when we rise above these relative ideas, we see, and ought to see, neither beginning nor end, neither origin, termination, nor arrival; neither past, present, nor future, but simply a harmonious whole. It must not be said that the universe has been constructed for a given end by stated means; nor that the means necessarily determine the end.

Mechanical and teleological distinctions are vain. They vanish in the absolute. As Bergson says, we thus come to ' a metaphysical system in which the totality of things is placed in eternity, and in which their apparent duration expresses merely the infirmity of a mind which cannot know everything at once.'

This is what Laplace had previously expressed in the well-known dictum that ' to an intelligence, which, at a given moment, should know all the forces which move Nature and the relative situations of all beings; and if, moreover, that intelligence were powerful enough to analyse these data, it would comprise under the same formula the movements of the greatest bodies in the universe and those of the smallest atom; nothing would be uncertain to its view, and the future, like the past, would be present to its eyes.'

What does M. Bergson object to in this ? That we cannot eliminate Time: ' Nothing in all our experience is more unquestionable than Duration. We perceive duration like a river which cannot change its flow. It is the foundation of our being, and, as we are well aware, the very essence of things with which we are in relation.'

This objection is certainly insufficient: if Time and Space are but illusions of our limited understanding, it is obvious that these illusions may be imposed on our understanding without therefore ceasing to be illusions.

It seems, then, to be true that mechanical or teleological metaphysics can neither be demonstrated nor refuted, because they are outside our modes of reasoning. Nevertheless they seem to receive unexpected support by the facts of prophetical lucidity, and a certain number of these facts are well established.

But even admitting the abstract and metaphysical possibility, this theory brings no concrete addition to the doctrine of evolution. Questions of transcendental ends and means are inseparable from consideration of the Absolute. It is above our intelligence, and cannot be discussed to any profit. We must be content to admit the necessity for a single evolutionary principle containing within itself all evolutionary possibilities, and merely endeavour to understand how these possibilities come into realisation.

Now it is quite certain that the classical naturalistic pantheism, or Monism, does not aid us here.

' This supreme law of Nature,' writes Hæckel, 'being laid down, and all other laws made subordinate to it, we have convinced ourselves of the

---

[1] Hæckel: *The Riddle of the Universe.*

universal unity of Nature, and of the eternal validity of natural laws. From the dark *problem* of Matter there issues the clear *law of Matter.* . . .'

In these words he only enunciates a formula which is very incomplete if not actually valueless.

The clear law of matter has in reality nothing clear about it except its affirmation of unity. It is quite dark as to all that concerns the essential factors and meaning of evolution.

CHAPTER III

I HAVE already, on several occasions, had to quote M. Bergson. It is now desirable to undertake a methodical study of his work with the view of ascertaining whether it brings us nearer a solution of the problem of evolution.

Although I wish to consider here only those ideas of M. Bergson which deal with evolution, I shall not be able to avoid some references to his general philosophical system. His theory of Creative Evolution is, no doubt, his masterpiece; but its leading idea cannot be grasped apart from his other works.

I shall therefore endeavour faithfully to reproduce the main outlines of his system without taking sides either with its obstinate detractors, or its devout disciples.

I.—SUMMARY OF THE BERGSONIAN THEORY OF EVOLUTION

M. Bergson admits transformism, he considers its proof sufficient and unquestionable. But, he adds, even if they were not, the evolutionary concept could not be put aside. He endeavours to demonstrate this necessity in pages which are certainly the most powerful, the most profound, and the most noteworthy of any that he has written.

'Let us suppose that transformism were convicted of error. Let us suppose that by inference or experiment, species were shown to arise by a discontinuous process of which we at present have no idea. Would this invalidate transformism in its most interesting parts—those which have most importance for ourselves ? The main outlines of classification would remain unchanged, there would be the same relations between comparative anatomy and comparative embryology. Thenceforward we could, and should, still maintain the same relations—the same parentage—between living forms as transformism presents to us to-day.

'These relations would, no doubt, be more of a parentage of idea than of a material filiation. But as the actual data of palæontology would remain, it would have to be admitted that the forms between which this parentage of idea subsists, have appeared successively and not simultaneously. Now the philosophical mind asks no more than this of the evolutionary theory. It is the function of that theory to verify the relations of parentage in idea, and to maintain that where there is what may be called a logical filiation between diverse forms, there is also a chronological sequence between the species in which those forms appear. This double proposition would remain, whatever causes might be in operation. And thenceforward it would still be necessary to suppose an evolution somewhere. This might be in creative thought in which the ideas of different species would have successively engendered each other, just as transformism maintains the species themselves to have been engendered on the earth. Or it might be in a scheme of vital organisation immanent in Nature, gradually becoming more distinct; the relationship of logical and chronological filiation between abstract forms being precisely those which transformism presents to us as the relationship of real filiation between living creatures. Or again, the same sequence would be seen in some unknown cause of life developing its effects *as if* one did actually engender another. Evolution would then only have been transposed. It would have passed from the visible to the invisible. Nearly everything that transformism asserts to-day would remain intact, only it would be interpreted in a different manner.

'Is it not well then to keep to the letter of transformism, as understood almost unanimously by men of science ? . . . For this reason we consider that the language of transformism is necessary in all philosophy, as its positive teaching is necessary in science.'

Evolution being definitely established with all the weight of sure fact, it is incumbent upon us to seek to understand how it is effected. For M. Bergson evolution is due to none of the factors to which it is ascribed by naturalists; these are all secondary.

'We in no way dispute that adaptation to environment may be a necessary cause of evolution . . . but it is one thing to acknowledge that external circumstances are forces of which evolution must take account, and another thing to maintain that they are its directing forces. . . . The truth is that adaptation explains the minor windings of evolutionary progress but not the general direction of the movement, still less the movement itself. The road which leads to a town is certainly compelled to go up hills and down slopes, it adapts itself to the ground, but the accidents of the ground are not the causes of the road, nor do they assign its general direction.'

What, then, is the essential factor ?
This essential factor is a kind of interior impulse, an original and undefined ' vital surge ' (*élan vital*).

This vital impulse pertains to an immanent principle which is life, intelligence, and matter. It transcends them all, in the past, the present, and the future. It presupposes them, contains them, and precreates them, so to say, in proportion as they come into realisation.

This immanent principle, however, has no final completeness in itself; it comes into existence progressively as it creates the evolving universe. It constitutes what M. Bergson calls 'Duration.' This 'Duration' is not very easily understood. An eminent disciple of M. Bergson describes it as follows.

> ' It is a melodious evolution of moments in which each has the resonance of the preceding moment and foretells that which will succeed it; it is an amplification which never stops, and a perpetual origin of new manifestations. It is a Becoming, indivisible, qualitative, organic, beyond Space, and not amenable to number. . . . Imagine a symphony which should be conscious of itself and creative of itself: it is after this manner that Duration is best understood.' [1]

It is duration, with its vital impulse, which is the essential cause of evolution, and not Darwinian or Lamarckian adaptation.

How are we to conceive of evolution from ' duration ? ' Everything happens as if there were a centre whence worlds are thrown off like fireworks in a vast illumination.

But this centre is not a concrete thing; it is ' a continuity of outflow.'

This centre is God; but ' God, thus defined, has no completed existence: He is ceaseless life, He is action, He is liberty. Creation, thus conceived of, is no mystery: we experience it in ourselves as soon as we act freely.'

[1] Le Roy: *Une Philosophie Nouvelle.*

Therefore there is no pre-determined finality; no scheme of evolution laid down in advance; there are only objectifications which involve and succeed each other; 'a creation which proceeds without end in virtue of an initial impulse.' This creation brings forth, not only the forms of life, but the ideas which allow the intellect to understand it, and the terms by which it is expressed. Its future goes beyond the present and cannot be described by any existing idea.'

M. le Roy[1] has summed up as clearly as may be the thought of M. Bergson on the creative *processus* and on the concepts of spirit and matter issuing from that *processus*.

' In this concept of Being, consciousness is omnipresent as the original and fundamental reality, always there under a thousand different degrees of intensity or of sleep, and under an infinitely diverse rhythm.

' The vital surge consists in an impulse to create. Life, in its humblest stages is a spiritual activity; and its efforts start a current of ascending objectification, which in its turn directs the counter-current of matter. Thus all Reality appears as a double movement of ascent and descent. The former alone, revealing an interior energy of creative impulsion, has endless duration; the latter might be said to be almost instantaneous, like the recoil of a spring, but each imposes its rhythm on the other. From this point of view Spirit and Matter do not appear as opposed entities—the statical terms of a fixed antithesis—but rather as movement in inverse directions; and in certain relations it would be better to speak of spiritualisation and materialisation, rather than of Spirit and Matter, the latter process of materialisation resulting automatically from an interruption

[1] Le Roy: *Une Philosophie Nouvelle.*

of the former. " Consciousness " or " Supercon-
sciousness " is the rocket whose extinguished remains
fall to earth as Matter.

    'Under what metaphor is the course of the
evolution of the universe presented to us ? Not
that of a deductive flow, nor of a series of stationary
pulsations, but as a fountain, which, expanding as
it rises, partially arrests or delays the drops which
fall back. The jet itself—the reality disclosed—is
the vital activity of which spiritual activity is the
highest form; and the drops that fall back
are the creative movement which descends with
its reality dissipated—they represent Matter and
Inertia.'

According to M. Bergson, ' Matter is defined as a
species of descent; this descent is defined as the interruption of an ascent, the ascent itself as a growth, and
thus a creative principle is inherent in all things.'[1]
We are then faced with the question of origin. How
can the universe have come from nothing ? How can
that which is have sprung from the void,—from that
which is not ?

According to M. Bergson that question should not
be asked.

    ' The idea of nothingness in the sense of being
an opposite to existence, is a pseudo-idea.' In
fact, ' nothingness is unthinkable, for to think of
" nothing " is necessarily to think in some way;
the representation of the void is always the representation of a *plenum*, which can be analysed into
two positive elements—the idea, more or less distinct,
of a substitution; and the sensation, real or imagined,
of a desire or a regret.'

    Hence ' the idea of absolute nothingness (under-
stood in the sense of the abolition of everything) is

[1] M. le Roy : *Ibid.*

an idea destructive of itself, a pseudo-idea, a mere word.'

' When I say, " there is nothing," it is not that I perceive " a nothing," I can perceive only what is; but I have not perceived that which I sought for and expected, and I express my disappointment in the language of my desire.'

In fine, it is only by an illusion of reason that the idea of Void is opposed to that of All. It is to ' oppose a *plenum* to a *plenum*,' and ' the question *why* a certain thing exists is consequently a meaningless question— a pseudo-problem built on a pseudo-idea.'

The creative *processus* cannot therefore not exist, and there is no mystery in verifying the existence of matter, life, or consciousness. They are functions of ' duration.'

The only mystery lies in the relations between Creative Evolution, matter, life, and consciousness.

M. Bergson rejects materialist theories. Consciousness is not the result of the working of the brain :—

' Brain and consciousness correspond because each measures the amount of choice which the living being has at disposal, the one by the complexity of its structure, the other by the intensity of its awakeness. But this correspondence is not an equivalence or a parallelism. Precisely because a cerebral condition merely expresses the action nascent in the corresponding psychological condition, the psychological condition vastly outstrips the state of the brain.'

M. G. Gillouin[1] says :—
' M. Bergson's writings abound in ingenious and striking similes to bring out the solidarity . *sui*

[1] *Essai sur les Données Immédiates de la Conscience.*

generis of the consciousness and the organism. Because, he says, a certain bolt is necessary to a given machine, which works when the bolt is in place and stops if it be removed, no one will maintain that the bolt is the equivalent of the machine. But the relation of the brain to consciousness may well be that of the bolt to the engine. Again, M. Bergson says, the consciousness of a living being is in solidarity with his brain in the sense that a pointed knife is in solidarity with its point. The brain is the sharp point by which consciousness penetrates the dense fabric of events, but it is no more co-extensive with consciousness than the point is co-extensive with the knife.'

Therefore the consciousness that resides in us is not bound to the organism, but enjoys liberty. But this word ' liberty ' must be taken in a very wide sense: that which is free, is the interior, complete self, rather than the individualised person.

' We are free,' says M. Bergson, ' when our acts emanate from our whole personality. Liberty is therefore a function of our power of introspection. . . . Liberty is something which continuously arises in us; we are liberable rather than liberated; and in the last analysis, it is a matter of duration, not of space and number, nor of our improvisation or decree; the free act has been long prepared, it is weighted with our whole past, and falls like a ripe fruit from our previous life.[1]

' What are we, in fact,[2] what is our *character*, if it is not the condensation of our history since birth, or even before birth, since we bring pre-natal dispositions with us ? No doubt it is but a small part of that past that enters into our thoughts, but

[1] Le Roy: *Ibid.* [2] *L'Evolution Créatrice.*

we desire, and will, and act, from the whole of that past, including the original bent of the soul.'

These general ideas being admitted, let us examine more thoroughly the mechanism of Creative Evolution. This evolution does not take place in a direct line. From the centre of origin there flow out many lines, at first interpenetrating, close, and parallel, which, according to their degrees of evolution, then separate and diverge like the trail of a group of rockets.

On the earth the chief lines of evolution end in the creation of plant life, of instinctive animal life, and intellectual human life. These forms are absolutely distinct; there is a chasm between the plant and the animal, and between the animal and Man.

M. Bergson writes:—

' The capital error which has vitiated naturalistic philosophy since the time of Aristotle, has been to see in vegetative, instinctive, and rational life three successive degrees of one and the same tendency, whereas they are three divergent directions of one activity which has become tripartite in process of its increase. The difference between them is one of essential nature, not of degree.'

He says, further —:

' Intelligence and instinct represent two divergent and equally elegant solutions of one and the same problem; . . . between animals and Man there is no longer a difference of degree, but of kind.

To meet the objection that intelligence is discoverable in animals and instincts in Man, M. Bergson says:—

' Having at first interpenetrated one another, Intelligence and Instinct retain something of their common origin. Neither the one nor the other are found in their pure state; there is no intelligence in which traces of instinct are not to be found; and, more especially, no instinct without a fringe of intelligence.'

But the essential characteristic of the animal is instinct, and that of the man is intelligence.

What is the part assigned to Man in the creation? His function is unique, he represents that which is essential in evolution as actually realised, vegetable and animal life being merely gropings after the human.

' Everything,' says M. Bergson, ' comes to pass as though an undecided and impressionable being, call him Man or Superman, as you will, had sought to realise himself, and had succeeded in doing so only at the price of leaving a part of himself by the way. These residues are represented by the animal, and even by the vegetable world.'

Man only has been able to acquire consciousness.

' In Man, consciousness breaks the chain (of material needs); in Man and in Man alone, it is freed. Till this point was reached life had been an effort of consciousness to raise matter, and consciousness was more or less crushed out under its weight. . . . The task to be accomplished was to use matter (which is necessity), to create an instrument for liberty, to make machinery which would triumph over mechanism, and to employ the determinism of Nature to pass through the meshes of the net which that determinism had spread. But in all cases except that of Man, consciousness has been caught in the net through which it would fain have passed.

' It has remained captive to the mechanism which

it invented. From the springboard whence Life took its leap, all the others failed to reach the bar; Man alone has leaped high enough.'

Is the human consciousness, thus formed and freed, indestructible or does it cease at death ?

To this grave question, which dominates all religions and philosophies, M. Bergson merely replies:—

'All Humanity is an immense army which presses forward in Space and Time, before, behind, and by the side of us all, in an impulsive charge that can overcome every resistance and clear many an obstacle, perhaps even death.'

Such is the summary of M. Bergson's chief teaching. We have now to discuss the method on which this teaching is founded.

M. Bergson's method for the solution of philosophical problems is to appeal to the intuition and not to the understanding.

He allots to intelligence the task of finding solutions of all problems which have to do with the relations of the Self to the universe, and with the knowledge of material and inorganic existence, nothing more. This is the domain of science.

As for the world of Life and the soul, it is amenable neither to thought nor to scientific knowledge, but to intuition.

What, then, is intuition, according to M. Bergson ?

The intuition is nothing else than instinct conscious of itself, able to consider its purpose and enlarge that purpose indefinitely.

'If the consciousness which sleeps in instinct were to awake; if it were to interiorise itself in knowledge instead of exteriorising itself in action; if we could question it, and if it could reply, it would give up to us the most intimate secrets of life, for it does but continue the work by which Life organises Matter.'

Unfortunately, as a consequence of the evolution of the animal to man, intuition is vague and discontinuous; 'it is an expiring lamp which burns up ,at long intervals and for a few moments only . . . it sheds but a feeble and flickering light on our personality, on the place which we hold in Nature, on our origin and destiny, but its rays scarcely penetrate the darkness in which our reason leaves us.'

The intuition, however, cannot dispense with reason, we must inevitably reckon with reason in some measure, and taking account of the lessons of fact, must submit them to the control of reason.

But 'the proper task of philosophy is to absorb reason into instinct, or rather to reintegrate instinct in Intelligence.' Thus understood 'philosophy includes, pre-supposes, and rests on science; and it further involves tests by experimental verification.'[1]

It has been objected that this concept of intuition and its relations to intelligence is paradoxical, the reasoning being in a vicious circle. Bergsonians have been told—'you claim, on the one hand, that intuition goes beyond intelligence in a domain proper to itself, and on the other you reserve to intelligence a right of control in this domain which is not its own!'

Bergsonians reply that the answer is that the intelligence to which they refer is not 'the critical and discursive intelligence, guided by its own power . . . and enclosed in an inviolable circle. We are speaking of something quite different—that intelligence should take the risk of a plunge into the phosphorescent water around it, which is not altogether strange to reason

[1] Le Roy : *Ibid.*

since reason arose from it, and since it contains the powers complementary to understanding. The intelligence can therefore adapt itself, and will have been only lost for the moment, that it may become greater, stronger, and enriched.'[1]

To break through ' the inviolable circle ' the intelligence must set aside its habitual methods of reasoning and give itself up to the magic power of intuition. Renewed, vivified, elated, and transformed by intuition, the intelligence will become a super-intelligence capable even of judging the results of intuition.

2.—CRITICISM OF THE BERGSONIAN PHILOSOPHY

The Bergsonian philosophy presents to criticism a method and a doctrine.

Let us examine the method in the first place.

According to Bergson the great philosophical problems on life, the nature of being—and of the universe, lie outside Science, and their solution depends entirely on intuition.

Intuition, as he understands it, is both instinctive inspiration and introspection. It admits of check by the intelligence, but only if super-intelligent, so to say —an intelligence exalted and vivified by intuition.

This method alone admits of our going beyond known facts and scientific ideas.

The first questions that arise are:—

1. Is this Bergsonian ' intuition ' something new, and does it inaugurate a new method not previously published ?

2. Must this method be specially retained for philosophy as philosophy specialises in this kind of method ?

[1] Le Roy : *Ibid.*

From the Unconscious to the Conscious

The answers to these two propositions are by no means established.

It is clear that all men of genius, all inventors, all the great minds which have added something new to human resources, were intuitive by nature.

But intuition cannot be reserved to philosophy. It belongs to many departments of life—philosophical, artistic, industrial, and scientific. Science depends on intuition as much as on reasoning. The great scientific discoveries existed in the understanding of men of genius before being adapted to the facts and shown to be true. There is as much intuition in the genius of a Newton or a Pasteur, as in that of a great metaphysician.

The distinction, and the only distinction, between philosophical and scientific method, is that men of science keep as much as possible within the limits of fact and take as their criterion concordance with facts or with rational inferences; whilst philosophers, although endeavouring to keep their intuitions in accord with facts, sometimes allow themselves to propose bold hypotheses which go beyond them.

This, and no more, is exactly what Bergson has done.

I know very well that some persons see in the 'Bergsonian intuition' something heretofore unpublished to the world. I humbly avow that I do not comprehend the discussions which have arisen on this matter between the partisans and the antagonists of M. Bergson, and I even find them tedious.

It is well to bring out clearly that this 'new' method which consists in putting intuition in contrast with reason and in referring to the former the sole origin of philosophic truths, has previously been definitely claimed and severely criticised, just as it is to-day.

'An endeavour is being made to smuggle palpable sophisms in place of proofs; appeal is made to intuition. . . . Thought, that is to say, reasoned knowledge, judicial deliberation, and sincere demonstration—in a word the proper and normal use of reason—is disliked: a supreme contempt is proclaimed for rational philosophy; meaning by that, all the series of linked and logical deductions which characterise the work of previous philosophers.

' Then, when the dose of impudence is sufficient, and encouraged by the ignorance prevailing in these times, we shall soon hear something of this sort: " it is not difficult to understand that the ' mannerism ' which consists in enunciating a proposition, giving the reasons which support it and similarly refuting its antithesis, is not the form under which truth should be presented. Truth is the movement of itself by itself." '

By whom is this biting apostrophe ?

No doubt, it will be thought to be one of Mr Bergson's detractors, criticising the philosophy of ' Duration.' . . . Not at all: it is Schopenhauer on Hegel.[1]

But the question of the novelty and the originality of the Bergsonian ' intuition ' is a quite secondary matter. Let us, for the moment, admit the novelty and content ourselves with a valuation of the method by what it teaches us. Our judgment will go by the results obtained.

If it is demonstrated that the teachings of M. Bergson's are of value only within the limits within which they can be checked by facts; that when they go beyond facts they are insufficient or erroneous, that will suffice to prove that the ' Bergsonian intuition ' has no special validity.

It will then be no longer permissible to contrast the intuitive to the scientific methods. It will be established

---

[1] Schopenhauer: *Parerga et Paralipomena.*

(yet once more) that there is one only method of reaching truth, that which brings the results of intuition into accord with logic and the study of facts. This is the positive method which admits only rational inductions as valid. M. Bergson's teachings may be placed in three categories :—

    (*a*) Those which are in accord with facts, and are therefore within the limits of scientific method.

    (*b*) Those which are not deduced from facts, and are undemonstrable.

    (*c*) Those which are opposed to well established facts, and are therefore erroneous.

We will now examine these three categories.

3.—TEACHING IN ACCORD WITH FACTS OR DEDUCED FROM THEM

This is the teaching relating to the proof of evolution as a general theory, and to the principle of the essential causality in evolution.

The reality of transformism and the impossibility of explaining it by the classical factors of selection and adaptation are brought into full light by M. Bergson with flawless logic and an irresistible power of persuasion. To those synthetic reasons which have been set forth in the earlier chapters of this work, he adds certain reasons of an analytical and special order, which will be found scattered here and there throughout his ' Creative Evolution.' He finds new proofs of the impotence of the classical theories in the study of certain details of comparative anatomy, such as the eyes of some molluscs compared with those of the vertebrates.

M. Bergson's analytical work is extremely conscientious, and the reasoning on the facts before him is exact and rigorous. If it is not of a kind to convince the disciples of naturalism (for discussion may continue indefinitely without reaching absolutely unanswerable conclusions), that is of little moment, since the synthetic study of evolution proves undeniably that the classical factors are secondary and there is some essential factor as yet unknown.

The necessity for this essential factor, being some kind of internal creative impulse giving rise to the ‘vital surge’ is evident from the study of the facts. M. Bergson’s teachings on this head, are strictly rational inferences which do not transgress the limits of scientific method. As such, and apart from other doctrines, they ensure a unique place to his philosophy in the higher walks of contemporary thought.

The notion of the ‘vital surge’ may be seen, in germ, in some naturalistic systems such as Nägeli’s, and in ancient and modern pantheistic philosophies, but the special merit of the Bergsonian system consists in the rigorous application of this idea to the facts, and in a presentment which is truly a work of genius.

4.—DOCTRINES WHICH ARE NOT DEDUCED FROM FACTS
AND ARE NOT DEMONSTRABLE

These include the teaching on God, the non-existence of void, the nature of matter and spirit, the relations of consciousness to the organism, the independence of consciousness and matter, on human liberty, and on the hope of survival.

All these are given without being based on facts, even when (as we shall see later) the facts are such as might be used partially to confirm the doctrines. The teaching on these points is of the intuitive order. There is no need to demonstrate their impotence. The classical physiological ideas which make consciousness dependent on the brain will never be upset by arguments drawn from the intuition. As long as the experimental idea of a psycho-physiological parallelism subsists in modern science, all the beautiful reasoning of a spiritual kind or the highest idealist hopes (apart from an act of faith), will alike be entirely inoperative against them.

M. Bergson's efforts to buttress intuitive arguments by ingenious similes will not do. He may compare evolution to a sheaf of rockets with God at its centre; intelligence to the ascending energy of the fireworks, and matter to the dead sticks falling back to earth; he may imagine many comparisons to make it understood how, in spite of a seeming psycho-physiological parallelism, consciousness is not limited by the organ of consciousness . . . all these similes, however ingenious, can only give a superficial and fugitive satisfaction—they prove nothing.

Not merely do they prove nothing, they are dangerous, because they bring errors in their train and give the illusion of proof to an investigation which is wanting in thoroughness.

The chief error in the Bergsonian philosophy, an error which we shall presently expose—its anthropocentric concept—is probably due to the initial simile comparing evolution to a sheaf of diverging rockets.

5.—CONTRADICTIONS AND INEXACTITUDES

Besides these illusory or dangerous similes, M. Bergson's philosophy shows obvious contradictions and inexactitudes posing as a system. The contradictions are striking.

M. Bergson makes out intuition to be a kind of dethroned instinct, a residue of the animal evolution. But he also makes it the basis of philosophic method; so much so, that, according to his system, Man, the privileged member of creation, can know truth only by the faculty which (again according to his system) characterises animal evolution! Then, in order to palliate the insufficiency of the former idea, he makes it a superhuman faculty, which nevertheless, is still only instinct.

He rejects the control of the intelligence in philosophical matters, but then finds himself obliged to have recourse to some kind of super-intelligence, different from intelligence itself.

He contrasts intuition and intelligence, but by most subtle reasoning, endeavours to bring them into unity; he places the criterion of truth in the intuition controlled by intelligence which is at the same time vivified by the intuition; so that in the last analysis the intuition is both advocate and judge.

He denies to logic the right to know that which deals with life and high philosophical problems, but in his work erudition and reasoning take a very prominent place.

He invents a new metaphysical entity—' duration,' but it so happens that this entity is founded on that which is least certain, most subjective, and most relative to our understanding—the concept of time!

The inexactitudes are yet more serious; through them M. Bergson's work leads to a vague idealism—an idealism which does not express itself frankly and clearly.

Difficulties seem eluded rather than solved. The old contradictions are not reconciled by a higher synthesis, which, whether true or not, might at least be precise; they are (we must venture to say) subtilised under confused and plastic formulæ.

This quasi-systematic lack of preciseness causes the earnest reader of M. Bergson's work to feel a discomfort which neither his genius nor his skill can dispel. It is hard to know whether one perceives the truth through a mirage, or is simply the dupe of illusion and paradox. The impression that remains is that of a splendid but phantasmal edifice, of gorgeous tapestries hiding an imperfect and defective structure whose foundations are insecure. We lie under the magic spell and fear to awake disillusioned.

M. Gillouin[1] says: ' M. Bergson carries us along with him round and over all obstacles, with an ease which makes us think of some high intellectual school of thought.' Unfortunately it also makes us think of skilful sleight of hand. . . .

The want of preciseness in Bergsonian philosophy makes it appear conformable, at least on a superficial survey, to the most opposite doctrines. It would be comical, were it not saddening, to see men who stand for the most opposed ideas placing themselves under M. Bergson's ægis. Deists and pantheists, orthodox and theosophists, neo-occultists, and even it would seem neo-syndicalists[2] all invoke his authority.

As for the philosophers, they are simply disconcerted by a system so pliable as, on the one hand, to allow of the assertion that[3] ' whatever may be the deepest essential nature of things we are a part thereof' (which seems a profession of pantheist faith conformable to the general spirit of Bergsonian metaphysics); and, on the other hand, to affirm that the whole of this metaphysic 'presents the idea of a God freely creating both matter and life, whose creative work is continued by the evolution of species and by the constitution of human personalities,' and also, that ' this work is the categorical refutation of both monism and pantheism! '[4]

6.—DOCTRINES CONTRARY TO WELL-ESTABLISHED FACTS

One of M. Bergson's principal doctrines is that the distinction between the animals and man is one of nature, not of degree.

[1] Gillouin : *La Philosophie de M. Bergson.*   [2] Idem.
[3] *Revue de Métaphysique et de Morale*, Nov. 1911.
[4] *Études*, 20th Feb., 1917.

This distinction is not supported by any facts, and contradicts the most certain data of contemporary psychology.

According to M. Bergson, the divergent lines of evolution have produced on the one hand, the animal instincts, and on the other, the human intelligence. Animal instinct has retained 'fringes of intelligence,' and human intelligence has kept a residue of instinct. But instinct and intelligence are separated by an impassable abyss, and Man alone is the essential and superior product of evolution, while the vegetable and animal world are its residual products.

This theory is profoundly distasteful to naturalistic philosophy which sees in it a return, whether sincere or disguised, to old anthropocentric ideas. If it were established on any positive data, it would profoundly disturb the whole evolutionary synthesis.

But these data do not exist and M. Bergson's teaching rests on an omission fatal to his theory. The concept of Creative Evolution takes no account of subconscious psychism.

The study of this subconscious psychism proves to the point of demonstration, as we shall see, the identity of the nature of animals and man.

There is no need to seek to discover whether there are in animals more than fringes of intelligence; comparative psychology is not sufficiently advanced to permit of this being established with any certainty. It will suffice to demonstrate that there is in man much more than residues of instinct; there is a vast subconscious domain which is instinct much more highly developed.

To this domain belong the automatism of the main functions of life which are identical in animals and men; the great instinctive impulses of self-preservation, reproduction, etc., equally potent in animals and Man though frequently masked in the latter; and finally the higher active subconsciousness, of which animal instinct is but the first manifestation, which has in human mental life a much larger field than that of the consciousness by which it is concealed from view.

Subconscious psychology dominates human and animal life alike, and consciousness appears only as an acquisition growing with evolution and proportional to the level of that evolution. There is therefore no difference in the essential nature of animals and man; from the psychic point of view both are governed by the subconscious. There is between them only a difference of degree, which is marked by the amount of conscious realisation.

The demonstration of this truth is of capital import, for it involves the failure of one of the chief doctrines of the Bergsonian system, and therefore invalidates its whole method.

This demonstration falls into three parts.

(*a*) Animal instinct is but the first manifestation of unconscious psychism, and is of an inferior kind.

(*b*) Human subconsciousness is the animal instinct developed, expanded, and enriched by progressive evolution.

(*c*) The degree of conscious realisation in the animal and in man, and from the animal to man, is purely and simply a function [1] of the evolutionary level attained.

(*a*) THE ANIMAL INSTINCT IS BUT THE FIRST MANIFESTATION OF SUBCONSCIOUS PSYCHISM OF AN INFERIOR KIND

Instinct, for the most part, obeys neither logic nor conscious reasoning, nor will. Its characteristics are those of human subconsciousness. It attains marvellous

---

[1] 'Function': here used in the mathematical sense—a quantity whose changes of value depend on those of other quantities called its variables.—[Translator's note.]

results superior to those of intentional and conscious thought; and this is precisely the case with human subconsciousness. It is essentially mysterious, and follows no known psychological laws; just like human subconsciousness. Finally it is connected to the human subconsciousness by that supernormal psychology which at the present time must always be taken into account.

In the manifestations of what is called accidental instinct a very marked and striking transition from instinctive subconsciousness properly so called, to supernormal subconsciousness may be observed.

Guided by this accidental instinct, animals sometimes behave with the certainty and lucidity which pertain to human somnambulism.

Fabre cites the following instances from his own observation.

A cat was taken from the house where it had lived to quite the other side of the town of Avignon, without any means of seeing the road by which it had been conveyed. It escaped, and very shortly afterwards reached its old home, having traversed the town nearly in a straight line, taking no account of any obstacles not absolutely impassable. It had to pass through a labyrinth of populous streets and did not appear to notice any of the dangers of the way from boys and dogs. It swam the river Sorgue, ignoring the bridges, which did not happen to be just on its line: in short, it acted just as if in the somnambulic state.

Another cat was taken by train from Orange to Serignan (over four miles). For the first few days it seemed to be getting used to its new abode, showing no tendency to escape. Then suddenly it showed an irresistible desire to return, and went back to its old home by the shortest line, crossing the river Aygues by swimming.

Many analogous cases of dogs returning to their masters' house after long and intricate journeys have often been reported. In these cases we touch what has been called 'metapsychic phenomenology.'

True supernormal manifestations, as well as hypnotic or somnambulic phenomena have been observed in animals. Some have strange premonitions; the 'death-howl' of a dog, once heard in tragic circumstances, can never be forgotten. I have myself heard it on more than one occasion, and have been vividly impressed by it.

For instance, I was one night watching, in my medical capacity, by a young woman who, in the midst of health, had been stricken down that very day by mortal illness. She was dying, and the death *râle* was in her throat. The family was present, silent and deeply distressed. The time was 1 a.m. (She died at daybreak.)

Suddenly from the garden which surrounded the house came the 'death-howl' of the house-dog—a long, lugubrious wail on one note, at first loud then falling diminuendo slowly to a close.

For some seconds there was silence, then the wail began again, as before. The dying woman had a gleam of consciousness and looked at us with an anxious expression. She had understood. Her husband went out in haste to silence the dog. At his approach the dog fled and hid, and in the darkness it was impossible to find it. As soon as the man returned to the house the wails began again, and continued for more than an hour till the animal could be seized and taken away.

Dr A. R. Wallace, and others have cited many cases of a metapsychic kind, still more mysterious, in which animals, especially dogs and horses, have been the agents. In this connection the case of the Elberfeld calculating horses may be mentioned; these have been observed and the facts verified by several men of science, among others Professor Claparéde of Geneva. All agree in authenticating the facts. M. de Vesme[1] has shown that the solutions (to mathematical questions

[1] *Annales des Sciences Psychiques.*

given by these horses) cannot be reasoned or conscious, but are of the metapsychic and subconscious order. I think it needless to insist on these and analogous facts known to all specialists of the subconscious.

Von Hartmann has already pointed out the similarity between instincts and supernormal manifestations in the case of presentiments, second-sight, and clairvoyance. Instinct, he remarks, and the unconscious, intrude their results on consciousness in each case with the same suddenness and precision.

To sum up, the final results of the analysis of animal instinct are, that it is of the subconscious order; that it is in essence the same as human subconsciousness; and that it is obviously only the first and lower manifestation of the subconscious psychism.

If it occupies the whole, or what appears to be the whole, of the psychological field of the animal, that is merely because in the animal consciousness is as yet undeveloped.

(*b*) HUMAN SUBCONSCIOUSNESS IS THE ANIMAL INSTINCT DEVELOPED, EXPANDED, AND ENRICHED BY PROGRESSIVE EVOLUTION

This law is the corollary of the last, and rests on the same arguments. All that essentially characterises human subconsciousness is found in animal instinct. M. Ribot says of inspiration that 'primarily it is impersonal and involuntary, it acts *like an instinct*, when and how it will.'[1]

It only remains to show that all particulars in which subconsciousness is superior to instinct, can be simply explained by difference in the evolutionary level. For this demonstration we must refer the reader to Book II. We shall there show the *processus* by which the

[1] Ribot: *Psychologie des Sentiments.* The italics are Dr Geley's.

progressive enrichment of the subconscious has come about, and how the inspiration of genius, with its higher intuition and creative faculty, is visible and already outlined, in the animal instincts.

It will be difficult for M. Bergson's partisans to revolt against this law, since they admit that intuition is essentially instinctive. Intuition can be very much better understood as an expansion and enrichment of instinct, than by considering it as a residue of an animal faculty.

(*c*) THE DEGREE OF CONSCIOUS REALISATION IN THE ANIMAL AND IN MAN, AND FROM THE ANIMAL TO MAN, IS PURELY AND SIMPLY A FUNCTION OF THE EVOLUTIONARY LEVEL ATTAINED

The demonstration of this law also is deferred to Book II., but the importance of this demonstration is lessened by reason of the fact that the major portion of psychology, whether animal or human, is subconscious and essentially the same in both. From this it follows that the capital distinction between animal instinct and human intelligence which M. Bergson labours to establish loses all importance.

Considering only the evolution of consciousness (taken separately), it obviously is merely a function of the evolutionary level, and equally obviously there is no impassable abyss between animal and human intelligence. It appears profoundly illogical and erroneous to say that there are in the animal only ' fringes of intelligence.'

From the lowest to the highest evolutionary types the conscious intelligence is observable as a development by stages. It is potential only in plants and in very inferior animals; sketched out in higher species; distinctly active in the highest animals, in which it begins to play an important part; still more distinct and active in the lower grades of Humanity; and expanded and developed in the highest human types.

It now only remains to draw a general conclusion from this study of M. Bergson's concepts as set forth in *L'Évolution Créatrice*.

Of all its doctrines the only ones which can stand criticism are those which are based on the study of facts or drawn by reasoned inference from the examination of facts. These are the teaching on the primordial cause of evolution, on the insufficiency of the classical factors of selection and adaptation, and on the need for recognising an essential and creative vital impulse.

The other doctrines, based on an alleged new notion of intuition, are either insufficient or inexact or, worse still, are contrary to the facts.

Whatever may be thought of M. Bergson's method, and however great our admiration for his incomparable talent of exposition and his persuasive eloquence, we cannot find in the system of Creative Evolution a solution to the great enigma. The truths which that system contains are eclipsed by a proved error bearing on an essential point, an error which radically vitiates all his metaphysic.

CHAPTER IV

IT has been shown that the principal error of M. Bergson's *Creative Evolution* and, generally, of his whole system, consists in his disregard of the psychology called sub-conscious or unconscious.

We shall now examine a philosophy which, in contrast with M. Bergson's, is based on the unconscious.

The expression, 'The Philosophy of the Unconscious,' was invented by von Hartmann; but the foundation of that philosophy, the notion of a creative, immanent, and omnipresent unconsciousness belongs to all ages and all civilisations.

The numerous metaphysical concepts of the human understanding on the nature of things come in the end to two classes, apparently contradictory; if indeed the contradiction is not really due to the limitations of our intellectual and intuitional faculties.

The one class admits a Creator and a creation, and understands the latter as the carrying out of the design of a sovereign and conscious will. These theories raise irreconcilable contradictions; such as the co-existence of providential foresight with the prevalence of evil; and of the soul of man as immortal but not eternal, having a beginning but no end. The other class places the Divine Idea in the universe itself; its theories seek to disentangle the one sole permanent divine essence from the infinite varieties of passing and ephemeral phenomena.

Those who belong to the latter class consider that the universe of matter, energy, and mind is made up of 'representations' or 'objectifications' of the creative immanence, but that these do not necessarily proceed from a deliberately willed design, because consciousness does not appear as a primordial attribute of Unity.

The One, the Real, as opposed to the many and the illusory, is the divine principle of the religions of India. It is the single principle of pantheism and Monism. It is the ' Idea ' of Plato, the ' Active Intellect ' of Averroes, the Natura naturans ' of Spinoza, the ' Thing in Itself ' of Kant; it is the ' Will ' as understood by Schopenhauer, and it is the ' Unconscious ' of von Hartmann.

I.—SCHOPENHAUER'S DEMONSTRATION

Until modern times this great concept rested on intuition alone. It was of a metaphysical nature, and was consequently enmeshed in obscurities and contradictions.

Only in our own day has it been more and more conformed to facts and has entered into the domain of scientific philosophy. It adapts itself to facts so well, that it is doubtless destined to reconcile the genius of the East and the West; to bring the highest truths within our reach; and to be the foundation and the framework of a structure both scientific and philosophical which will extend its shelter to all aspirations and ideals.

Schopenhauer has the high merit of being the first who sought to adapt this system to facts. No doubt his system contains serious errors, referable to the insufficient biological and psychological data at his disposal; but by the clarity and precision of his mind and by the depth of his genius, his work deserves to be taken as the point of departure for every modern study on the nature of things.

From the Unconscious to the Conscious

In order to understand the remainder of the present work, it is necessary that Schopenhauer's thesis should be kept in mind.

But 'The World as Will and Representation' cannot be given in a summary. It must be studied and meditated upon as it stands. The primary idea which reduces the innumerable appearances of things to one single, essential, and permanent principle, cannot be detached from its intuitive and logical demonstration and its development by a masterly inspiration; in a word, from the magical framework in which this great philosopher has set it. This framework is necessary to the comprehension of its power and to the manifestation of its value and beauty.

An analytical summary is, however, indispensable, as I am well aware. I must, however, beg the instructed reader to pardon its inevitable insufficiency, and to excuse what seems to me like a profanation.

Schopenhauer's system does not claim to explain everything. He declares that certain questions of high metaphysics, such as the beginning and end of things, are incapable of complete solution. He does not ask whence came this world nor how it will end. He only inquires what it is.

To him the world is at once will and representation; a real will and an illusory and factitious representation.

Why does he select the designation of 'Will' to describe the real essence of things? Because Will—

'is something that we know directly; something that we know and understand better than anything else . . . the concept of Will is the only one among all known concepts which does not take its rise from phenomena and intuitive representations, but comes from the depths of the individual consciousness which recognises itself essentially, directly, without any forms, even of subject and object, seeing

190

that here that which knows and that which is known coincide.'

Will is the sole thing which really exists. It is the Divine Absolute. It is one, indestructible, eternal, outside Space and Time. It implies neither individual-isation, nor beginning, nor end, nor origin, nor annihilation.

Will, in objectifying itself produces the diverse and innumerable appearances of things. 'In the multiplicity of phenomena which fill the world, which co-exist or succeed one another as the succession of events, it is Will only that is manifested. All these phenomena do but make it visible and objective; it remains immovable in the midst of all these variations. It is the Thing in Itself; and, to take the words of Kant, every object is manifestation and phenomenon.'[1]

Will is primitively and essentially unconscious. It needs no motives for action. We see it active in animals; active without any kind of knowledge, under the impulsion of blind instinct. In man, Will is unconscious in all the organic functions, indigestion, secretion, growth, reproduction, and all vital processes. 'It is not only the actions of the body, it is the whole body itself which is the phenomenal expression of Will, it is Will objectified and become concrete; therefore everything which happens in it must have emerged from Will; and here, however, this will is not guided by consciousness nor regulated by motives; it acts blindly . . .'

Will shows itself as unconscious in the vast majority of its representations; in the whole inorganic world, in the plant-world, and in nearly the whole animal world.

That which we call consciousness has nothing in itself of an essential nature. It does not belong inseparably to will. It is but a temporary realisation, ephemeral and vain.

[1] *The World as Will and Representation.*

' Will, without intelligence (and in itself it is no other), blind, irresistible, as we see it in the inorganic and in the vegetable world and in their laws; as we see it also in the vegetative life of our own bodies, this Will, I say, thanks to the objectified world which lies open to it and develops in order to serve it, comes to know that it desires, and what it desires; and this is the world as it is, it is life as realised in the world.'

But this limited consciousness which the will thus acquires is still more ephemeral, and does not overstep the temporary boundaries of individualisation. It is only whilst individualisation lasts that it has a part to play, and this part is only to substitute an intentional and limited activity for its unconsidered and boundless impulses.

It is therefore necessary to distinguish accurately between the unconscious will and its conscious expression. That which is really superior in man, his eternal essence, his genius, his inspiration, his creative power, all these are impersonal, all belong to the unconscious will.

The domain of consciousness, created by the objectification of the attributes of the will, attaches to the cerebral psychism only. Consciousness in the higher animals and man is bound to their organic representation, it is born and dies with it.

Death brings it to annihilation. As a set-off, that which is the essence of Being, the Will, is not affected.

' When we lose intellect by death, we are thereby carried back into the primitive state, devoid of knowledge, but not absolutely unconscious. It is doubtless rather a state superior to the state of unconsciousness, in which the distinction between subject and object disappears. . . .

'Death shows itself openly as the end of the individual; but in this individual there is the germ of a new being. Therefore nothing that dies in it, dies for ever; but nothing that is born receives an essentially new existence. That which dies, perishes; but a germ remains whence arises a new life which enters on existence without knowing whence it comes, nor why it is what it is. This is the mystery of *palingenesis* (re-birth).

'The human being may therefore be considered from either of two opposite points of view. From the first he is an individual beginning and ending in Time, a transitory phenomenon. . . . From the other he is the original indestructible being which is objectified in every existing person. No doubt such a being could do better than manifest himself in a world like this—a finite world of suffering and death. That which is in him and proceeds from him must end and die. But that which never leaves him nor desires to leave him goes through him like a lightning stroke and then knows neither Time nor Death.'[1]

Thus, then, the individual consciousness, like the universe, has no real and proper existence. It is a temporary function of will. It is born of the will to live.

And the will to live is the consequence of an unfortunate illusion of the will.

2.—SCHOPENHAUER'S PESSIMISM

This pessimism, which is expressed in pages of great eloquence, follows with rigorous logic on his premises.

If individualisation and consciousness are but passing illusions soon to disappear, all effort, troubles, and sufferings end in nothing. The injustices endured are

[1] Schopenhauer: *Religion.*

193

without compensations. Life is objectless. The hopes
of religion are absurd, since, apart from their dogmatic
difficulties, they are all based on the insensate concept that
the individual soul, a thing which had a beginning,
should nevertheless have no ending.

There is therefore no hope, neither in a future world,
nor in this present one.

The will to live does but engender effort without
a goal and suffering without result.

'In considering inanimate nature we have already
recognised as its inmost essence continuous, objectless, reposeless effort; but in animals and man the
same truth is even more obvious. For every act
of willing starts from a need, from a lack, and therefore from a pain; it is therefore a necessity of nature
that the creatures should be a prey to pain. But
when will comes to have no object, when prompt
satisfaction removes all motive for desire, they fall
into emptiness and weariness; their nature, their
mere existence weighs on them intolerably. Life
then, swings like a pendulum from right to left,
from suffering to weariness: and, in fine, these are
the two elements of which life is composed. Hence
comes a very significant fact, the more significant
by its strangeness—man, having placed all pain
and misery in hell, has found nothing to put in
heaven but monotony!

'Now this incessant effort, which is fundamental
to all forms which Will puts on, finds at last, at the
top of the scale of its objective manifestations, its
real general principle; there Will is revealed to
itself in a living body which imposes an iron law
—to provide it with nourishment; and that which
enforces this law is just the will to live, incarnate.
. . . Add a second need, which the first brings in
its train, that of perpetuating the species. At the

same time unending perils assail man from all sides, perils from which he escapes only by perpetual watchfulness. . . .

'For the most part, life is but a continuous struggle for mere existence, with the certainty of being defeated in the end. . . . Life is a sea full of reefs and perils; man, by dint of care and prudence avoids them, but knows all the while that his success in steering between them by skill and energy does but bring him nearer to the great total and final shipwreck, for he cannot escape death.'

Efforts, sufferings, and death! It is of these only that will acquires knowledge, and it is for these that after having 'affirmed itself,' it comes to negation. This is the fruit of individual existence.

'What a difference,' exclaims Schopenhauer, 'between our beginning and our end. Its opening scenes are characterised by the illusions of desire and the transports of voluptuousness; its close by the destruction of all our members and the odour of the grave! The road that separates these is a descending slope of lessening happiness and well-being: the happy dreams of childhood, the gaiety of youth, the work of manhood, the decrepitude of age, the tortures of the last illness and the final struggle with death!'

The pessimism of Schopenhauer is not only the logical consequence of his philosophic premises; it is founded also on a clear insight into life. This insight fills him with an immense pity: pity for the animals which, when they are not devoured by each other, suffer untold miseries in 'a hell where men are the demons!' Pity for men, whom the will to live leads to trouble and sufferings not compensated for by sparse pleasures which are mostly illusory.

How, too, should man take pleasure in these brief

joys when he has attained consciousness of his essential identity with a world in which evil reigns supreme? How should he not suffer in sympathy with the vast and general pain?

How is it that he does not understand that the will to live is a misfortune, and should be annulled by the abdication of desire and by renunciation of the illusory motives with which intelligence rocks itself to sleep, in order to find a sufficient reason for living? It is only by attaining to this, that the reason for life and suffering can be understood.

The sufferings of animals are explained 'by the fact that the will to live, finding absolutely nothing beyond itself in the world of phenomena, and being a famished will, must devour its own flesh.' For the higher consciousness of man 'the value of life consists entirely in learning not to desire it.' Existence is nothing but a kind of aberration of which a better knowledge of the world should cure us.

3.—VON HARTMANN'S SYSTEMATISATION

Von Hartmann has taken up Schopenhauer's thesis, adding thereto certain data derived from the natural sciences and psychology.

Besides and above the causes admitted by the mechanical concept of nature, he finds a superior principle which he calls the Unconscious. The Unconscious is that which is essential and Divine in the universe. In it will and representation exist potentially. Everything therefore that comes into realisation does so by the will of the unconscious.

In evolution the unconscious plays the primary part: natural selection does not explain the origin of new forms: it is but a means, one of the means by which the unconscious attains its ends.

The unconscious has the predominant part in the vital phenomena of the individual; in it is the essence of life; it forms the organism and maintains it, repairs internal and external injuries, and is the ultimate guide of its movements.

It plays an essential part in psychological phenomena. It is the source of instincts, of intuition, of the æsthetic sense, and of creative genius.

Finally, the unconscious is the basis of 'supernormal phenomenology,' which is a mere manifestation of its divine power, independent of contingencies relating to time, space, psychological, dynamic, and material representations.

For Von Hartmann, as for Schopenhauer, there is an abyss between the unconscious and the conscious.

The former is divine, and the latter purely human.

Nevertheless, consciousness (when sufficiently developed) permits us to pass judgment on the universe and on life. And this judgment is not favourable. As consciousness is both ephemeral and unproductive, it cannot participate in the divine infinite.

It suffers from a limitation without compensations and without hope, from many painful contingencies, more painful in proportion to its degree of development, in individual existence. Its last resource would be self-extinction; but perhaps even this sacrifice would be useless, as the indestructible unconscious creator would no doubt recommence another evolution destined to end in the same conscious realisation with the same desolating results.

4.—CRITICISMS OF THE SPECIFIC DISTINCTION BETWEEN THE CONSCIOUS AND THE UNCONSCIOUS

Two things strike one at the outset in the systems of Schopenhauer and von Hartmann, in the first place the clarity of the reasoning and its quasi-scientific rigour;

in the second, the pessimistic conclusions which seem to flow naturally and of necessity from it.

This conclusion does, in fact, necessarily follow if it be admitted, as Schopenhauer and von Hartmann maintain, that there is an impassable abyss and an essential difference between the unconscious and the conscious.

This essential difference takes away all ideal purpose and all meaning from the universe and from life.

And while the other postulates of the German philosophers are deduced with mathematical precision, the alleged essential difference between the unconscious and the conscious rests on nothing.

The assimilation of consciousness to a mere ' representation ' is not logical.

Why should consciousness be exclusively bound to the temporary semblances which make up the universe ?

Why should not all that falls within its domain be registered, assimilated, and preserved by the eternal essence of being ?

What! The divine principle, the will or the unconscious, is to be allowed all potentialities except one, and that the most important of all—the power to acquire and retain the knowledge of itself.

How much more logical it is to presume that this real and eternal will which is objectified in transitory and factitious personalities, will keep integrally the remembrances acquired during these objectifications, thus by numberless experiences passing from primitive unconsciousness to consciousness.

Certainly the human personality which covers the period from birth to. death of the body is destined to perish and to have an end as it had a beginning; but the real ' individuality,' that which is the essential being, keeps and assimilates to itself, deeply graven in its memory, all states of consciousness of the transitory personality.

When, conformably to the palingenesis of which Schopenhauer speaks, it builds up another living personality, it brings to the latter all its permanent gains, and is further enriched by those of the new objectification.

It is thus that the will, originally unconscious, becomes a conscious will.

It is curious to note that Schelling and Hegel, whose systems preceded those of Schopenhauer and von Hartmann, but are much less precise, had nevertheless declared this progress from the unconscious to the conscious and had drawn idealist and optimist conclusions from it. The metaphysics of the two last-named philosophers though more precise and better supported from the scientific point of view, show an unfortunate regression regarded from the idealist standpoint.

Schelling's universe is the result of an ‘ activity ’ essentially unconscious. This activity becomes at least partially self-conscious in man.

For Hegel the essential unconscious activity, however, possesses some kind of reason. The creation which it brings into existence is rational, and we may find in evolution and the progress it implies, some reasonable finality. Thus reason gradually grows into consciousness. Evolution is the means which the universal and creative reason uses to acquire self-consciousness.

No positive objection can be taken to this concept, but that does not suffice for its acceptance; it is necessary to co-ordinate it with facts.

In the light of the new facts the errors, the contradictions, and the lacunæ, as well as the heartrending pessimism, all disappear. These new facts and the inferences they carry with them, allow us to replace the Philosophy of the Unconscious which, though marred by these errors and omissions, is a truly great work of genius, by another, similar indeed in its premises and its essence, but leading by a different development to

conclusions quite other than the pessimism of Schopenhauer.

Different in its development, because it takes note
of all the available facts, and conforming strictly to
reason while avoiding dogmatic assertion, it assigns a
place to all that can be explained, and to that which
necessarily transcends our powers of understanding and
knowledge.

Different in its conclusions, which are diametrically
opposed to Schopenhauer's distressing pessimism, because
it fills in the artificial chasm which he has made between
the unconscious and the conscious.

BOOK II

FROM THE UNCONSCIOUS TO THE CONSCIOUS

SKETCH OF A RATIONAL PHILOSOPHY OF EVOLUTION AND OF THE INDIVIDUAL

FOREWORD

We can now attempt to outline a general theory of collective and individual evolution based on all facts at present known, whether of the naturalistic or the psychological order, and on the deductions they involve. We shall also draw certain inferences that are strictly dependent on the facts.

We shall put aside, systematically, everything which pertains to pure metaphysics: the question of God, of the Infinite, of the Absolute, of beginning and end, and of the essential nature of things.

We shall consider only what it is permitted to us to know and understand on the destiny of the world and of the individual according to the degree of intuitive and intellectual faculty which evolution has actually attained.

This is relatively little, but it is much more than the classical naturalistic philosophy teaches.

It is henceforward possible to understand the mechanism and the general trend of collective and individual evolution; the degree to which individual consciousness is dependent on, or independent of, the material organism; and the ' wherefore ' of Life.

When these notions are clearly established they carry with them a lesson of idealism which is no longer vague, but precise, and is based, not on an act of faith, nor on a supposed ' intuition,' but on an estimate of probabilities.

The preliminary limitation which we have here laid down, is not founded on the old and obsolete distinction between ' the knowable and the unknowable,' but only on the verification of the relative incapacity of our actual powers of knowing and understanding.

Strictly speaking, there is nothing that is unknowable. That which is called the region of the unknowable is continually being lessened as evolution proceeds. The simplest metereological laws were unknowable to our cave-dwelling ancestors; the laws of gravitation, the physical constitution of the stars, and the origin of animal species were unknowable before the development of modern science. It must be the same for the great laws of life and destiny, whether of the universe or of the individual.

As for the problems which are necessarily still above all attempts at explanation, they can be resolutely and systematically put aside; they will constitute the philosophy of a more highly and ideally evolved humanity.

The sacrifice which modern scientific philosophy makes in thus limiting its aims to that which falls within the bounds of reason, has great compensating advantages.

To begin with, this sacrifice, resolutely and courageously accepted, clears out of our way those two stones of stumbling—mysticism and despondency—which encumber the path of idealism. The thinker will avoid mysticism, for he will be able to avoid that intoxication of the personal imagination which is always most luxuriant when dealing with the subliminal. He will be released from ancient and modern forms of dogmatism, and will no longer look for a Messiah or a Magus to guide him, nor yield to the puerile attractions of so-called initiations into occult mysteries.

He will be saved from despondency, and will not be led to say, like Herbert Spencer, who has paraphrased and extended a celebrated dictum of Pascal:—

' Then comes the thought of this universal matrix, itself anteceding alike creation or evolution, whichever be assumed, and infinitely transcending both, alike in extent and duration; since both, if conceived at all, must be conceived as having had beginnings, while

Space had no beginning. The thought of this blank form of existence which, explored in all directions as far as imagination can reach, has, beyond that, an unexplored region compared with which the part which imagination has traversed is but infinitesimal—the thought of a Space compared with which our immeasurable sidereal system dwindles to a point, is a thought too overwhelming to be dwelt upon. Of late years the consciousness that without origin or cause infinite Space has ever existed and must ever exist, produces in me a feeling from which I must shrink.' [1]

The mental vertigo produced by consideration of the Infinite and the Absolute does not affect the philosopher who has clearly recognised the actual limitations of his work. On the contrary, he finds serenity of mind in resignation to these limitations, and to the wholesome and fruitful discipline which they impose upon him. This sacrifice has also the supreme advantage of ruling out all those vain and pretentious discussions, the sterile formulæ and contradictory systems, by which the highest minds have entered the lists against each other. All such systems have now only a historical or a literary interest.

This resignation to the actual limitations of human intelligence enables him to dispense altogether with metaphysical entities—'the Thing in Itself,' 'non-Being,' 'Will,' 'the Unconscious,' 'Duration,' etc., etc.—which in the end are but empty words.

For these factitious entities and pure abstractions we propose to substitute a concrete thing—the notion of an essential concrete dynamo-psychism, which can be verified as a reality, even though its metaphysical nature cannot be formulated, and though research into its metaphysical essence may even be inadvisable.

To this concept, the objection will at once be made

[1] Herbert Spencer: *Facts and Comments* (1902 Ultimate Questions).

that this essential dynamo-psychism, by the very fact
that it is something concrete and conceivable and that
we can in a measure understand it, is no longer the
thing in itself, abstracted from all representation, which
is, as Kant finally proved, essentially inconceivable.

We reply that the same objection can be raised
against all systems based on the distinction between the
divine essence of the universe and its phenomenal
manifestations. Schopenhauer thought to elude this
difficulty by making the Thing in Itself a ' Will '
unconscious of itself, having neither substratum nor cause
nor end, because it is ' outside the realm of pure reason.'
Thus deprived of all attributes the ' Will,' which knows
not what it wills, nor how, nor why it wills, nor even
the fact of its willing, is an abstraction as inconceivable
as the ' Thing in Itself.'

Hartmann's Unconscious is more conceivable simply
because our understanding naturally, spontaneously, and
necessarily, attributes to the unconscious a concrete
substratum, and makes of it the very thing that we
here unequivocally advance—an unconscious dynamo-
psychism.

This dynamo-psychism also is, if we will have it
so, a ' representation,' but it is the only means by which
we can understand ' the nature of things.' For a relative
intelligence to endeavour to understand the Absolute
is, we must always remember, to limit the Absolute.

What does it matter that the thing in itself should be
inaccessible to us ? We can at least reach it under a
first limitation. Under the immeasurable variety of
transitory and phenomenal appearances which constitute
the physical, dynamic, and intellectual universe, there
is one essential, permanent, and real dynamo-psychism.
Its immanent activity is revealed to us in the immense
series of facts which evolution presents; and Evolution
itself is, as we shall see, nothing else than the transition
from unconsciousness to consciousness.

Foreword

The two bases and primordial postulates of the philosophy which this second part of our work will set forth and sustain, are the following:—

1. That which is essential in the universe and the individual is a single ' dynamo-psychism ' primitively unconscious but having in itself all potentialities, the innumerable and diverse appearances of things being always its representations.
2. The essential and creative dynamo-psychism passes by evolution from unconsciousness to consciousness.

These two propositions rest on facts. They can to-day be made subjects of exact demonstration, first in the individual, and can then, by an extended induction be referred to the universe.

PART I

THE INDIVIDUAL, AND INDIVIDUAL EVOLUTION

OR

THE TRANSITION FROM UNCONSCIOUSNESS TO CONSCIOUSNESS IN THE INDIVIDUAL

CHAPTER I

THE INDIVIDUAL CONCEIVED OF AS AN ESSENTIAL DYNAMO-PSYCHISM AND AS REPRESENTATION

I.—THE SCIENTIFIC BASIS OF THIS CONCEPT.[1]

OUR physiological study of the individual, starting from all known facts, has demonstrated the distinction between his essential and real dynamo-psychism and its visible representations.

We have established by those facts, the illusory nature of the appearances on which the general concept of classical physiology is built—the concept of the living being as a simple cellular complex, organising itself by means of specifically distinct tissues, and having in itself the reason for its being, its origin, and its end, the cause for its form, its mechanism, and its functions; all these properties arising only by heredity from generative cells.

At the outset we have shown that it is not possible to find the cause of specific form, nor the origin, the essential cause, nor the purposes of its different modes of activity, either in the organism itself or in the fact of its cellular association.

We have been obliged to admit that the corporeal form is but a temporary illusion; that organs and tissues have no absolute specificity; that these organs and tissues, even though proceeding from the single primordial substance of the ovum, can even in this life be disintegrated into a unique primordial substance, which

---

[1] The whole of this and succeeding chapters are closely connected with the physiological and psychological demonstrations of Book I. They will not be understood apart from this connection.

can then reorganise itself into new and distinct forms and build up temporarily different and distinct organs and tissues.[1]

In a word, we have been compelled to surrender to the evidence, that the body, the organic complex, has neither definitive and absolute qualities nor a specificity proper to itself. Its origin, its development, its embryonic and post-embryonic metamorphoses, its normal functions and supernormal potentialities, the maintenance of its normal form, and the possibilities of metapsychic' dematerialisation and re-materialisations, all show that this organism is separable from a superior dynamism which conditions it.

It no longer appears as the whole individual, but as an ideoplastic product of that which is essential in the individual—a dynamo-psychism which conditions all, and essentially is all.

In philosophic language, the organism is not the individual; it is but his representation.

By this concept all the physiology of the physical being and all its normal or so-called supernormal capacities can be understood; whereas, without this concept the most familiar organic functions and the most unexpected phenomena of mediumship are alike mysterious.

In reality there is neither normal nor supernormal physiology. All is limited by representations; some usual, some exceptional, both equally conditioned by the essential dynamo-psychism which is the reality. If embryonic metamorphoses and the histolysis of the insect seem to us mysterious; if the interpenetration of solid matter by other solid matter, and organic materialisations and dematerialisations seem impossible, this is only because we attribute final reality to the characteristics and properties by which we represent matter to ourselves. If, on the contrary, we understand that these

[1] *Vide* Part I., Chapter II.

characteristics and properties are factitious and unreal, the mystery and the impossibility disappear; or become merely correlatives of our ignorance and weakness. The changes presented by both normal and supernormal physiology have no other philosophical meaning than changes in the external appearance of things. The causality which makes them what they are, and the explanation by which they are understood, lie in the dynamo-psychism which conditions them.

What is true in this matter from the physiological point of view, is even more decisively true from the psychological standpoint: the supernormal only becomes comprehensible when we distinguish the essential dynamo-psychism from its representations. In order to conceive of the possibility of action from mind to mind it is necessary first to admit the reality of a superior psychic mechanism (psychism) detached from the usual contingencies which pertain to psychological representations.

In order that vision at a distance beyond the range of the senses, or the lucidity which presents the past, the present, or the future, may no longer seem incredible miracles, it is indispensable that we should first understand that time and space are but the means of our representations and are as artificial and illusory as the representations themselves.

Thus the concept, which has found its best expression in the works of Schopenhauer,[1] must henceforth quit the realm of metaphysics for that of science.

That which is real and permanent in the individual, which Schopenhauer called Will, we designate as essential dynamo-psychism, and the distinction between this and its temporary representations is founded on facts. At least everything occurs as if this were so.

---

[1] Schopenhauer had already seen the importance of the phenomena known as supernormal to his metaphysical scheme. (Parerga and Paralipomena.)

We can now make a step forward in our search for truth; and, keeping steadily to facts and within the limits of the possible, we can distinguish that which belongs to the essential dynamo-psychism in the individual from that which pertains to its representation.

2.—THE INDIVIDUAL CONSIDERED AS REPRESENTATIONS

Schopenhauer, adopting the biological ideas then current, laid down a very simple concept of individuality. Apart from his metaphysical theory, his concept was in accord with the materialist thesis which taught that the organism *is* the individual. To this Schopenhauer added that 'the individual is Will objectified in an organism'; and he regarded the organism as the unique individual representation of that will. For Schopenhauer, as for the materialistic physiologists, the organism —that unique representation—contains within itself all manifestations of individual activity, and these remain strictly within the limits of time and space which condition the body. They are born and die with the individual, and cannot transcend the range of his physical and sensorial capacities. His psychism is the pure and simple product of the activity of his nerve-centres. The consciousness that belongs to him is a function of that activity. All the attributes of the individual are passing and ephemeral attributes created by the objectification of 'will' in an organised being.

This concept of Schopenhauer's was in agreement with the biological knowledge of his day. It is so no longer. The facts now known traverse this simple aspect of the individual; they prove that individual activity may surpass the limits and the framework of the organism. They prove, in philosophic language, that there are in the individual 'representations' of the creative dynamo-psychism which differ from the organism itself, are superior to that organism and condition it, in place of being conditioned by it.

In fact, as we shall show, everything occurs as if the essential dynamo-psychism objectified itself to create the individual, not in one unique representation—the organism—but in a series of graded representations successively conditioning one another.

In treating of physiology we have seen that the organism is directed by an organising, directing, and centralising dynamism able to act outside the organism, to disintegrate it and reconstitute it in new and distinct forms. Therefore we can, and should, conclude that the organic representation is itself conditioned by a higher representation—the vital dynamism.[1]

Physiology, considered by itself alone, does not admit of any other inference.

But the study of the psychology of the individual allows of new and larger ideas.

These ideas may be summed up as follows.

The semblances, according to which the psychological individuality would seem to be merely the sum of the consciousness of its neurons and its cerebral psychism, are false.

In reality the cerebral psychism, like that of the whole organism, has its origin, its ends, and its most intimate conditions of function, in a superior dynamo-psychism, which is, for the most part, subconscious. It has been demonstrated that in the psychological individuality there is a superior psychism independent of the functioning of the nerve-centres and free of all organic contingencies, and that this superior psychism forms the very foundation of the living being; it centralises and directs the psychic whole; it binds together all

---

[1] Schopenhauer admitted the existence of a 'vital force' but he did not make it a distinct and superior objectification.

present states of consciousness by an activity, which is immanent though mostly latent, and links them to the past by its cryptic memory; in fine, it possesses the so-called supernormal faculties.

If we would express the new psycho-physiological concept in philosophical terms, we must say that the organic representation, far from constituting the whole individual, is only the lower and coarser objectification of his essential dynamo-psychism. Above the organic representation (*i.e.* the organism) and conditioning it, is a superior representation—the 'vital dynamism.' Above the representations known as the 'organism' and the 'vital dynamism' there is a third and yet higher representation belonging to the mental order.

These concepts are not new. Pythagoras and Aristotle distinguished between the body and the vital dynamism which they called the psyché, and between the psyché and the mental dynamo-psychism which they called the Nous. Similarly animists and spiritualists of the old school admitted analogous categories. But there is a great difference between the old and the new ideas. In the first place the new idea is based on facts and demonstrated by facts. As we shall see more clearly in the sequel, it rests also upon reasoning—everything occurs as though things were thus.

Then further, the new idea does not imply differences of essence between the body, the vital dynamism, and the mental dynamo-psychism. All are graded representations of the same essential principle. Their differences are only in degree of evolution, of activity, and of realisation.

But this cannot be fully understood till we have completed our study of the Self. Let us therefore put aside for the moment the analysis of the representations, and pass on to the investigation of the Self considered as essentially a dynamo-psychism.

3.—THE SELF CONSIDERED AS ESSENTIALLY A DYNAMO-PSYCHISM

Is the Self distinct from its representations ? Where is the Self apart from its representations ? Until now the answers to these questions could only be of a metaphysical nature.

Let us consult the facts alone and see what they tell us.

Taking into account only facts the question takes shape as follows.

Is the Self, as taught by classical psychology, the sum of the states of consciousness, or is it separable ? Can it be conceived of as separate from those states of consciousness ?

We shall see that the answer is not in doubt—the Self is not to be confused with states of consciousness. But a certain effort is needful before this can be understood. We can admit without much difficulty that the Self cannot be identified with the material body, but it is much more difficult not to identify it with the mentality. It is much less easy to distinguish oneself from the mental, than from the organic representation. This can be done only by modifying our habitual and inveterate intellectual habits, and by applying the whole power of reason to get beyond the Cartesian axiom—'I think, therefore I am,' and to admit another—'I am, even apart from my thoughts; they represent me, but my mental representations are not the whole of Myself.'

Nevertheless facts prove that nothing is more certain. The induction is exact : if the Self were but the sum of states of consciousness it would be incomprehensible how, these states of consciousness being intact, the Self, which is by the hypothesis their synthesis, could lose that which is most essential and important—the notion of its unity and the possibility of control over the psychic whole. Now it is a commonplace fact that this integrity of states of consciousness coexists with the disappearance of the synthetic unity and the centralising directive power.

The diminution or the disappearance of control by the Self is the fundamental fact in all supernormal psychology and of all the psychological anomalies which nevertheless coexist with the unimpaired anatomo-physiological condition of the nerve-centres.

Whether we consider a pure neurosis such as hysteria, or insanity, or double personality, or mediumship, the first fact observed is always the disappearance of the control and centralising direction of the Self. In hysteri-form disturbances and in dementia, the states of consciousness are intact and remain so for long periods; the faculties, taken separately, are not affected—memory, imagination, feelings, etc. . . . are the same, but the central direction is replaced by anarchy or polyarchy.

In hypnosis, double personality and mediumship, we find that faculties and knowledge, and the most varied states of consciousness—in fact all the mental sequences —persist integrally. But here also the habitual central direction by the Self has disappeared and is replaced by a heterogeneous direction. In a word, the states of consciousness, faculties, and knowledge can be dissociated and separated from that which is essential in the Self—the consciousness of its unity and reality.

Therefore the Self is distinct from the constituent states which represent it.

The most typical phenomenon from this point of view is that of alterations of personality. These modifications of the personality prove two things:—

1. The existence of mental groups of stratification, as Jastrow[1] puts it, constituting as many subconscious formations.

[1] Jastrow: *La Subconscience.*

2. The existence of a centralising psychic direction of these mental groups, since it is precisely the failure and the want of this central direction that is the basis and *sine quâ non* for alterations of personality and for the appearance of secondary states.

Jastrow says, 'When the dominant Self abandons any considerable part of its sovereignty, it may be that the organised activities are freed.' . . . It is then seen that 'the altered Self maintains relations so special, so incomplete, and so indirect, with the normal Self, that we must admit that the mind is dissociated. *The psychic autocracy is overthrown and gives place to an enfeebled rule exercising power over a reduced area.*'[1]

To sum up: The real Self conditions and directs the mental dynamo-psychism.

Therefore that which is essential in the Self must not be confounded with subordinate and secondary states of consciousness.

As in the organism, so in the mentality the permanent essence must be distinguished from temporary 'representations.' The states of consciousness are but representations of the Self. But the Self—an individualised portion of the universal dynamo-psychism—cannot be confounded with its representations.

Moreover, there is a further proof of this assertion. Facts show that there are in the Self capacities which outrange the limits of states of consciousness and dominate all its representations.

Intuition and creative genius very greatly transcend the intellectual faculties. In these there is nothing like the linked sequences which mark logical deductions, they are superior faculties, deriving evidently from the divine essence of the Self.

Still more obviously the supernormal psychic faculties, and more especially lucidity (which is independent

---

[1] Italics are mine, G. G.

of all contingencies) cannot be attributed to the intellect.

Therefore, once more, the real and essential Self is distinct from the states of consciousness and the mental processes which represent it at any moment.

But it will be said:—'so be it; but what are we to understand by the real Self apart from its representations?

'Is it the Creative Essence, Will, the Unconscious, the essential dynamo-psychism (the name matters little), but is it the Creative Essence devoid of any individualisation, acquiring this individualisation only in and by representations, and losing it when these representations cease?

'Is it a part of the essential dynamo-psychism which retains individualisation, remembrance, and self-consciousness even after the cessation of the representations which it has passed through?'

To answer this question, let us consider the second part of our demonstration, viz., that the essential dynamo-psychism passes by individual evolution from unconsciousness to consciousness.

CHAPTER II

IN INDIVIDUAL EVOLUTION THE ESSENTIAL DYNAMO-
PSYCHISM PASSES FROM UNCONSCIOUSNESS TO CON-
SCIOUSNESS

Up to this point our demonstration has been rigorously scientific and rests entirely on facts, or on inferences closely following on the facts.   In that which follows we shall be obliged, though keeping to the same method, to allow a slightly larger margin for hypothesis.   But we must ask the reader to hold judgment in suspense till the whole theory developed in this work has been completed.   None of its details should be considered separately or apart from the general synthesis.   This synthesis, as we shall see further on, is such that, as a whole, it appeals with all the weight of truth.

For Schopenhauer and von Hartmann consciousness is inseparable from its representations.   Between the conscious, on the one hand, and the will or the unconscious on the other, there is, according to them, an abyss which cannot be filled; there is an essential differentiation.

We desire to establish on the contrary:—

1. That there is no such abyss between the conscious and the unconscious, for, in the individual, they constantly interpenetrate and mutually condition each other.

2. That there is an uninterrupted transition from unconsciousness to consciousness; and that the primitive unconsciousness tends more and more to become conscious by an undefined and uninterrupted evolution.

From the Unconscious to the Conscious

I.—THE CONSCIOUS AND THE UNCONSCIOUS INTER-
PENETRATE AND MUTUALLY CONDITION EACH OTHER

To consider the Unconscious first:—
In the analytical study of its constituent elements
we find some that are innate, which we shall consider
further on, and some that are acquired. These latter
were at first conscious; then they passed from the
field of consciousness into subconsciousness and became
cryptomnesic. Part of the subconscious cryptomnesia
is made up of former states of consciousness. There
is, therefore, a current setting continually from the
conscious to the unconscious.
Let us now consider the Conscious:—
In the analytical study of its constituent elements
we found that there are acquired elements which we
know well, and innate elements which are more obscure.
These latter are at first subconscious, then they pass
from the field of subconsciousness and become conscious;
from being cryptopsychic they become psychic.
Thus the very structure of the conscious being—his
essential character—is made up of subconscious capacities.
The conscious psychism is therefore in main part
constituted by the subconscious which conditions and
directs it. There is therefore a continuous current
setting from the unconscious to the conscious.
In fine, there is a double, reciprocal, and continuous
influence from the unconscious to the conscious, and vice
versa—a complete interpenetration.
Not only is there no impassable abyss, but the
connection is close and direct.
In conditioning the conscious the unconscious
partly loses its character of unconsciousness, and acts
not as unconsciousness but as a cryptoid consciousness,
sometimes active, sometimes latent.
In its turn the conscious partly conditions the

unconscious by pouring into it the stream of psychological acquisitions. Finally, these acquisitions, once
conscious and now become subconscious, may, under
favourable conditions, re-emerge into consciousness.

What are we to conclude? Simply this:—

That which we in daily experience call 'consciousness' is but a part of the conscious—the part immediately
accessible within the given limits of time and space;
but a large part of the conscious normally remains
latent.

That which we in daily experience call 'unconsciousness' is but a part of the unconscious, of the true
unconscious—that which remains inaccessible and
unfathomable. The greater part of the unconscious
rises daily into consciousness; it makes that consciousness and directs it. It is not even occult, it is merely
anonymous: its activity from day to day is constant and
cryptoid.

From this point our demonstration will proceed
easily.

2.—THE UNCONSCIOUS OR SUBCONSCIOUS DYNAMO-
PSYCHISM TENDS TO BECOME A CONSCIOUS DYNAMO-
PSYCHISM

The leading proposition may be established by a
reasoned study of the individual psychism.

Analysis of the higher subconsciousness permits us
to distinguish in it two main categories of powers and
knowledge.

(*a*) The first category has no analogy in conscious
powers and conscious knowledge. It includes
the so-called supernormal faculties, which are
creative and are able to bring to the living being
knowledge independently of his habitual means
of cognisance and understanding.

This category, this portion of the Self, necessarily remains mysterious; it is of the very essence of the unconscious, and brings the individual into touch with that which is divine in the universe. It eludes investigation by reason, and is incapable of any complete interpretation.

(*b*) The second category includes those faculties and that knowledge which are essentially analogous to the conscious faculties and knowledge, differing from them only by variety and extent. This category is more easily interpreted.

We can verify in the first place that it is composed partly of psychological experiences acquired consciously or even unknown to ourselves, which have passed, integrally, below the threshold of consciousness.

Everything occurs as though the multitude of daily experiences had as their end or their result, an uninterrupted enrichment of our subconsciousness during the whole of life.

No remembrance, no vital or psychological experience is lost. In the course of life the organism undergoes immense modifications, and is doubtless renewed several times molecule by molecule. States of consciousness all more or less different, succeed one another. A life is really made up of a series of lives; the life of infancy, of childhood, of adolescence, of adult age and of old age; quite distinct lives though united by a substructure common to them all.

These successive lives are more or less affected by seemingly complete oblivion, so that for the living being they are like so many partial deaths.

But throughout the renovation of organic molecules, and of renewed states of consciousness, there persists a deep, superior psychism which has registered these states of consciousness and retains them indelibly.

They are therefore not lost though they are in great

part latent. But this is not all. The subconscious psychism which is thus enriched throughout life, by all these states of consciousness, does not merely register them, it also assimilates them.

All conscious acquisitions are assimilated and transmuted into faculties. This is noticeable in the course of existence. The being 'develops,' and acquires new or extended powers of feeling, knowing, and understanding. Psychological progress can be the result only of this transmutation of knowledges into faculties. And this transmutation is subconscious. It does not take place among the unstable and ephemeral cerebral molecules; it necessitates a deep-seated and continuous elaboration in the essential and permanent part of the being; that is, in his subconscious dynamo-psychism.

Thus the perpetual disintegration of the conscious personality is of small importance. The permanent subconscious individuality retains the indelible remembrance of all the states of consciousness which have built it up. From these states of consciousness which it has assimilated it constructs new capacities.

During the course of life the individual subconsciousness has made a new stride towards consciousness.

We have henceforth a firm basis whence to proceed higher and further in our discovery of truth.

Cryptopsychism is only in minor part composed of the experiences of this present life. The greater part is inborn. Whence does this come ?

The most natural and reasonable hypothesis is that which is based on facts. Since cryptopsychism and cryptomnesia are both partially constructed out of daily experiences which have passed into the subconsciousness which they enrich, it is legitimate to infer that they are entirely constructed from past experiences.

Since then in the course of our existence we find the origin of a part only of the contents of subconsciousness, it is at least permissible to seek the remainder in anterior experiences and to push back the cryptomnesia and the cryptopsychism of the individual beyond the present existence.

Obviously this is a very wide inference to draw. To many readers it will at first sight seem, if not absurd, at all events out of proportion to the facts on which it is based.

It must not, however, be considered by itself, but in conjunction with all the preceding demonstrations.

It then has more weight. It is not hard to understand how the essential dynamo-psychism objectifying itself in new organic representations should retain the deep memory of experiences realised in previous representations. If in place of a single existence, we include a series of successive existences, the acquisition of consciousness by the primitive unconsciousness can readily be understood.

Each of these innumerable and various experiences would have been impressed on the essential dynamism of the being, and would be transformed into a state of consciousness; that is into a remembrance and a capacity.

It is thus that the living being passes little by little from unconsciousness to consciousness.

Against this inference of re-birth, no objections of a scientific kind can be raised. We may seek in vain for a single one in the whole stock of knowledge. Forgetfulness of previous existences has but slight importance for modern science. Remembrance plays but a secondary part in normal psychology; forgetfulness is habitual and is the rule.

In the course of a lifetime, the greater part of our experiences disappears. During regular and normal life the personal memory of the brain—memory—is altogether weak, unreliable, and fails us continually; it is still more defective in abnormal cases caused by ' secondary states ' whether spontaneous, hypnotic, or mediumistic.

On the other hand, above this cerebral memory is

the subconscious memory—the infallible memory of the true and complete individuality, as indestructible as the being itself.

In this essential memory there are engraved permanently all the events of the present life, and all the remembrances and conscious acquisitions of the vast series of antecedent lives.

In the light of the two propositions just stated, individual evolution can be understood and all naturalistic and philosophical problems relating to the individual can be resolved.

No doubt from the metaphysical point of view the concept gives a large range to hypothesis, but from the psychological standpoint, there is no enigma on which it does not shed light.

CHAPTER III

THE SYNTHESIS OF THE INDIVIDUAL

I.—PRIMORDIAL AND SECONDARY REPRESENTATIONS

THE rational concept of the individual in accord with all the facts is as follows.

For the genesis of the individual the essential dynamo-psychism objectifies itself by graded primordial representations successively conditioning one another.

According to our present knowledge the primordial representations are:—

1. The purely mental;
2. The Vital Dynamism;
3. The single organic substance.[1]

These primordial representations constitute themselves into secondary representations: the mental, by states of consciousness and thoughts; the unique substance by cells and organs. These primordial representations are 'cadres' which remain the same from the birth to the death of the grouping which constitutes the individual.

The secondary representations, on the contrary, are perpetually renewed. The cells of the organic complex, are born, die, and succeed each other very rapidly. The states of consciousness and thoughts follow on one another in the same way, associating, opposing, converging or diverging in a chaos which is co-ordinated only by the directing Self.

---

[1] It is curious that the schools of thought called occultist have reached by intuitive or mystical paths a systematisation not unlike this, and describe each of the primordial representations as having each a concrete presentment, by means of an organic or fluidic substratum.

228

The last terms of these representations, whether cells or thoughts, have a collective self-activity, a dynamism proper to themselves, and the rudiments of consciousness. Cells and thoughts are ' wholes,' fragmentary dynamo-psychisms, or monads.[1] The graded ' hierarchies ' which exist between the primordial representations exist also in principle between the secondary representations. There is a hierarchy of the tissues and a hierarchy of mental groups; and in the ' cadres ' of primordial representations which are fixed and unchangeable during the continuance of the life-group, there exists a possibility of representations different from the normal secondary representations. Thus, the tissues and organs of the unique substance can be reconstituted by metapsychic materialisation into new forms, and the mental representations can be reconstituted into secondary personalities by an abnormal psychism.

This clears up the concept of the individual both as such and in the many details of his physiology and his psychology.

We will now return to the analysis of the individual and his representations, in detail.

2.—THE BODY AND THE VITAL DYNAMISM

The body, which is the lower objectification and the ideoplastic representation of the self, can no longer be considered as playing the primordial and essential part that was assigned to it by classical psycho-physiology.

The known facts of supernormal physiology seem to establish definitely that the diverse anatomical modalities of the organism are reducible to a unique representation—the primordial substance, which is not nervous,

---

[1] The celebrated experiments of Dr Carrel have positively demonstrated this as regards the cells.

R

muscular, or osseous, etc. . . . but is substance pure and simple.

This opens a vast field; and the study of organic modality must be resumed on an altogether new basis.

This organic substance is built up, developed, maintained, and repaired by the higher active principle—the vital dynamism—which conditions it.

In our study of physiological individuality we have sufficiently demonstrated the reality of this vital dynamism considered as independent of the organic complex, and as an organising and directing principle. There is no need to revert to this demonstration.

The vital dynamism, moreover, has its own proper, autonomous existence, shown by its limitations in time and space, as distinct from the higher dynamo-psychic principles in the individual, which are above time and space. The apparent manifestations of its organising, directive, and reparatory powers do not extend beyond the birth and death of the organism which it conditions. All available evidence shows that these manifestations are restricted within narrow limits.

In building up the organism the vital dynamism is under a double influence: the influence of the higher dynamo-psychism of the Self, and the hereditary influence which seems to be linked to substance, *i.e.* the active ideoplastic influence of the living being, and the passive ideoplastic influence which is the mental imprint given to the substance by progenitors.

Schopenhauer had already conceived of the sequence of organic edification as really proceeding from the active ideoplastic power.

' The different parts of the body must correspond perfectly with the principal appetites by which the Will is manifest; they must be their visible expressions in being. The teeth, œsophagus, and intestinal canal are hunger objectified; similarly the genital organs are the objectified sexual instinct; the hands which grasp, the feet which move, correspond to the less urgent desires of the Will which they represent. As the human form as a whole corresponds to the human will as a whole, so the form of the individual body (which is consequently very characteristic and very expressive) corresponds to the individual modifications of the will and to a particular character.'

To this concept of the ideoplastic activity we have only to add that the objectification of the essential dynamo-psychism is not primarily and immediately an objectification in matter. It is primarily mental. Then the mental objectification is transferred into dynamic objectification, and this again into organic representation.

The passive ideoplasticity is the mental imprint received from progenitors, and is the sum total of heredity. It plays an important part in the building up of the organism, because the directive will of the Self is not powerful enough at the existing level of evolution to modify the main physiological functions. The body and the vital dynamism form a kind of lower self, having a will of its own, over which the control of the higher Self is only a partial and relative.

The influence of the active ideoplasticity is none the less the preponderant influence. It determines the destiny and the purpose of the organism and adapts human cerebration to its normal use.

Deprived of this higher direction, the action of the vital dynamism in highly evolved creatures, and especially in man, may be perverted, warped, or weakened, and may produce abortions and monsters.

The embryonic growth of an organism is manifest as a regular and normal 'materialisation,' while metapsychic materialisation is only an irregular and abnormal ideoplastic growth.

The building up of an organism, moreover, can occur

normally, otherwise than under the usual conditions which govern generation in highly evolved creatures. In parthenogenesis, in reproduction by budding, the grouping of organic and dynamic monads takes place otherwise than by the conjunction of an ovum and spermatozoön. These facts, which seem disconcerting, can easily be explained by the new ideas; they simply prove that the conditions which govern cellular and dynamic groups are not restricted to fertilisation.[1]

Once constituted, the vital dynamism represents a storage of power, confined within narrow limits both as to its duration and its potentialities.

In its duration, because the powers of organic repair diminish with maturity and do not prevent the body from slow disintegration under the wastage of old age.

In its potentialities, for an organic injury may be beyond the power of repair and may bring about the premature end of the corporeal grouping.

It is to be remarked that the limitations of the vital dynamism are more pronounced in the higher than in the lower forms of life. It may be, however, that in these latter the case is rather one of less restricted specialisation than of greater power.

In any case, a special study of the vital dynamism in the lower grades of life, such as plants and protozoa, will be necessitated by reason of the great differences in its qualities and modes of action as shown in them. It seems certain, however, that in the more highly evolved forms the reparative action of the vital dynamism

---

[1] We may remark, *passim*, that there is a curious analogy between reproduction by cuttings, and especially by buds, and the metapsychic materialisations. Materialisation often proceeds (as we have seen) by a kind of budding or prolonging of the primary substance exteriorised by the medium, this bud developing into a being or the fragment of a being. The difference is in the duration, and that is only a matter of time and modality. There is nothing to prove that in the end the materialisation may not prove to be separable from the medium, and given a separate existence, just as the cutting or the bud is separated from the parent stock. Impossible! it will be said. By no means. The rashness would lie with those, who, knowing what we now know, affirm the impossibility.

is very much more restricted than in the lower forms because of the high centralisation in the former which monopolises the greater part of the energy for the functions of the nervous system.[1]   Certainly in these more evolved forms it has far less than the amazing power observable in the invertebrates and even in some lower vertebrates; a power which extends to the renewal of members or even of viscera.

Even such as it is, it is capable of unexpected marvels, and if it is premature to anticipate a new system of medicine based on a deeper study of the vital dynamism, at least its possibility may be foreseen.

The function and purpose of the body and the vital dynamism which, together constitute the lower self of the individual, seem to be to limit the activity of the Self and give it a specific direction—to specialise it, so to speak. Everything occurs as though each terrestrial existence, each organic objectification, each ' incarnation ' if the term is preferred, were for the real being a limitation in time, space, and means. It would seem to resemble a compulsion to a restricted and specialised task, an effort directed to a single aim exclusive of others. Sharply defined as this is from the physiological point of view, this limitation is still more strict psychologically.

This limitation is the cause of the impotence of the supernormal faculties. It trammels the manifestation of the inspiration of intuitive and creative genius. It is the cause of the forgetting during organic life of the immense majority of acquired experiences in their quality of remembrances as distinct from capacities developed; it

---

[1] It is not absurd to surmise that prolonged artificial quiescence of the nervous system, say by a long period of special hypnosis, might render possible a quite unexpected extension of the healing and reparatory power of the vital dynamism.

This power is actually shown, exceptionally, in abnormal states and in the cures which are called miraculous.

is the dominant cause of ignorance in the individual of his real position in the evolutionary scale.

The cerebral organ is, of course, indispensable for psychological function in relation to the external world. But this organ is capable only of a restricted activity and has but a limited amount of that storage power which we call memory. As the passing impressions which it has received are effaced, the memory of these impressions tends to disappear from normal consciousness.

This is very obvious in the normal course of life, and, *a fortiori*, the brain when newly acquired cannot vibrate in harmony with impressions long past, which, even in normal life, only occasionally reach the threshold of consciousness.

This forgetfulness, however, is only apparent, since the remembrance remains in the essential memory of the Self; and in the lower phases of evolution it is salutary, for it necessitates a multiplicity of experiences under continually changing conditions. This forgetfulness, moreover, allows the Self to pursue its line of development without being embarrassed or turned aside from its aim. Like death itself, it is a factor favouring evolution.[1]

And further, the usual inaccessibility of the faculties of instinct, intuition, and the supernormal powers generally (which pertain to the unconscious), compels constant considered effort, and thus it also favours evolution.

3.—THE REAL SELF AND ITS MENTAL REPRESENTATIONS

We have now considered the body and the vital dynamism which constitute the lower self of the individual. We shall now study the higher group—the mental dynamo-psychism and the Self.

[1] See Part III.

Everything that is essential in the being—the innate faculties, the intellectual aptitudes, and the primordial powers—belong to this group.

The central monad, the real Self, is the source and principle of creative genius and inspiration. Its function is to centralise and direct the psychological whole. It ensures individual permanence in spite of the perpetual renewal of states of consciousness during one life and the changes of personality in successive lives. It retains integrally the remembrance of all its acquisitions, and assimilates them to itself. By this assimilation of past states of consciousness, the consciousness which represents and synthetises all past realisations, develops little by little. In it resides the whole of the latent consciousness, made up of a vast mass of experiences, acquisitions, and realisations.

The mentality which the Self directs is made up of states of consciousness not as yet assimilated, but which it regulates and uses. There is in it an extensive group of intellectual monads—'elementary dynamo-psychisms,' at a high evolutionary level and possessing a marked degree of self-activity, autonomy, and individualisation.

In the psychic whole these elements form secondary groups determined by affinities and associations which all tend to independence. Thus there are in the psychism two constant currents—the one centrifugal and decentralising in its action, tending to anarchy or polyarchy; and the other centripetal, tending to centralisation and governance by the Self.

The general grouping is determined by affinities; the psychic elements which form a new being are grouped by the tendencies and the aspirations which mark the evolutionary level reached by the Self.

We are here dealing with a primary fact, on which special stress is to be laid, that the total psychism is closely bound up with and limited by the cerebral psychism for all manifestations in its relations with the external world. The expression of thought, and all manifestations of mental activity have to flow along the cerebral channel; and this channel, which is both narrow and fixed in its direction, limits and determines the whole activity of the Self in that same direction.

The close association of the Self with the lower group implies a restriction of the activity of the Self; whereas all dissociation from the lower group implies its extension. The total psychism therefore differs from the psychism of normal life, which is limited by the cerebral conditions.

In this concept there is one point to which we must call special attention in order to avoid false and misleading interpretations; this concerns the subordination of the cerebral to the higher psychism. This concept must by no means be understood in the sense that there are in the individual two beings, distinct in their essence and destiny. This misapprehension is, unfortunately, nearly universal. It dominates the systems both of Schopenhauer and von Hartmann.

'We may be consoled,' writes Von Hartmann, for having minds so low and absorbed in material things, so devoid of poetic and religious sense; there is deep within us a marvellous subconsciousness which dreams and prays while we work for our livelihood.'

Certain mystics fall into the same error when they gravely teach that all acts, both those which are most meritorious or most guilty, have little importance because they do not proceed from the real Self, and have no effect upon it.

This is radically false.

The Self is not a duality, it is a unity. But during terrestrial life cerebral conditions only allow of a restricted and truncated manifestation of the total psychism. This limitation hides from the person not only his metaphysical essence, but also the greater part of his conscious realisations.

In abnormal states, when the subconscious part manifests itself more or less distinctly, this creates the illusion of duality, just because being outside and above temporary limitations, it appears quite different from the normal psychism.

But the conscious and the unconscious constitute one and the same individuality in which the interplay from one to the other is correlative and unceasing.

It is, moreover, extremely difficult, for want of a definite criterion, to state exactly what are the limits of contribution by the subconscious, and in what measure this contribution is conditioned by organic factors and cerebral heredity.

According to the notions put forward above, there are constant alternations of ' associated life ' and ' dissociated life ' in the permanent and indestructible existence of the individual.

The phases of associated life—the association of the Self with organic and material life—imply a process of analysis, a perfecting of detail, a progress towards consciousness by restricted efforts directed in a special sense which is imposed by the present objectification; efforts which are concurrent with those of the other ' monads ' constituting the dynamic and material organism.

The phases of dissociated life imply a progress by contemplation, by deep inward assimilation, working towards synthesis.

Myers believed also in a special development of the faculties called supernormal during these phases of ' discarnate ' life. These faculties, however, which pertain to the divine essence of the unconscious, must really be immutable; but it is quite possible that the

Self, passing beyond terrestrial existences, may learn to use these supernormal faculties, and to understand them sufficiently to bring them little by little under the dominion of its will.

The hypothesis is a large one, but its study must be left to future research in the metapsychic domain, by which it may, perhaps, be confirmed. With more certainty we may infer that the being in its discarnate phases, freed from cerebral conditions, can and should, when it has reached a sufficiently high level of consciousness and liberty, know itself better and better.[1] Its past should be accessible to him within the limits of its evolution as actually realised, and it might even be able consciously to prepare its future.

4.—METAPHYSICAL INFERENCES ON THE ORIGIN AND END OF INDIVIDUALISATION

This paragraph has no claim to be scientific; the hypotheses which it puts forward are only intended to offer matter for discussion.

THE ORIGIN OF THE INDIVIDUAL

At the beginning of evolution, as far as we may be able to conceive of such beginning, there is neither consciousness nor individualisation. Schopenhauer expressed this as follows:—

‘ Thus in the lowest forms of life we have seen Will appearing as a blind impulse, a dumb and mysterious effort far from any direct consciousness. It is the simplest and weakest of its objectifications.

---

[1] We have shown in *L'Être Subconscient* that liberty and consciousness are correlative to each other.

238

It is manifest as a blind impulse and an unconscious effort in all inorganic nature and in all the primary forces whose laws it is the task of physics and chemistry to seek out. Millions of phenomena, show each of these laws as altogether similar and regular, bearing no trace of any individual character.'

It may be admitted that wherever a rudiment of consciousness appears in the primitive unconscious, individualisation has begun. This rudiment of consciousness is at first extremely minute and inappreciable. It existed, however, doubtless, as soon as the universe showed a trace of organisation—sooner, perhaps, than Schopenhauer thought.

However this may be, once this rudiment of consciousness has been acquired, it will be indelible, and will henceforward continue to increase without limit.

Thus are constituted individual 'monads' by rudimentary accessions of consciousness. This old term 'monad' may be kept, restricting it to the general meaning of a dynamo-psychic individuality—a part of the universal creative dynamo-psychism; having, like it, all potentialities of realisation and the characteristic of divine permanence.

The objectification of these monads, and their subsequent evolution, are the resultant of the continuous effort of the unconscious dynamo-psychism in its tendency towards consciousness—an effort which necessitates an immense total of sensations and acquisitions.

From this continual work of analysis and acquisition there result groups of monads which constitute the whole organised representation of the universe.

In the universality of things there are therefore only everlasting monads, and temporary groupings of them in ephemeral 'representations.'

That which is called the formation of a living being, would thus be only the complex association and formation of a group. That which is called its death would be in reality only the dissociation of the group. It is not the annihilation of the constituent monads, which, according to affinities determined by the past or by the necessities of future evolution, go to form a new being by a new grouping.

These individual monads are identical in potentiality but not in realisation. By reason of the rudiments of consciousness they have acquired, the evolutionary impulse becomes more and more susceptible to the influence of acquisitions. The factors of adaptation and selection come into play; they make effort obligatory— an effort which is at first purely reflex, then instinctive, then reasoned; and effort necessarily causes inequalities of consciousness and consequent inequalities in realisation. These inequalities of evolving parts are, however, kept within limits by the original and essential solidarity of those parts.

Thanks to that all-powerful solidarity, the growth into consciousness cannot be purely individual, it is necessarily in very great measure, collective. Thus the evolution of the more conscious monads favours the evolution of the less conscious; and the retardation of these latter slows down the evolution of the former.

This solidarity which is evident in the sum total of beings and in the whole universe, is especially visible in those complex associations which constitute animal colonies and still more so in those graded (hierarchised) associations which we have already studied as constituting living beings.

THE FUTURE OF THE INDIVIDUAL

If now, having considered past and present evolution, we seek to predict what its future will be, we are led to an important inference.

From the Unconscious to the Conscious

As the reversion from the conscious to the unconscious illuminates the latter more and more, there will necessarily come a time when nothing will be mysterious or obscure.

At what we will call the summit of evolution, as far as it is possible to conceive of this, the apparent separation and the temporary scission between the conscious and the subconscious will no longer exist. All the capacities and all the knowledge that go to make up the living being, all its vast past, will henceforward be integrally, directly, regularly, and normally accessible. Similarly the supernormal powers will be under the control of the conscious will.

The subconscious being will have disappeared and only the conscious being will remain. Then, but only then, the essential dynamo-psychism will deserve the name of Will.

If we did not fear to lose our way in the metaphysical realm, we might permit ourselves another inference, but one which we can merely indicate with caution and with large reservations.

This infinitely vast expansion of consciousness should necessarily result in the disruption of those factitious and transitory groupings which make individualisation.

The monads would then return to the original unity from whence they were derived.

But this unity, this synthesis of all consciousness, will absorb them all into itself, while leaving each indelible and eternal.

Arrived at its *summum*, each individual consciousness will be expanded to total consciousness; it will have become the total Consciousness Itself.

The ' summit ' of evolution may then be imaged as a kind of ' conscious nirvana.'

CHAPTER IV

INTERPRETATION OF PSYCHOLOGY BY THE NEW IDEAS

IT remains now to adapt the preceding notions to psychology as a whole.

The simplicity of this interpretation compared with the lamentable impotence of classical psychology, will afford a conclusive and palmary proof of its truth. To the classical psychology all the states and all the facts which we are about to discuss are so many pure mysteries.

I.—THE PSYCHOLOGY CALLED NORMAL

Let us imagine a certain person in whom the synthesis of the different constituent principles is well established. They are linked together by satisfactory affinities and none is out of harmony.

The centralisation is strong and the homogeneity obvious.

The central monad—the Self—directs the mental dynamo-psychism, and has complete control over all its elements. Through the mental dynamo-psychism it directs the vital dynamism and the body, within the limits prescribed by the evolutionary level attained. It must be remembered that this evolutionary level does not allow of consciousness of the vital functions and does not give the power to act on the main bodily functions— the vital dynamism retaining a large measure of self-activity.

The individual so constituted is in stable equilibrium. His psychic health is perfect. But at the same time he finds himself severely limited by organic conditions.

The solidarity of his superior psychism with his cerebral psychism being absolute, all the activities of the former are limited by the extent of the latter and restrained within its conditions.

Such an individual cannot be conscious of his latent powers, nor of anything which concerns his higher psychism. In him the products of higher inspiration and of his brain are closely unified and make a harmonious whole. His psychology is *normal*—typical—marked by the equilibrium of his faculties and their regular output, but also by their narrow limitations.

These well-balanced individuals may be at very different evolutionary levels. There are among them many mediocrities, but also some very intelligent men. Their intellectual output is regular and contains no surprises. They never perceive any subconscious contributions, these being too closely connected with the results of voluntary effort. They know nothing of intuition; they are never original. If they understand art they are never artists in the higher sense of the word; still less are they inventors or creative. They have no genius, and none of the higher kind of inspiration.

Well-balanced minds play a useful part in science and social life by their poise and the correctness of their reasoning on ordinary matters; they are also detrimental by their hatred of innovation and their immovable attitude.

Their opinions are generally those of their surroundings. They do not seek to improve on these, and are inclined to accept any prevalent idea, which seems to them established by the mere fact that it is prevalent. They are impervious to philosophy, or are satisfied with a dull commonplace philosophy conformable to established ideas. They tend strongly towards materialism, for the close fusion of the constituent principles and their limitation by matter do not allow them to look beyond material things. That in them which is above

243

material limitations, is entirely unknown to them; and they have no real philosophical curiosity. To them everything is relatively simple because they avoid going to the bottom of anything.

2.—ABNORMAL PSYCHOLOGY

In place of the previously described harmonious and well established synthesis and the perfect blend of the different constituent principles of the Self, let us now suppose an unstable synthesis, having some lack of union or affinity between the ' cadres,' involving a disharmony. The whole phenomena of abnormal psychology result from such conditions.

Where there is a break of equilibrium or want of harmony between the body and the vital dynamism which directs and conditions it, we have the origin of all hysteriform manifestations of a physiological kind. Where there is a break or want of harmony between the mentality and the Self, we have the cause of all kinds of mental instability from simple neuroses to disintegration into multiple personalities, or dementia.

Theoretically, want of equilibrium could only exist between any two of the constituent principles of the Self; but in fact no want of balance is partial only; by reason of the essential solidarity of the individual grouping, every cause of disharmony between any two ' cadres ' reacts on the whole of the groups forming the individual. This is the reason why there is no hystero-physiological disturbance without mental disturbance, and no mental trouble without some hysteriform repercussion.

The same causes which produce abnormal psychology —a want of perfect equilibrium between the constituent principles of the individual grouping—permits of the isolated manifestation of one or other of these groups by its ' secession ' or even its ' exteriorisation.'

It has one good result; it diminishes the limitations of the higher psychism, and permits it to appear.

Thus the same factor is the source of psychological morbidity, and of high psychic manifestations: it opens the door to mental disorder, but also to crypto-psychism, cryptomnesia, to the manifestations of genius, to intuition, and to supernormal states. It allows the individual flashes of insight into his real state and his destiny.

These general notions being admitted, we can now enter more fully on detail, and shall successively consider :—

Neuropathic states;
Neurasthenia;
Hysteria;
Dementia;
Hypnotism;
Alterations of personality;
Intellectual work by the higher subconscious psychism
     and genius;
Crypto-psychism and cryptomnesia;
The Supernormal; and
Mediumship.

All these abnormal psychological states have reciprocal relations and inevitable points of contact, both by their original nature and by their particular conditions. They often interpenetrate.

3.—NEUROPATHIC STATES

Instability in the equilibrium of the individual grouping is at the root of all neuropathic states, causing a relative and partial disorder which is the origin of all nervous troubles.

Contrariwise to what we have noted in the well-balanced man, we find a want of homogeneity and dependence between the different constituent principles.

The centralising direction is imperfect; there is no harmonious fusion between the Self and the mentality, between the mentality and the vital dynamism, and between this last and the organism.

This state of unstable equilibrium allows of momentary and partial decentralisations which are indeed sources of disorder, but are also conditions in which the lessened limitations imposed by the body, allow of the possibility of bringing to light everything which in the normal psychic being is cryptoid or occult, whether of the nature of faculty or of knowledge. But this manifestation is never regular; the intellectual output is occasional and sporadic; it requires a collaboration of the conscious and the subconscious; and the modalities and difficulties of this collaboration are well known. Persons so constituted are, like the well-balanced, at very various levels of evolution.

There are among them mediocrities, in whom, however, a tinge of originality corrects psychological monotony.

There are inferior neuropaths who drag out a morbid existence of semi-insanity or semi-imbecility, showing the mental and physical defects which are now called degeneracy.

There are also superior neuropaths whose talents or genius are inseparable from similar defects. These defects cause great suffering; the superior neuropath finds it hard to govern his grouping, to direct his body and even his mentality. Often this mentality escapes more or less from his control and he then skirts the edge of total disequilibrium or insanity. Over and above his psycho-physiological defects, he feels dimly the limitations imposed on him by his nerves and brain, and thence arise his greatest sufferings, even though he is not fully aware of their cause.

How much suffering is involved in these limitations, in the intuitive perceptions of genuine intuitive faculty which nevertheless are not at his free disposal; in the desire to reduce large abstract perceptions to concrete analytical work; in the effort to express in words that which he conceives of so well without words; in the necessity which obliges him to submit the work of his highest and conscious Self to the lower organic mechanism.

Guyau has described this state very vividly.

'We suffer from a kind of hypertrophy of the intellect. All those who are in travail of thought, all who meditate on life and death, all those who philosophize, end by experiencing the same pain. And so there are great artists who pass their lives in the endeavour to bring to realisation an ideal which is more or less inaccessible to them. They are attracted from all sides, by all the sciences, by all the arts; they desire to enter into all, and are obliged to refrain and to divide themselves. A man feels the greedy brain draw to itself the energy of the whole organism, and he is impelled to subdue it, and to resign himself to vegetate instead of living. He does not so resign himself, but prefers to give himself up to the inner fire which consumes him. His thought becomes enfeebled, it stresses the nervous system, feminizes him; though it does not touch his will which remains virile, unsatisfied, and always on the stretch. From all this arises a long struggle of himself against himself, a weary conflict between the alternative of muscle or nerve, to be a man or a woman. The thinker, the artist, is neither the one nor the other.

'Oh, if we could only once, and by one huge effort, give birth to the whole world of thought and feeling that we carry within, with what joy would we welcome that power even though the whole organism were to be broken and destroyed in the pangs of creating. But no! We must give our-selves by small fractions, spend ourselves drop by drop, and endure all the trammels of life. Little by little the whole organism is wearied out in this struggle between the body and the ideal, then the intellect itself is obscured and fails—it is a living and suffering flame which flickers in a wind which blows ever more strongly till the vanquished spirit is borne down.'

The co-existence of neuropathic disturbance, or even of insanity, with the inspiration of genius does not then prove that this latter is derived from the former. It simply proves that the want of equilibrium in the individual grouping which is the first condition of the decentralised manifestations, is at the root of genius. And indeed this psychological decentralisation in a man of genius is sometimes pushed so far that he may behave as a visionary, may exteriorise his inspirations and objectify them till they become hallucinations.

Another type of neuropath not less curious than the man of genius is the medium.

The essential characteristic of this type is an excessive tendency to decentralisation in the individual grouping. It is by reason of this tendency that phenomena of exteriorisation, the isolated action of constituent elements, the activity of cryptoid faculties, and the incursions of the supernormal become possible.

The decentralising tendency is the origin of most neuropathic defects, but in this, more than in other neuropathic types, it withdraws the individual grouping from the directive action of the Self. The medium is not master in his own house; and thence, from the psychological point of view, three characteristics follow:—

He is extremely impressionable;

He is very suggestible;

He is very unstable in his temper and his ideas.

These characteristics are found, more or less, in all mediums of whatever intellectual level.

The psychological instability of mediums does not prevent strength of will and perseverance, at least among those of a superior type, but both strength of will and perseverance only appear when supported by a suggestion or an auto-suggestion. If these are not present, a strange falling off may be manifest; the opinions of the medium are unstable and eminently open to surrounding influences when he is not on his guard. One may hear him with the utmost good faith from one day to another, sustain quite diametrically opposed opinions; indeed it often happens that in a short space of time he passes from one extreme of opinion to another.

The want of regulating power of the Self on his mentality is shown by marked tendency to disjunctions in the latter. These disjunctions sometimes end in the formation of secondary personalities, following a sequence which we shall study later on, and more frequently to incipient duplications; owing to which the medium is essentially complex, difficult to judge, and capable of extremely contradictory words and acts.

In daily life the sudden predominance of some single pervading idea, impression or feeling, may constantly be observed; and then, all the psychological powers escaping from the control of the Self, group themselves round the usurping idea and give it unexpected force. It is for this reason that mediums make exceedingly good actors.

This dominance by a single idea may have fruitful results; but in most cases the pseudo-centralisation round the idea lasts but a short time. A new idea takes the place of the former, and determines a new grouping and a new impulse. Being at the mercy of the momentary impressions, the medium is liable to a sudden throwing out of gear of the psychic forces, thus producing a disproportionate effect in the sense given by the impression which has brought about the disturbance. He then is impervious to any exterior influence and to all reasoning. At such times an external contradiction is never accepted.

When mediums are persons of high intellectual type the concentration of the psychic powers on ideas succeeding one another rapidly and reinforced by this concentration, makes them brilliant speakers and wonderful improvisers; but the quality of their intellectual output is extremely diverse, varying from high inspiration to commonplace fluency, and mere incontinence of thought.

Just as the neuropathic defects of men of genius do not explain genius, so the characteristics or defects of mediums do not explain mediumship, they are its accompaniments.

4.——NEURASTHENIA

It may seem strange to refer neurasthenia to a disequilibrium in the individual grouping, but nothing is more true.

Neurasthenia is essentially due to a want of correspondence between the vital dynamism and the organism.

This disturbance can hardly exist without a congenital predisposing cause, but it may be provoked by some proximate cause, a slight infection or toxic influence, a defect of glandular secretion, some organic defect or a reflex action. Whatever the immediate cause may be, there is no proportion between it and the symptoms produced.

The defective action of the vital dynamism appears first as a feeling of fatigue. The vital functions, the regular play of the organs, all which normally take place unnoticed and regularly, require a painful effort in the neurasthenic.

His sleep is disturbed, there is always insomnia, or hypo-somnia, which does not completely arrest the activity of the brain, so that sleep does not renovate, and fatigue is experienced on awaking. During the day cerebral work is slow, laborious, and marked by a difficulty in associating ideas and concentrating attention.

The want of equilibrium between the organism and the vital dynamism reacts more or less on the whole grouping.

Thus neurasthenia is not the consequence of nervous exhaustion; that is secondary; it arises from a disturbance in the action of the vital dynamism on the body.

To cure it, ' tonics ' are useless; what is required is to regularise the relations of the body with the vital dynamism, while suppressing also the immediate organic cause.

This latter is readily accessible to medical science, and neurasthenics are always benefited when the immediate cause is known and treated. But the more important point—the regularising of relations between the body and the vital dynamism—should be studied with a view to more precise knowledge of this latter and its essential nature. It would be well to try physical agents whose dynamism is powerful. Already the sun-cure, and life in the open air have produced distinctly good results, and indicate a wide field for experiment.

Curative mediumship deserves to be thoroughly studied. Some persons seem to be able to exteriorise part of their own dynamism to reinforce the failing powers of the sick. Some surprising cures have been thus effected, some of which seem to go beyond the class of nervous ailments.

5.——HYSTERIA

Hysteria is brought about by want of harmony between the constituent principles of the individual

251

grouping and the want of subordination to the central direction of the Self.

From the physical and physiological point of view this disharmony, this want of affinity and concord between the organs and the vital dynamism, explains all the varied symptoms and morbid localisations of hysteria —anæsthesia, hyperæsthesia, cramps, paralysis, and nutritive troubles.

The symptoms of this neurosis are unstable and changeable, just because they are not of organic origin but result from imperfect regulating power of the vital dynamism.

From the psychological point of view, the disharmony between the mentality and the Self and imperfect control by the latter, explains all those psychic defects which are so common and well known. The hysteric is usually an ' inferior neuropath,' incapable of fulfilling his duties —an engineer who cannot control his machine.

Suggestibility and ' pythiatism ' are consequences of the feeble control of the Self; they are not the causes, but the results, of the hysterical condition.

6.—DEMENTIA

If we take one step farther and imagine a want of equilibrium which is not merely relative but absolute or nearly absolute—a total or nearly total want of direction —we have dementia.

Dementia is primarily anarchy of the mental elements, on which the Self has no longer any action; not even the limited, enfeebled, and intermittent control which it still retains in the hysteric.

What comes to pass when mental anarchy is firmly established by the absence of control by the Self ?

The psychic functions and faculties, the acquired knowledge are intact but undirected. They may show only incoherence, but more frequently some idea, some feeling, some elementary psychic grouping, is formed and tends to become permanent, producing fixed ideas and systematic delirium.

The mental disharmony is not an isolated symptom, but by reason of the fundamental solidarity of the constituent principles, it is always accompanied by a total want of equilibrium of the individual grouping. Mania may be ascending or descending, it may arise in the mentality or it may end there. Very often it is started by some toxic, infectious, or reflex trouble attacking the brain. In these cases the symptoms are often mental confusion, maniacal excitement, or melancholia, sometimes alternating with circular delirium. The frequent inheritance of insanity proves the importance of the physical factor in its genesis.

In other cases the origin may be purely mental, and when that is so the insanity is generally partial only; a certain amount of control by the Self persists; not sufficient to arrest the tendency to delirium and the abnormal grouping round a predominant idea, but enough to leave some appearance of reason and to permit the continuance of psychic function.

There are many degrees in the insanity which has a mental origin and we find every grade between mere mental instability and complete dementia. There are not only the half-mad, but 'quarter and one-tenth mad.'

The control of the Self over the mentality at the actual evolutionary level that humanity has reached is so imperfect that it is seldom perfectly regular; and in this sense there is no man who is completely free from some mental disequilibrium. Some mental irregularity is almost the rule, perfect psychic health the exception.

Whether the exciting cause be of organic or of mental origin, essential insanity is not strictly speaking a disease of the brain. It is simply the partial or complete absence of the control of the Self over its mentality.

253

The elementary groups of the latter are intact and long remain so; but if the superior control is not re-established the prolonged disorganisation reacts on cerebral function and ends in the brain lesions of degeneracy.

7.—HYPNOTISM

Hypnotism and its modalities are capable of very simple explanation. Its manifestations are analogous to those of hysteria, with this difference—that they are artificial and generally wider in scope. Hypnosis demands a certain predisposition to decentralisation, such as the mediumistic temperament. It comes about by a factitious rupture in the equilibrium of the individual grouping.

The real and true cause and primary condition is the decentralisation of the individual grouping.

All the usual phenomena are then easily understood —automatism, suggestibility, modifications of personality, the substitution of an inner or outer direction for the central control, mono-ideaism, etc, etc.

The isolated cerebral psychism is remarkably suggestible and automatic. Its manifestations appear as a kind of inferior subconsciousness, very passive, and unable to go beyond its acquisitions and habits.

The extra-cerebral psychism shows itself in cryptomnesia and cryptopsychism, and its grouping into very diverse personalities. Sometimes it will reveal higher powers and supernormal flashes due to decentralisation, and therefore to the momentary and relative release from organic limitations. Hypnotism resembles a half-opened door on the cryptoid portion of the Self.

What part is to be referred to suggestion in the genesis of hypnosis? Simply that it is a frequent and useful, but by no means an indispensable factor. Suggestion, by itself, explains nothing; it is a secondary reaction resulting from lessened or suppressed control by the higher direction of the Self over the decentralised individual grouping. Hypnotism may act, exceptionally, on the mental elements, but it seems unnecessary to point out that it acts chiefly on the cerebral psychism.

The commonplace hypnotic state referred to in classical theory is primarily due to the secession of the lower group (the vital dynamism and the body) from the higher group (the mentality and the Self). This lower group acts as an automaton, slavishly, under the suggestion of the magnetiser. The automatism and the extreme suggestibility are thus easily comprehensible.

Both in hypnosis and somnambulism the automatism acts with remarkable precision.

In *L'Être Subconscient* I explained this precision of action by the fact that all the vital forces grouped round a single idea without consideration or distractions give great power and sureness of action. This, no doubt, is true, but there is more in it than this; there appears to be a curious regression towards animality. The lower group, deprived of conscious direction, seems to recover for the time the sureness characteristic of animal instinct.

8.—ALTERATIONS OF PERSONALITY

Nothing puts the truth of our concept of the individual in a clearer light than the ease with which it enables us to understand alterations of personality.

These manifestations have, up to the present, been either absolute riddles or have received pseudo-interpretations which have been crude or meaningless when they have not been empty verbalism—distinguishing the subconsciousness from infra-consciousness, super-consciousness, or co-consciousness!

The root and original cause of the phenomenon is the setting aside of the central direction of the Self.

The factitious personalities are due to isolated

manifestations in the psychological groups detached from the Self.

Isolated activity of the cerebral psychism is shown by automatism; or by pseudo-personalities aroused by suggestion—personalities of a commonplace kind and inferior order, devoid of originality.

Isolated activity of the mental elements of the extra-cerebral psychism is the origin of the multiplication of personalities of higher and more complex kinds.

The phenomenon of incipient mental dissociation with a tendency to duplication, is frequent in normal life, by reason of the complexity of the mentality, of the alternating predominance of certain groupings which may be rivals or antagonistic, and the inability of the Self to bring them into harmony.

But in abnormal states and in certain predisposed persons this duplication of personality goes to unexpected lengths.

That true multiple personalities should appear, two conditions are essential.

Firstly, a liability to decentralisation, and a certain instability of the central direction—a weakness in the individual ' autocracy.'

Secondly, a defect in assimilation of the mental elements by the Self. This second condition is a chief one. Without this defect of assimilative power, there may be decentralisation, but no ' personality ' worthy of the name will appear.

We have seen that the Self retains the complete knowledge of states of consciousness and assimilates them. If this assimilation is imperfect, these states of consciousness retain an irregular and centrifugal self-activity which tends towards isolated and distinct manifestations.

The genesis of a secondary personality is then easy to follow. To begin with, there is abnormal activity, a ' parasitic budding ' in the mentality. An ill-assimilated grouping takes place round some specially active thought, some emotion, tendency, impression, suggestion, or auto-suggestion, as a nucleus. This primary group partly escapes from the directing centralising control, and collects round it secondary and weaker mental elements.

From this point there arises in the depths of the mentality a silent struggle between the parasitic personality and the Self. Most frequently the former is vanquished, disintegrates, and is assimilated by the Self. But sometimes by reason of insufficient directing power in the latter, because its evolutionary level is low, or through a want of affinity (original or acquired), or through a congenital tendency of the grouping to decentralisation, the parasitic personality prospers and develops.

It groups around itself a larger and larger part of the mental activities, annexes imaginative elements, strengthens by daily use, and soon a rupture becomes possible; a new confederation is formed in the mentality and there is a secession from the Self.

Thenceforward there begins open strife, with variable results, with alternations of failure and success, between the Self and the factitious personality or personalities for the possession of power, for the integrity or the disintegration of the whole, for domination of the psychological field.

There is no known case of secondary personality which cannot be explained as the result of this process.

It might be possible to go further still, and to suppose a defect in assimilation of the mental elements by the Self not only within the period since the birth of the actual vital group, but in some anterior grouping. On this hypothesis (which would have to be brought to the test of facts), the possibilities connected with the genesis of secondary personalities would be greatly enlarged.

Such a one or another of these secondary personalities

might be the unassimilated 'representation' of the Self in a preceding life. . . .

Among secondary personalities mediumistic personalities should be placed in a distinct class. By their self-activity, their originality, their permanence, and their definite affirmations as to their origin, and finally by the supernormal powers they sometimes manifest, they must be made the subject of a special and separate study. We shall consider them last.

9.—THE MODALITIES OF INTELLECTUAL WORK— GENIUS

Ordinary intellectual work is essentially the result of close collaboration between the cerebral and the superior psychism.

In the normal man during waking hours, the two psychisms are fused, united, and homogeneous, and their output is regular, but limited as to quality by the cerebral capacity. The superior faculties are manifest only by innate proclivities, general capacity, and individual character.

During the repose of the brain the superior psychic activity persists, but it is not perceived or remains entirely latent. Its action is manifest however in the well-known mechanism of subconscious elaboration, which is wrongly attributed to automatism of the brain. This latter automatism only produces ordinary, incoherent, and futile dreams of a commonplace kind.

Logical, coherent dreams, and those which show genius, are due to accidental repercussion on the cerebral psychism of the superior psychism which is always active, though unperceived.

We may place reverie side by side with dreams. Reverie means the relaxation of all intellectual effort and of the full control by the Self. Ideas pass through the mind according to habitual associations and affinities, and the Self looks on as at a play; not interfering unless to set aside a disturbing idea from time to time, to direct ideas in a prescribed sense, or to make imaginative additions.

In order that intellectual work may reach its greatest output and to ensure the full collaboration and direction by the superior and extra-cerebral psychism, it is necessary that there should be some relaxation in the centralised direction of the individual grouping.

It is for this reason that the extension of subconscious collaboration and the occurrence of inspiration are nearly always associated with the abnormal and neuropathic states which this momentary and relative decentralisation brings about.

Now and then it seems that the limitation imposed by cerebration is broken through; then the higher faculties appear, but these will always be impeded or even diverted by the alternations between effort (*i.e.* centralised action), and relaxation of the synthesis, which latter implies relaxation of cerebral limitations.

Crypto-psychism and cryptomnesia, so incomprehensible as mere cerebral faculties, are readily explained by the fact of the higher subconscious psychism. Though not directly accessible to the will and knowledge of the person, which are normally bounded by cerebral limitations, they none the less contribute greatly, though in an occult fashion, to the extension of the field of psychic activity, of which they constitute the main part.

Innate proclivities, powers which are not inherited, inspiration, talent, or genius appearing apart from voluntary work, are all explicable by the essential nature of the subconscious psychism and the part it plays in the origin, the development, and the functioning of the normal individual.

Inspiration is the result of the free activity, increased by liberation, of this higher extra-cerebral psychism. But, by the very fact of the decentralisation which liberates it, this activity only reacts on the normal consciousness by flashes, intermittently or fragmentarily, in an inconstant and irregular manner.

That which is called ' unconscious work ' is, moreover, rarely pure inspiration. Most frequently it is, we repeat, the result of a kind of collaboration of the conscious with the higher subconscious psychism.

Consciousness elaborates or starts the work; but the limitations of cerebral capacities do not allow of its satisfactory conclusion, whatever efforts may be made. Then the collaboration of the subconscious sets in by a latent process. It is continued during, and especially during, the repose of the brain ; for the subconsciousness is then detached from the physiological contingencies which affect that organ, and transcends its limitations. The fact that this collaboration is unperceived causes its results to appear sometimes like a revelation.

Genius takes its creative power from the very essence of the Self. It is well to observe that theoretically, genius does not necessarily imply a high degree of mental evolution for its manifestation. But practically, in order that its creations may be durable, genius requires an extended knowledge of the mutual relations of things, and this conscious or subconscious knowledge implies a high evolutionary level. It must also be remarked that genius does not imply perfection. The diverse manifestations of genius—scientific, philosophical, artistic, religious, and so on—are not protected from disharmonies and errors. Reasoned control is indispensable, as we have before observed. It is for this reason that a man of genius can produce nothing of use to humanity unless he is also at a high evolutionary level.

10.—THE SUPERNORMAL

The appearance of the supernormal resembles that of creative inspiration and genius—it is conditioned by a degree of decentralisation sufficient to break for the moment the cerebral limitation of the individual. From the depths of the subliminal consciousness there will sometimes issue, as from a window suddenly opened in the opaque enclosing envelope, dazzling flashes of divination, powers of action from mind to mind, or powers superior to matter, released from the contingencies of Time and Space.

This lucidity, these apparently unlimited powers, are not really marvellous; or at least they are neither more nor less marvellous than all the phenomena of life and thought.

There is no hard and fast line between the normal and the supernormal; both have their origins in the vital *processus*, and the only difference is that the one is familiar to us and therefore gives us the illusion of understanding it, while the other derives its occult character from the fact that it is unusual.

Supernormal physiology presents exactly the same mystery as normal physiology: the normal formation of a living being is neither more nor less marvellous, neither more nor less comprehensible than the abnormal formations which mediumship presents to our view. It is, we repeat, the same ideoplastic miracle which forms the hands, the face, the tissues, and the whole organism of the child at the expense of the maternal body; or the hands, face, and organism of a ' materialisation ' at the expense of the body of a medium.

The psychological supernormal is but one aspect, a hidden aspect, of the normal conditions of the individual, whose apparent consciousness is only the limited reflection of his total consciousness. There is the same mystery in the creations of genius as in lucidity, the same independence of contingencies, the same divine reflection.

In the sum total of the phenomena of life, of consciousness, and of the evolution of the individual, either one apprehends nothing or one apprehends all. We apprehend nothing when we seek to refer the whole being to one of its principles, more especially to the crudest—the material body; we apprehend everything when we consider the divine and permanent Self in its passing and diverse objectifications.

In fine, there is no supernormal, as there are no miracles! The supernormal is but the unusual manifestation of the Self, released by decentralisation, revealing itself by all its powers, even those that are highest and most latent; in contrast with normal psychic life which only allows of narrow manifestations, strictly confined within bounds of material ' representation.'

Emergence of the ' supernormal ' merely proves that there are in the Self higher powers which are unused and unusable during terrestrial objectification; powers of action from mind to mind (mento-mental), extra-sensorial powers of divination and clairvoyance, and finally powers of dominating matter.

We may admit, with Myers, that these higher faculties which escape our will during earth-life, and are accessible in a relative and fragmentary manner in proportion to the abnormal decentralisation of organic limitations, are more completely accessible to us after the final rupture of those limitations by death. Especially does it seem reasonable that these faculties now in process of development should, some day, be fully available to the Self. Their regular and normal use will denote the superior and ideally evolved life in which consciousness will have won its final triumph over the original unconsciousness. Then there will be no ' limitation ' of the Self by the individual grouping which it directs. The

Self will know all and have power over all. It will have realised its diverse and unlimited potentialities.

II.—MEDIUMSHIP

Mediumship puts great problems before us; but these become relatively easy in the light of the preceding ideas.

The mechanism of mediumistic action may be summed up as decentralisation of the individual grouping of the medium and isolated manifestations of the decentralised portions.

Sometimes these isolated manifestations are carried on in the grouping itself, intrinsically; sometimes they take place extrinsically, by an actual exteriorisation. It can be seen how vast is the field covered by mediumistic action:—

> Motor, sensorial, dynamic, and intellectual exteriori-
> sations;
> Different kinds of automatism;
> An immense variety of manifestations of a psycho-
> logical order;
> Isolated action of the cerebral psychism; mental
> disjunctions and personifications of very various
> natures and levels; Pythian or suggested
> phenomena; crypto-psychic or cryptomnesic
> manifestations, and those called supernormal.

Thus understood, mediumship is a whole world; one that defies any partial and fragmentary exploration and is concealed from those who merely look into a few details, but which reveals itself to the high and clear vision that contemplates the sum total of the complex factors of Being.

To seek to explain mediumship, as some psychologists do, by a series of fragmentary hypotheses adapted to a few of its phenomena, is useless. None of these partial explanations on points of detail can have any value at all. Mediumship, in all its prodigious diversity can be understood only by the knowledge of the actual psychological constituents of individual man, what the individual grouping consists of, and its possibilities of relative and momentary dissociation; and, especially, by knowledge of its metaphysical essence, and of the creative dynamo-psychism objectified in it.

If, and only if, we take our stand on this new concept of the Self, it becomes easy to comprehend the endless diversity of mediumistic action. Nevertheless, even if we take these precise notions on the constitution of the individual as our point of departure, there will always remain questions open to controversy on the subject of mediumship.

Among these reserved questions two, more especially, are open to discussion—the personalities manifested, and the teachings given by these personalities.

1. Mediumistic personalities. In all manifestations of mediumship is to be observed a marked tendency to ' personification.' The mental disjunctions, exteriorisations, cryptomnesic and crypto-psychic phenomena, and powers over matter, are not usually anarchic or incoherent; they denote a purpose and show direction. This direction is by a secondary personality distinct from the Self.

Often this secondary personality is insignificant and ephemeral. Just as elementary exteriorisations and incipient mento-mental action or clairvoyance—the 'small change' of mediumship—are usual in the normal existence of mediums, so also the tendency to disjunctions and autonomous personifications appears as a commonplace and uninteresting phenomenon.

But in the favourable atmosphere created by spiritist séances, or following on frequent use or impulse, or sometimes spontaneously, these manifestations become more precise and accentuated, and the directing

264

personification then sometimes acquires truly remarkable power, and deserves the closest attention.

What is the origin and nature of these mediumistic personalities ? In ordinary disjunctions, the secondary personalities which appear as a consequence of mental decentralisation behave as usurpers of the place of the Self. They seem to aim at replacing the legitimate government; they declare themselves to be the true Self. In mediumship, their behaviour is different—they declare themselves foreign to the Self; they claim to be distinct entities. Usually, at least in our day and in the west, they claim to be the 'spirits' of the dead, and say that they only borrow from the medium the vital dynamism and organic elements which they need in order to act upon the material plane.

The proofs given by them in support of their statements are generally vague and will not bear examination; but sometimes they are singularly clear; they recall the personality of the deceased, they give minute and unknown personal details, his native language, his features (in teleplastic cases), his signature, etc.

What are we to think of these affirmations ? Are they always false ? Is mediumship but the domain of deceit and illusion? Many students of psychism do not hesitate to say so. Let us reproduce some of their arguments. They say:—

'Mediumistic personalities may well, in spite of their affirmations, be only secondary personalities, their genesis being analogous to these latter. As they start from a suggestion or an auto-suggestion, whether conscious or subconscious, their development and their acquirements would be under the same mechanism.

'None of the proofs of autonomy and independence can be formal. The psychological differences in faculties and knowledge from those of the

medium can be explained simply by the complex
nature of mentality and the extension of crypto-
psychism; the contradictions in ideas, character,
and will, may represent merely interior tendencies
repressed by daily life and escaping violently by the
safety-valve of mediumship. The supernormal may
belong to the mediumistic subconsciousness.

' None of the proofs of identity can be completely convincing; the origin of all knowledge,
even the most unexpected and secret, even that of
a language of which the medium is ignorant, may
be in cryptomnesia, thought-transference, or clairvoyance.

' The new tests invented by English and American
investigators (cross-correspondences, communications
of the same entity to different mediums who have no
relations with one another) are evidently at first sight
somewhat disconcerting to our thesis. It is clear
that facts as precise and extraordinary as those for
instance, observed by Madame de W.,[1] seem to
indicate an independent and autonomous directing
will. But is not that another illusion? Who can
say if the personality may not acquire by mediumistic
culture, besides great autonomy, a transitory
dynamism, at all events while the experiment lasts,
a dynamism borrowed from the medium and giving
it the power of acting on other mediums at a distance?'

Of course, anything may be possible. But when
arguing on mediumship, all the notions which we have
established on the constitution of the individual must
be borne in mind. These notions which (accepted in
their entirety) have extricated us from the chaos of

[1] *Annales des Sciences Psychiques*: 'Contribution a l'étude des corre-
spondances croisées' (In this case 'Rudolph,' the alleged communicator,
in order to prove his separate existence, gave parts of a message to one
automatist in Paris, and other parts to another at Wimereux, near
Boulogne, within the same hour; the parts making no sense till combined.
[Translator's note.]

classical psycho-physiology, and have enabled us to understand the general meaning of the individual and the universe, also permit the affirmation of the survival of the Self, and its endless evolution from unconsciousness, to consciousness. It should be beyond doubt that the Self both pre-exists, and that it survives the grouping which it directs during one earth-life; that it more particularly survives its lower objectification during this life. This may at least be admitted, if not as a mathematical certainty, at least as a high probability.

If so, the manifestation of a ' discarnate spirit ' on the material plane by the aid of dynamic and organic elements borrowed from the medium then appears an undeniable possibility.

In face of a fact apparently of a spiritist nature, one attitude only befits the instructed investigator—to take good sense as his guide. It is for good sense and sane judgment to appraise the statements of the communicator.

It is in the name of good sense that English and American investigators, weary of strife, and well aware of the disconcerting subtleties which have been advanced to explain the mental side of mediumship, have ended by accepting, with striking unanimity, the categorical and repeated affirmations of the communicators.

After Hodgson, who, starting from absolute scepticism, declared after twelve years of study that there was in his mind no room for even the possibility of doubt of survival and on the reality of communication between the living and the dead, Hyslop, Myers, and more recently Sir Oliver Lodge, have plainly given utterance to the same conviction.

I refer the reader who desires to form a reasoned opinion, to the publications of these psychologists, that he may weigh the value of their arguments.[1]

[1] See the *Proceedings* of the English and American Societies for Psychical Research, and Sir Oliver Lodge's recent book, *Raymond.*

For my own part, if I may give a personal impression of what I have observed in the domain of mediumship, I should say that even if in a given case spiritist intervention could not be affirmed as a scientific certainty, one is obliged, willingly or unwillingly and on the aggregate of cases, to admit the possibility of such intervention. I think it probable that there is, in mediumship, an action of intelligent entities distinct from the medium. I base this opinion not only on the alleged proofs of identity given by the communicators, which may be matters of controversy, but on the high and complex phenomena of mediumship. These frequently show direction and intention which cannot, unless very arbitrarily, be referred to the medium or the experimenters. We do not find this direction and intelligence either in the normal consciousness of the medium, nor in his somnambulistic consciousness, nor in his impressions, his desires, or his fears, whether direct, indirect, suggested, or voluntary. We can neither produce the phenomena nor modify them. All happens as though the directing intelligence were independent and autonomous.

Even this is not all. This directing intelligence seems to be deeply aware of much that we do not know; it can distinguish between the essence of things and their representations; it knows these sufficiently to be able to modify at its will the relations which normally govern these representations in space and time. In a word the higher phenomena of mediumship seem to indicate, to necessitate, and to proclaim direction, knowledge, and abilities which surpass the powers—even the subconscious powers—of the mediums.

Such is the deep impression resulting from my own experiments as well as from the reports of experiments by other metapsychologists. If my impressions are correct it can readily be understood why certain series of celebrated experiments (such as those of Crookes and Richet), seem to have had but one outcome: to bring these eminent men to an unexpected conviction by the methods most likely to produce a strong impression.

2. In what concerns the 'teaching' given by the communicators, the difficulties of an estimate are no less considerable.

These teachings are too variable in nature and value to be made the basis for rational beliefs.

The contradictions which M. Maxwell[1] has taken pains to set forth are very disconcerting to any one who thinks to base his beliefs on them. But it is not less obvious that these contradictions are both natural and inevitable.

Bearing in mind the notions which have been demonstrated above, a mediumistic communication may be conceived to have either of two origins:—

(a) The communication may come entirely from the medium.

In this case it may be due to cerebral automatism, or to a mental disjunction and a factitious personality, or it may be a manifestation of crypto-psychism or cryptomnesia. . . . Obviously then its value will be very variable. Intellectual mediumship will be sometimes the source of wonderful foreknowledge or revelations; or sometimes, and more frequently, of platitudes, falsehoods, and errors. It may show a superior inspiration; it may also display a disconcerting and silly incoherence. There are all degrees and categories in the products of mental disjunction; and only those who are ignorant can be surprised or moved by them.

'We are incarcerated prisoners,' Mæterlinck[2] exclaims poetically: 'with whom he (the real Self, the unknown guest) does not communicate whenever he will. He prowls round the walls, he cries,

[1] Maxwell: *Les Phénomènes Psychiques.*
[2] Mæterlinck: *L'Hôte Inconnu.*

269

he warns, he knocks at all doors; but nothing reaches us but a vague disquiet, an indistinct murmur which is sometimes translated to us by a jailer only half awake, and, like ourselves, captive till death. . . . In other words, and without metaphor, the medium draws from his habitual language, and from that which the sitters suggest to him, materials wherewith to clothe and identify the presentiments and the unwonted visions which come he knows not whence.'

This unknown guest, this subconscious person is not in reality a single and homogeneous being. It would be better named 'the subconscious complex,' which can reveal itself to us under the most diverse forms and attributes.

Unity belongs to the real Self only, as distinct from the mental process as from the organic form, but retaining in itself the memory-total of all representations.

In order that the Self, abstracted from organic limitations, should be able to reveal its higher powers and the immensity of its latent conscious acquisitions, it must be able sufficiently to master its own decentralised mentality.

Such a condition rarely comes about, and it is for this reason that crypto-psychic manifestations are usually fragmentary and erratic.

(*b*) Even if the communication proceeds from an intelligence distinct from the medium, it may itself be imperfect or falsified, frequently both and in varying degrees.

Passing through the mediumistic channel it will necessarily be limited by the mentality and the cerebration of the medium; and as the intrinsic subconscious inspiration has such difficulty in reacting accurately on the brain, there is all the more reason why an extrinsic inspiration should be limited, lessened, or deformed.

Not only so; by the very fact of communicating, the communicator experiences a psychic disturbance; a fact which has been specially noted by English and American investigators. In borrowing substance from the medium, the being takes on limitations as it does at birth by taking on a body of the substance of his mother. By the fact of communication on the material plane he undergoes a kind of relative and momentary reincarnation; accompanied, as in normal reincarnation, by oblivion of his real situation and by the suppression of the greater part of his conscious acquisitions.

If the spiritist explanation be accepted, one is obliged to suppose that during the time of manifestation through the intermediary of a medium, the communicator finds himself irresistibly brought under conditions which were characteristic to him in earth-life. For these reasons, and because of these primary difficulties, communicators may abound in details of their identity but find great difficulty in giving precise notions of their actual conditions.

These ideas, if they were capable of proof, would tend to establish the existence of an ' other side ' not very dissimilar to this side. The ' representation ' which the discarnate spirit would make of it would at least recall the 'representation' which the incarnate Self does actually make of the material world, though on ' planes ' more subtle and related to all we have previously noted of the individual constitution of Man.

The information given relating to evolution and the transition from unconsciousness to consciousness are more precise.

If, as is logical, we take account only of the messages which bear marks of high inspiration and superior will, most of the contradictions disappear.

All the higher communications without exception, affirm the survival of that which is essential in the Self,

and also unlimited evolution towards greater consciousness and greater perfection. They all place the ideal
and the purposes of Humanity above any dogmatisms.
All proclaim a high morality of goodwill and justice.

Progressive evolution from the unconscious to the
conscious is not however always referred to palingenesis.[1]
The plurality of existences is never denied in the higher
type of communications, and it is often implied. It is
so in the admirable messages received by Stainton
Moses.[2]

But this is of small importance. It will evidently
be wise to take account only of facts and reasoned
deductions from facts in constructing a philosophy of
individual evolution. It is on them only that the
sovereign beauty and the shining truth of evolution
by palingenesis should be based. It needs no other
revelation.

[1] *Palingenesis.* Gr. πάλιν =again; γένεσις =production. Used in
modern biology for hereditary evolution not modified by adaptation.
Here used in its philological meaning of re-birth.—[Translator's note.]

[2] Stainton Moses : *Spirit Teachings.*

PART II

EVOLUTION OF THE UNIVERSE

CHAPTER I

THE TRANSITION FROM THE UNCONSCIOUS TO THE CONSCIOUS IN THE UNIVERSE

I.—THE UNIVERSE CONCEIVED OF AS AN ESSENTIAL DYNAMO-PSYCHISM AND AS REPRESENTATION

WE can now, by a wide induction, refer back to the Universe what we know of the individual; for what is demonstrated for the individual—the microcosm—cannot but appear true for the universe—the macrocosm.

Like the individual, the universe should be conceived of as a temporary representation and an essential and real dynamo-psychism.

Just as the individual organism is but an ideoplastic product of his essential dynamo-psychism, so the universe appears as a vast materialisation of the creative principle.

Finally, like the individual, the universe passes by evolution through the fact of experiences acquired by and in representations, from unconsciousness to consciousness.

2.—EVOLUTION IS THE ACQUISITION OF CONSCIOUSNESS

Let us consider the universe under this aspect:—

In the living being we have seen the original and creative unconscious dynamo-psychism enriched and enlightened, so to speak, by conscious acquisitions. We have noted the progressive and unlimited tendency to unification, to harmonious fusion of unconsciousness with consciousness, and have been able to infer that the multitude of evolutionary experiences integrally retained and transmuted into new capacities, has, as its result, the greater and greater realisation of consciousness which absorbs the primitive unconsciousness.

In the evolving universe the process is the same. At first it represents a very ocean of unconsciousness; then, from that ocean, there emerge islets or icebergs of consciousness. These are at first very small, very few, and isolated; the waves of unconsciousness frequently submerge them. But the evolutionary impulse continues; the islets grow, are multiplied, and join. They form great continents whose summits shine in full consciousness; but their base and foundations lie deep in the Unconscious whence they arose and of whose nature they partake.

Later on, in higher evolutionary phases, the domain of consciousness will in turn have absorbed into itself the primitive ocean of unconsciousness whence it was derived.

That these propositions are of the philosophic order is undeniable; but they are not metaphysical in the proper sense of that word, because their data are scientific and rational.

When it is said that evolution is the transition of a potential and unconscious dynamo-psychism to a realised and conscious dynamo-psychism, this is not metaphysical: it is only the expression in philosophic language of an obvious scientific truth. It is a general conclusion of a higher order drawn from verified facts.

3.—EVOLUTIONARY LAWS, AND THE PROBLEM OF FINALITY

If we consider the details of evolution we shall see that the transition comes to pass very simply.

The primitive evolutionary impulse which is manifest in the first appearance of vegetative forms and those of the lowest animals, is obviously unconscious. The experiments of De Vries show that it is anarchic and without order. There is an exuberance of life in all directions.

But the secondary factors, especially adaptation and selection appearing at the same time as the forms themselves, come into play. They do not cause evolution, but evolution takes place conformably to their influence. They bring about the persistence or the extinction of the forms which have appeared. They aid the evolutionary process by regularising it.

To this primitive phase, a second succeeds: as soon as a rudiment of consciousness appears, it also has a part to play. The acquired consciousness reverts to unconsciousness; which it fertilises and enlightens. Thenceforward the creative impulse is not anarchic, little by little it becomes regular and concentrated; it obeys in some measure environing necessities in order to facilitate adaptation.

It is, however, not yet conscious in any way: even the appearance of the main species, the transition from the fish to the batrachian, from the reptile to the bird, from the anthropopithecus to the man, were not transitions deliberately planned. The fish could not have understood that the batrachian is a relatively higher form; the reptile did not consciously desire to acquire wings and become a bird; the anthropopithecus did not understand that the species Man would involve a higher total of psychic realisations.

But these transitions came to pass as if by the obscure influence of a need; as if the function, potentially anterior to the organ, had conditioned the organ which was to appear; as if, in a word, evolution had obeyed a marvellous instinct.

If there are still gropings and errors in this evolutionary phase, that is because instinct is not infallible.

Instinct represents the first manifestation of the subconsciousness collectively, as it does in the individual. As in the individual, so collectively, the subconsciousness appears as the intermediary between the primitive unconsciousness and the still future consciousness.

The subconscious is no longer a dark and chaotic unconsciousness; it is the unconscious already illumined by the reflection of realised consciousness.

From the unconscious it holds all potentialities; from the conscious it draws the general knowledge acquired through vital 'experiences' and instinctive or intentional aspirations towards the light.

The reversions from consciousness to unconsciousness which we have studied in the individual, greatly transcend the limits of individuality. By reason of the essential solidarity of all, the consciousness individually acquired reverts both into individual unconsciousness and into the collective unconsciousness.

Thenceforward evolution, even of inferior species, is in some degree guided by a superior and deep-seated influence which causes them to participate in the general progress that has already come into realisation.

The appearance of principal species and principal instincts, seemingly conforming to some kind of terminal state, which is not pre-established but acquired, can thus be understood.

At the beginning of these principal species and principal instincts there is a seeming effort of 'lucid' subconscious activity which creates them with a given form, and with characters having certain capacities, but also with their special limitations in space and time. This effort of lucid subconscious activity by reason of the acquired purpose (*finalité*), is always largely accordant with the demands of the environment in which new species will be evolved. The creation of a new species appears, in a word, as a result akin to genius in the unconscious, working towards consciousness.

Acquired purpose—this is the key to the enigma of transformism.

The totality of evolution, like its details, reveals an obvious purpose which neither selection nor adaptation nor any of the classical factors can sufficiently explain. But this evident purpose is certainly not a pre-established purpose, for if it were, the plan on which it proceeds would not allow of gropings or errors.

It is an acquired finality, relative, and explicable by the reversions from the conscious to the unconscious, and is simply proportional to the level of consciousness collectively attained.

By reason of the ideal adaptation which it implies, this acquired purpose alone allows of the complete operation of the classical factors—natural selection, influence of the environment, sexual selection, segregation, migrations, etc. Only this can explain how, wherever life is possible—in water, earth, and air, the most diverse forms of life appear; only this can explain the infinite variety in the forms of life and their narrow specialisation. Only this allows of comprehension how the appearance and the development of new organs corresponds exactly with precise needs.

Only this also can explain how the development of these organs sometimes goes beyond the need and is effected outside of adaptation, as we see in ornamental characteristics.

The tendency towards consciousness is not only a tendency towards intelligence, but a tendency towards all that constitutes a conscious psychism, including the affectional and the æsthetic senses. Affectional and æsthetic instincts which are realised in the more highly evolved individuals, revert into the collective unconsciousness, and reappear as an instinct towards organic perfection in the acquired finality and thus have important functions.

Finally, it is only the purely relative power of acquired

finality that enables us to understand the reasons for errors, gropings, and regressions.

In this lengthy phase of evolution, pure unconsciousness is represented by the automatism of the main vital functions, and (more especially) by its infinite potentialities.

Subconsciousness predominates in the invertebrates in which it plays an almost exclusive part. They act practically without any thought and are guided almost entirely by instinct.

Among vertebrates there appear large ' fringes ' of intelligence, but these fringes are not, as Bergson would have them, a ' relic ' abandoned in the transition from the animal to the man; there are no cast-off relics in this evolution. These fringes of intelligence are consciousness in rough draft.

Consciousness develops little by little as vital and psychological experiences accumulate and revert into the unconscious which they illuminate.

In the superior animals—the horse, the dog, the monkey, the elephant, etc. . . . . realisation of consciousness has made immense progress; the logical and reasoning faculties already play an important part. Simultaneously the function of instinct seems to diminish, its manifestations are no longer continuous and dominant, they have become limited and intermittent. Consciousness, in fact, tends by its gradual realisation, to break the bonds wherein the tyranny of instinct confines the activity of the being, and to become the substitute for instinct. The predominance of the logical and reasoning faculties over instinct is indispensable to the evolution of consciousness, for the exclusive use of instinct, or even its predominance, implies stagnation in intellectual progress.

The testimony of the insect which we have already had occasion to invoke from another point of view, again illustrates our position; it proves that organic progress and bodily complexity are not closely associated with mental progress. Physically, the insect is very highly evolved, but its consciousness is very greatly in arrear. The exclusive predominance of instinct has put the brake on its progress towards consciousness. There has, in this case, been what looks like a spurring of nature on a wrong road.

It is indispensable that instinct, sure but limited, should give place to reason, which is indeed hesitating and fallible, but contains infinite capacities for development.

It is also indispensable that instinct, fertilised by conscious acquisitions, should evolve by transformation. This is what has occurred in the transition from animality to humanity.

In Man, accordingly, instinct is duplicated. There remains in him an animal and physiological instinct which plays a less and less important part. There is also a higher instinct which is but another name for intuition.

Intuition is instinct renovated, idealised, and transformed.

As soon as this has appeared, consciousness has played a great part. Conditioned by the subconscious, it conditions it in turn. From the subconscious it receives its principal capacities and to the subconscious are returned the acquisitions of consciousness; leaving to subconsciousness the duty of preserving these and transmuting them into new capacities.

But consciousness is still very limited by the conditions of cerebral organisation, which is the instrument for psychic activity on the material plane. It can only partly utilise the unconscious potentialities. It can know scarcely anything of the cryptomnesic reserves. *It does not know itself.*

The result of this limitation and ignorance is to favour evolution by causing many efforts in all kinds of directions, thus producing a multiplicity of new experiences; whilst knowledge of its real state and full remembrance of the past would, in the present phase of evolution, be a restraint and an impediment to the thinking being, as likewise the regular use of the higher subconscious capacities would limit effort.

But this limitation and this ignorance must be passing: all past phases of evolution remain deeply imprinted on the parts as on the whole.

The interpenetration of the subconscious and the conscious, which is becoming more and more marked, will necessarily bring about a perfect fusion between them in higher evolutionary phases. The complete memory of the evolutionary past, the free disposal of original and acquired capacities, an extended knowledge of the universe, and the solution to the highest metaphysical problems, will all become regular and normal.

The unconscious will then have become the conscious.

If we would take a comprehensive view of evolution such as it is presented by the new notions, we shall see organic realisation proceeding according to the classical simile, as an immense tree of life, not as Bergson would have it, as a sheaf of diverging rockets.

Its principal and secondary branches represent the diverse groups of plant and animal life, all derived from the trunk common to all.

The realisation of consciousness is effected from complete unconsciousness to complete consciousness by a series of broken lines, which, starting from the base converge to a common summit.

These broken lines represent the perpetual passing and repassing from life to death and from death to life of ' the essential ' in the psychological elements individualised in the Self. The theory of palingenesis enables us to understand the return, by death, of the individualised monad to the central energy, and its restoration by life to the place which it fits according to its rising degrees of conscious realisation.

The infinite series of broken lines thus rises directly and logically from the primitive unconsciousness to consciousness.

The human form represents to-day the top of the evolutionary scale. How will future realisations of consciousness appear ?

Will they be correlative to a new complexity in the present physical organisation ? Or will they necessitate new and more perfect forms ?

Will the 'superman' retain the present human form ?

To such questions it is impossible to reply. There are as many arguments to be found for as against any answer that can be given.

The fact that we cannot discover any outline of a future organisation, carries no weight if the theory of mutations is true. There may be in our subconsciousness or in the subconsciousness of the universe, some latent preparation, some slow elaboration of a new form which will appear suddenly when the favourable conditions obtain.

This new form would be in conformity with all our conscious aspirations carried back into the subconscious. It would appear with an organism less gross, less subject to material needs, more free in time and space and reflecting at last our ideals of intelligence, balance, youth, strength, and health, our hopes of liberty, beauty, and love.

This form of life and consciousness would dominate matter instead of being as it is now, in servitude to it.

But is a more subtle organisation than the human body compatible with the needs of the terrestrial environment ?

Will it be realised only in other worlds ? Is it already realised elsewhere ?

These are insoluble problems, and more tempting to poetical than to philosophic minds.

CHAPTER II

EXPLANATION OF THE EVOLUTIONARY DIFFICULTIES

IF we look back at the difficulties in explaining evolution by the theories of classical transformism we shall see them disappear in the light of the concept which has now been set forth.

We may understand that the birth and evolution of a world is a vast materialisation of the universal dynamo-psychism.

We may understand how the greater can proceed from the less, since the creative Immanence which is necessarily the essence of all things, contains all potential capacities for realisation.

We may understand the origin of species and instincts by the vital surge of creative evolution. Evolution is thus distinguished as a genuine materialisation of the Idea, a materialisation which is progressive and discontinuous; an impulse at first anarchic and unconscious, then subconscious and ' lucid,' conforming to evolutionary necessities, and coming about according to a kind of acquired (though unreasoned) purpose, finally developing in the future into one which is consciously willed.

We may understand the sudden transformations which create species, and the immediate and definite crystallisation of the essential characteristics of new species, by the fact that the creative impulse, if not actually discontinuous, is (at least apparently) intermittent. It is easy to answer the question, Why should the creative impulse be intermittent ? It is so only in its visible manifestations; it is continuous, though latent, in the intervals between manifestations. Thus the appearance of a new species is prepared and determined by a subconscious elaboration which passes unperceived. It ripens in the directing idea before being abruptly transferred to matter.

This fact is not extraordinary. If nature does not actually proceed *per saltum*, it is not the less certain that in nature all manifestations of activity seem intermittent, being preceded and followed by seeming repose, during which a renewal of activity is obscurely prepared.

The work of nature may be compared to that of an artist; and the comparison is not idle or illusory, but really instructive because the works of nature, like those of the artist, are founded in the subconscious. Both put on modalities of the same order.

Case 1. The artist welcomes all his varied subconscious inspirations without seeking, controlling, or judging any. His productions will be characterised by a luxuriant, unco-ordinated, and disordered exuberance. It will be the task of the critic to select among them; only a few will go to posterity; the greater part will be forgotten or will remain imperfect or abortive.

This is what comes to pass in nature in the primary phase of evolution; the creative impulse is at first anarchic and disordered; there is an exuberant appearance of primary forms both in the plants and among the lower animals. Then the natural forces, represented by the classical evolutionary factors, do their work of selection, and permit only a part of the primitive forms to survive.

Case 2. The artist does not always consciously direct most of his inspirations, he is subject to them. But these inspirations are no longer anarchic, they obey in great measure the many unperceived suggestions of the environment in which the artist lives, his considered or unconsidered intimate desires, his ambitions and his needs. They are subject to a thousand contingencies of time, place, and racial proclivities by which he is governed unawares. The   work of the

subconscious

artist in this case, even if it is not directed by a precise effort of his will, is nevertheless in great measure ordered and regularised; concentrated, so to speak. There will, however, still be room, side by side with magnificent realisations, for errors, exaggerations, and omissions, and trials of effect which bear no fruit. And further, surrounding influences will necessitate long subconsciousness brooding over new works which will come to realisation. His work will be intermittent and unequal.

It is the same in Nature after the first degree of conscious realisation. Her creations are no longer exuberant and anarchic. The intermittent appearance of chief species and instincts are in conformity with environing necessities and vital needs, they obey the purpose acquired. But as in the work of the artist, side by side with the realisations which genius bring to perfection, there will be errors, imperfections, omissions, exaggerations, and gropings. . . .

Case 3. Lastly let the artist control his productions, and let them be perfectly conformed to the æsthetic sense, to high moral and intellectual purpose, to superior knowledge, to all that makes genius luminous, creative, and conscious.

Such a one does not yet exist. In the same way this ideal phase is not yet realised in Nature.

Conscious genius and the higher creation truly penetrated by the divine, will be the result of future evolution when the unconscious shall have been absorbed into the conscious. It will bring into realisation forms of life rigorously in conformity with the higher law, at last released from restrictions and precise in aim; it will avoid all gropings, errors, and evil; it will know all and accomplish all.

In fine, collective evolution, like individual evolution, may be summed up in the formula—transition from the unconscious to the conscious.

From the Unconscious to the Conscious

The individual—the visible person—subject to birth and death, limited in powers, ephemeral in duration, is not the real being; he is only its attenuated, fragmentary, and illusory representation.

The real being, learning little by little to know itself and the universe, is the divine spark on the way to realise its divinity, of unlimited potentialities, creative and eternal.

In the manifested universe, the different appearances of things are only the illusory, attenuated, and restrained representation of the divine unity coming into realisation by endless evolution.

Thus the constitution of worlds and individuals alike, is but the progressive realisation of eternal consciousness in the progressive multiplicity of temporary creations or objectifications.

PART III
THE INFERENCES
PESSIMISM OR OPTIMISM

CHAPTER I

UNIVERSAL PESSIMISM AND ITS REFUTATION

A GREAT Arab prince of the tenth century, whose reign marked the climax of the Caliphate of Cordova, thus began his last will and testament:—

> ' I have now reigned more than fifty years, always victorious, always fortunate: cherished by my subjects, feared by their enemies, and surrounded by general reverence. All that men desire has been lavished on me by Heaven; glory, science, honours, treasure, riches, pleasures, and love; I have enjoyed all, I have exhausted all!
> ' And now, on the threshold of Death, recalling to remembrance all the past hours in this long period of seeming felicity, I have counted the days in which I have been truly happy: I have been able to find only eleven!
> ' Mortals, appraise by my example the exact value of life on earth! '

This appalling cry of pessimism from one of the great and exceptionally privileged ones of earth enables us to understand the constant and monotonous complaint of the intellectually highest and best of mankind.

M. Jean Finot has collected from all epochs and all civilisations, the testimonies to the endless pessimism which seems to oppress him also with its irresistible gloom.[1]

> ' Behold a cheerful nation with an easy philosophy. It passes for being a generous purveyor of remedies

[1] J. Finot: *Progrès et Bonheur.*

against the ill-humour from which its neighbours suffer. To this nation is attributed a smiling and harmonious concept of life.

'This nation is France. Nevertheless, to read the words of its most representative minds is to see them oppressed by ill, beginning with the suffering of thought, and ending with the suffering of love. Whether we take Musset, Taine, Baudelaire, Maupassant, Dumas fils, Renan, Zola, the Goncourts, Leconte de Lisle, Anatole France, or Sully Prudhomme; Parisians or provincials; cosmopolitans, poets, thinkers or philosophers; all show us a troubled soul behind their melodious phrases and their conventional smile. . . .

'Their predecessors, Chateaubriand, Sainte-Beuve, Lamartine, show similar tragedies present to their consciousness. What are we to say of Bossuet, Racine, Corneille, and so many other illustrious writers ? From all the heights of French thought comes the same note of sadness. Voltaire, of all men the most poised and attached to life, says somewhere quite seriously, " Happiness is but a dream, but pain is real." Elsewhere he says, " I do not know what eternal life may be, but this life is a bad joke."

'For Diderot " we exist only amid pain and tears. . . . We are the playthings of uncertainty, of error, of necessity, of sickness, of ill-will, and of passion; and we live among rogues and charlatans of every kind."

'The moralists join in the chorus of disgust with life. Larochefoucauld, Charron, La Bruyère, Chamfort, and Vauvenarges, all make the same complaint: " Life is not worth the trouble of living!" And the writers of other lands are marked by a despair which is perhaps louder and less musical. . . .'

From the Unconscious to the Conscious

M. Finot takes in turn the dominant note in the state of mind evidenced by the literatures, the philosophies and the religions of all times and all places, and finds everywhere and always the same pessimism outweighing the optimism of the few who are happy or illusionised.

The works of Schopenhauer merely condense all this general pessimism. His philosophy, which sums up the truths known to his time, and is their natural and true expression, could not but be pessimist. ' To work and suffer in order to live; to live in order to work and suffer,' seemed to him the emblem, not of humanity only, but of all life.

Since Schopenhauer, new truths have illuminated natural philosophy; evolution has been the leading idea.

What are its conclusions to be? Will they also yield to pessimism? Do they allow us a rational anticipation of a reign of happiness?

For von Hartmann, evolution and pessimism go together.

M. Harald Hoffding[1] remarks:—

' The ethic of Hartman is closely connected with his pessimistic theories. He sees an inevitable incompatibility between civilisation and happiness. The progress of civilisation is marked by a reduction of happiness. The more complicated the mechanism of life becomes, the more chances of misfortune there are. Sensibility to pain becomes greater, and increasing capacity for thought only perceives illusions the more surely. Civilisation increases wants more rapidly than the means of satisfying them. Therefore it becomes necessary to choose between civilisation and happiness—between the theory of civilisation and that of happiness. Happiness presupposes calm and peace, and for this reason

[1] Harald Hoffding : *Histoire de la Philosophie Moderne.*

brings stagnation and extinction; Evolution leads us on until all possibilities are exhausted.'

M. Jean Finot has vigorously traversed the concepts of pessimistic evolution. He thinks that evolution, properly understood, leads to optimism; not the sanctimonious optimism of Sir John Lubbock, but a rational optimism, based on the progress of humanity from all points of view. Indeed, if we consider all the aspects of progress—social, individual, scientific, legal, medical, hygienic, etc. . . . we see clearly a very considerable reduction in the causes of suffering as time goes on.

Humanity has carried on a more and more successful struggle against harsh nature, against cold, heat, hunger, distance, sickness, and so on. Above all, customs have become more humane. Everything shows this; and concurrently with a diminution of suffering, evolution implies an increase in the power of knowing and in the capacity for feeling.

Joy—the predominance of happiness—ought to result mathematically from this double and inverse movement—enlargement of the field of consciousness and the faculties of sensation, and consequently of the sources of happiness; and a correlative reduction in the causes of pain.

We have then before us two opposite theses, both based on evolution. Which of them is true?

An impartial examination of the facts can alone decide.

If we consider only the actual state of humanity, it is clear that the pessimistic theory is still the only one that can be sustained. There is no need of prolonged reasoning or pathetic rhetoric in its support. We need not even appeal to the present spectacle of the limitless folly of man, putting the whole power of science into the service of Evil in a world-wide war destructive of all beauty and all joy; nor even the individual catastrophes which are the common events of life.

It will suffice to take an average normal human life, that of a man placed in ordinary circumstances and of ordinary understanding; and to consider it coolly.

What does his existence consist in ?

During one quarter of a century he works to acquire the means of livelihood; for another quarter he struggles amid perpetual anxieties to make these means of life give a sufficient return; then he dies without knowing exactly why he has lived at all. 'To will without motive, always suffering, always struggling, then to die, and so without end, century after century, until the crust of the planet breaks into pieces ! ' cries Schopenhauer.

What pains and sorrows, what anxieties and disappointments during the short quarter century during which the man 'enjoys' his gains; ephemeral youth with its short-lived illusions; a life worn down by preparation for living; hopes always disappointed and always renewed; a few flowers culled by the wayside of life and soon faded; a few instants of repose, and then the weary march forward again. Personal anxieties; family worries; heavy and ceaseless work; vexations, disillusions, and deceptions; such is the common lot of mortals. For those who have an ideal it is even worse; some intoxications in the pursuit of illusions and heart-breaking discovery of impotence to attain them. Where is the man who, like the great Caliph, on reckoning up his days of complete happiness could count on finding eleven ? Who is he who could find one single day of undiluted happiness.

If we consider life as it actually is to be the summit of evolution, Schopenhauer's pessimism is justified a thousand times over. Yes, it is replied, but humanity and life have as yet realised but a small part of their possibilities of happiness. Progress is continuous. Comparison with past centuries gives a glimpse of future ones. Better still, it is not forbidden to hope from human evolution a triumph over matter itself—an organism less liable to sickness, and the incidence of old age put back; a psychism more conscious, more detached not from ignorance only, but above all from the base and wicked sentiments which still pervade humanity as it is. We may hope for an era with fewer sufferings, less poverty, and fewer repulsive diseases. From the night of misfortunes and sufferings, lightened by a few passing rays of joy we may catch a glimpse of a dawn of happiness in which the pale shadows of residual pain will but bring into relief bright and harmonious beauty.

We may hope all this! We may imagine humanity one day reaching this ideal; but such a humanity will establish its victory only on hecatombs of vanished men. Thus for centuries and centuries men will have suffered in order that their privileged descendants may at last reach happiness; a happiness which they will have deserved no more than their progenitors had deserved their miseries!

All the efforts, the sorrows, the infinite pains of the former will have ended in this single result—the monstrous building up of this privilege for their posterity.

There is in this concept such injustice as would suffice to bring us irresistibly back into philosophic pessimism.

But this is not all. Even the concept of an ideally privileged humanity, highly evolved and happy, is weak in its foundations. This humanity would see its happy life poisoned by the idea of inevitable and approaching annihilation. The thought of death as the end of all would be unendurable to hypersensitive beings unprepared by daily trials for the renunciation of life itself.

The man of the future, we are told, will travel on a wide and easy road through a dream-country in which every one of his senses will bring him joy! Vanity!

From the Unconscious to the Conscious

He will but catch a glimpse of that dream-country between the tombs which border the way—tombs of ancestors, of parents, of dearest friends, sometimes of his children, and straight before him there will be his own, which will gape, great and terrifying, growing larger at every step he takes and hiding the view and the horizon. At every turn and stage of life, in the midst of every joy, his ear will hear the knell—'Brother, thou must die.'

In order that the vision may change; that the thought of death may lose its sterilising character and its apparent curse, the evolutionary idea must receive its natural complement—the teaching of re-birth. Then all becomes clear—the tombs are no longer tombs; they are but transitory harbours after the voyage of life,—beds of repose for the closing day. They will neither inspire fear nor hide the horizon; they only mark a stage accomplished in the blessed ascent towards consciousness and life. Beyond the tomb, with unfailing prescience we see henceforth the march resumed, less weary, with new horizons, a larger outlook in a more intimate, purer, happier communion with the Infinite.

And as with the idea of palingenesis the funereal attributes of death disappear, so also the monument of injustice raised by classical evolution crumbles down. In evolution there are no longer those who are sacrificed and those who are privileged. All the efforts, both individual and collective, all the sufferings will have ended in the building up of happiness and the realisation of justice; but a happiness and a justice for all.

The end and purpose of life are henceforth comprehensible, and we find them conformable to our dearest hopes.

In our concept of the universe there is no place for a pessimist philosophy which was derived only from a false outlook on things. No! the Single Essence, by whatever name it may be called, creative of numberless representations, does not end in materialising itself in a vain phantasmagoria of worlds, of forms, of beings— without past and without future, absurd representations, incoherent, nonsensical worlds, empty phantoms gone almost as soon as created, and vanished without leaving a trace!

No! And, *a fortiori*, that essence does not materialise worlds of pain serving no purpose but as theatres for a drama of universal, undeserved, useless, and fruitless suffering!

The fugitive representations are neither incoherent nor unfortunate; it is through them and by them that the one essence which is the sole reality, comes at last to self-knowledge, through the innumerable experiences which it brings with it, individually and collectively, in its parts and as a whole.

These representations, at last understood, reveal a governing harmony; from them issues the supreme end, a purpose truly divine. This harmony is the immanent concord of each with others, the close solidarity of the individualised parts of the one principle, and their inviolable union in the All. The aim is the acquisition of consciousness, the unlimited transition from the unconscious to the conscious; this transition is the release of all potentialities; it is the realisation in evolution of *Sovereign Intelligence, Sovereign Justice, and Sovereign Good.*

CHAPTER II

THE REALISATION OF SOVEREIGN CONSCIOUSNESS

That which is ' essential' in the universe is eternal and indestructible; permanent through all the transitory appearances of things.

That which is essential in the universe passes, by evolution, from the unconscious to the conscious.

Individual consciousness is an integral part of that which is essential in the universe, and itself indestructible and eternal, it evolves from unconsciousness to consciousness.

THE first of these three primordial data of our philosophy is unanimously admitted. At all events it is the foundation of all the great philosophical systems belonging to all ages of the world.

To deny it would imply the absolute bankruptcy of the philosophical mind; it would be to deny philosophy itself. This premise, moreover, is no longer an *a priori*, a postulate by the mind of genius: it rests, as we have demonstrated, on a solid and positive basis.

Intuition, reason, and facts, show us with one accord under innumerable formal representations which are temporal and spatial and therefore (like Time and Space) illusory, a dynamo-psychism which alone is endowed with unity and permanence; that is to say, which alone is real.

The second idea, though more open to question, is really forced upon us by all considerations relating to evolution. The transition from unconsciousness to consciousness is the one thing which is most striking and undeniable in evolution. The procession of forms of life admits of gropings, mistakes, arrest, and even retrogression; but the development of consciousness as a whole is continuous. There is more general consciousness in the reptiles of the secondary epoch, than in the invertebrates and fish of the primary epoch; still more general consciousness in the mammals of the tertiary; and yet more in the quaternary when man appears.

Comparing one species with another, there is only one certain criterion of evolutionary superiority—the degree of consciousness acquired. That superiority consists neither in organic complexity nor in its perfection; it is not physical power; nor adaptation to some privileged function such as flight; it is only the degree of consciousness acquired.

To evolve is really to develop consciousness of one's real state, of the state of the environing world, of the relations established between the living being and his surroundings, between the immediate surroundings and the whole environment.

The development of the arts and sciences, the perfecting of the means to diminish pain or to satisfy human needs, are not in themselves the purposes of evolution. They are but consequences of the realisation of the essential aim, which is the acquisition of a larger and larger sphere of consciousness; and all general progress has the enlargement of the field of consciousness as its preliminary condition.

All this is undeniable and undenied, and it is only a perfectly legitimate inference that the summit of evolution, in the measure that we can conceive of this summit, should be the realisation of a general consciousness unbounded and quasi-omniscient—a consciousness truly divine and bringing with it the solution of all problems.

It is the province of the Conscious to subdue to itself, little by little, the vast area of the Unconscious from which it arose.

From the Unconscious to the Conscious

If the two first data of our philosophy are undeniable and generally undenied, this is not the case with the third. The permanence and unlimited development of the individual consciousness are denied by most philosophers, even by those who have admitted our general concept of things.

Averroes and Schopenhauer are in agreement with contemporary materialists on this point. For them, personal consciousness is a cerebral function appearing with the organism and disappearing with it. Like the body, that consciousness is a passing and ephemeral phenomenon indissolubly linked to its proper representation.

We maintain on the contrary that the individual consciousness is an integral part of that which is essential and permanent in the living being, that it pre-exists and survives all successive organisations—all objectifications or representations of the eternal essence; keeping the entire remembrance of these representations, and growing step by step with all the experiences which they involve.

Doubtless the permanence of the individual consciousness is contrary to appearances, because the major part of its gains remains subconscious and latent during the period of a terrestrial life; and it is not surprising that this should appear an absurdity to the vulgar crowd, unless indeed it be made into an article of faith for them.

On the other hand, it is as regrettable as it is surprising that a philosopher of Schopenhauer's genius should have shared the opinion of the crowd without discussing it.

The permanence of the individual consciousness has a double demonstration to support it—the scientific and the metaphysical.

It is quite natural that the scientific demonstration, being based on facts still unknown in Schopenhauer's day, should have escaped his notice, but it is all the more difficult to understand his blindness to, or his prejudice against the metaphysical demonstration.

The metaphysical proofs for the permanence of the individual consciousness are two.

The first is presented to our view by the field of nature. Schopenhauer remarks that nature seems everywhere and always to consider death, which is apparently so much to be dreaded, as an unimportant incident. She expresses this

' by delivering over the life of every animal and of man himself to the most insignificant accidents, without interfering to save any. Think of the insect placed on your path; the least deviation, the most involuntary movement of your foot decides its life or its death. Look at the slug, deprived of all powers of fleeing, resisting, defending itself, or hiding—a prey to the first enemy that comes. Look at the fish playing unconscious in the net about to close; the frog, whose mere indifference is the bar to its escape; look at the bird unconscious of the hawk that hovers over it; the sheep whom the wolf watches from its hiding-place. Provided with only the shortest foresight, all these creatures play in the midst of dangers which menace their every moment. These creatures, made with such consummate art, are abandoned, without hope of return, not only to the violence of the stronger, but to the merest chance, to mischievous instinct of the first comer, to the waywardness of children.

' Does not this amount to a declaration by Nature that the annihilation of the individual is a matter of indifference. Nature very plainly declares this, and she never lies. Well, if the Mother of all things cares so little as to throw her children into the midst of a thousand environing dangers, that must be only because of the certainty that if they fall, they fall back on her own breast, where they are in shelter; so that their fall is but a jest. . . . If our sight could penetrate to the foundation of things we should think as Nature does. Fortified by this thought, we should explain the indifference of Nature to the death of individuals, by the fact that the destruction of phenomena in no way touches the true and real essence.'

The argument of this great thinker does not concern life alone; it adapts itself wonderfully to consciousness. Personal consciousness is as ephemeral as the earthly life to which it seems to be linked. Yet more, nature seems to set no special value on the perfection or the extent of personal consciousness. The intellectuality of the senseless crowd, of the formless mass and mere dust of humanity are under the same chances as the higher intellectuality of the great men who seek to guide the masses; the rudimentary consciousness of the Russian peasant, little above, if it is at all above, animal consciousness, and that of a Newton, a Pasteur, or a Schopenhauer, are treated alike. If these marvellous intelligences whose entrance on life has required indescribable efforts of evolution prolonged through centuries —intelligences that actually sum up all the perfection that evolution has as yet engendered, are abandoned without hope of return to the merest chance, to contamination of the body by a microbe, or even to senile decay, does not this amount to a declaration of Nature that the disappearance of personal consciousness, however elevated it may be, is a matter of indifference, or, which comes to the same thing, that this disappearance is only seeming disappearance ? Yes! If the Mother of all things cares so little for her highest realisation—personal consciousness —that can be only because of the certainty that when this personal consciousness seems to vanish, it returns to the shelter of her own breast.

If our insight penetrates far enough to the foundation of things, we think as Nature does.

We then know how to explain the absolute confidence, this complete indifference of Nature to the disappearance of personal consciousness; the seeming end is not really the end, for it cannot touch the true and real essence of the individual, nor his realised consciousness, which, like that essence and with that essence,—the divine spark—is pre-existent, surviving, and eternal.

What, then, does death matter? It destroys only a semblance, a temporary representation. The true and indestructible individuality assimilates and so preserves all the acquirements of the transitory personality; then bathed for a time in the waters of Lethe, it materialises anew in personality and thus continues its evolution indefinitely. Yes, that is what Nature teaches us very clearly and Nature never lies.

To this first metaphysical proof, another, not less remarkable, may be added. If the realisation of consciousness is really the undeniable end of evolution, it is not possible to imagine the disappearance and annihilation of individual consciousness.

Let us imagine general evolution very far advanced; let us suppose it ideally developed to a point not far removed from omniscience, as it must necessarily be some day. Nothing in time or in space could escape such a universal consciousness, to which time and space would be relatively meaningless.

Would this universal consciousness have all knowledge with the one exception of the individual states which it had passed through in its evolution? That is impossible; the universal consciousness must necessarily contain the sum of individual consciousnesses, it would, in fact, be their sum and totality.

We have then the choice of alternative—either

evolution is not the realisation of consciousness, or, if it is, it necessarily implies the remembrance and the knowledge of all past states of consciousness.

It matters little from the philosophic point of view that this remembrance and knowledge should be acquired late and at the ideal summit of evolution; the essential thing is that they be not destroyed. Time does not affect the question. Philosophy may maintain no more than this—that the consciousness of individuality may be lost temporarily by the destruction of the organism but that it cannot be annihilated; that it becomes latent, and remains latent, till the height of consciousness attained revives it by awakening it from its sleep.

This concept differs from the one which has been set forth in the preceding chapters only under the mode of time, which is of no philosophical importance. Essentially, both concepts are the same.

These are the metaphysical proofs for the permanence of the individual consciousness. They have obviously no more weight than attaches to metaphysical proofs generally; however undeniable their cogency, they cannot stand in lieu of scientific demonstration.

The whole of this book in its entirety is that scientific demonstration. By referring to the preceding chapters the reader will see the steps by which we have been able to deduce clearly and positively, at least as a rigorous estimate of probabilities, that the individual consciousness is indestructible and permanent, even when it becomes latent in subconsciousness.

Every new life necessarily implies a temporary restriction of the individuality. Every embodiment, or representation on the material plane implies a limitation of all psychic activities by the field of cerebral action and its organic memory.

But below that cerebral memory, the profound memory remains indelible and permanent, retaining all its

305

past acquisitions, though these are for the most part cryptoid.

This has been demonstrated and there is no need to go back to that demonstration.

From the point of view treated of in this chapter, which is the contrast between an optimist or a pessimist concept of the universe, we have only to ask ourselves whether the limitation of being, in and by reason of material representation, is for the better or the worse. We do not doubt that it is for the better. It is so if we consider the whole being in his past, his present, and his future.

For the present, ignorance is an advantage. It is necessary that a man should think his field of action limited to the period between birth and death, and that he should be ignorant in the main both of his anterior acquisitions and of his latent capacities.

To begin with, the fear of death concurrently with ignorance of the real position, is indispensable. Without this salutary fear a man would not exert his best efforts in actual life. He would only too readily look for change. Any check, or disease would be unendurable; suicide would be of daily occurrence.

Ignorance of anterior acquisitions is not less indispensable. In its absence the man would have an irresistible inclination to work always in the same direction, to follow the line of least resistance. He would hardly bend his mind to new tasks involving an increase of labour, and would almost inevitably be led into a one-sided evolution which would end in an abnormal and hypertrophied specialisation.

Ignorance of the faculties which are called transcendental is a yet more imperative necessity; for the regular, normal, and daily use of these faculties would virtually eliminate effort. The workings of instinct are exceedingly instructive on this point. Instinct is only the lower and primary form of intuition; like the latter it implies a kind of divination.

Now what do we see in the comparative psychology of animals?

That wherever instinct predominates it has arrested intellectual evolution. Insects possess marvellous instincts which they obey blindly. The insect has evolved perfectly steadily, but its evolution has led it into a blind alley where all conscious progress seems absolutely shut out.

On the other hand, consider the vertebrates. Infallible instinct has given place to thought; fallible indeed, but fruitful in that it implies and necessitates effort. In them accordingly, the progress towards consciousness is uninterrupted and allows all things to hope. That which is true of instinct is still more true of the mysterious faculties which are independent of time and space. Imagine a man who could avail himself of these faculties in daily life, exercising at will the power of reading the thoughts of others, of vision at a distance, and of lucidity. Where would be the need for reflection; why should he calculate the effect of his actions, foresee or strive? He would make no errors but also no efforts; and without effort there is no progressive consciousness. Like the insect, the man would become but a marvellous piece of mechanism.

An evolution thus impelled would not have resulted in a higher degree of consciousness, but in some kind of hypersensitive somnambulism allowing of man knowing everything without understanding anything: the superman so produced would have been a kind of transcendental automaton. At the present stage of evolution it is therefore not merely well, but indispensable, that the highest faculties, and all other psychological wealth accumulated by man in his evolution should remain subconscious and latent. Their latency does not prevent these subconscious faculties from playing a considerable, and even a primary part in man. They are the very foundation of his being—they make its essential characteristics. Their manifestations are sufficiently latent not to impede effort while sufficiently active to aid and guide it.

This marvellous equilibrium is rarely perfect. Most men ignore these faculties too much, and leave them lethargic. Others know them too well; they suffer from the conscious inability to realise their highest aspirations.

This suffering is the price paid for genius.

Ignorance of the past is as great a blessing as ignorance of the present. Only the ideally evolved being will find no drawback in knowing all the vast accumulation of experiences—sensations and emotions, efforts and struggles, joys and pains, loves and hates, high and low impulses, self-sacrificing or selfish acts—all, in fact, which has gone to build him up through the multiple personalities which have each specialised in some particular way.

If the commonplace man had but a flash of this knowledge he would be dumbfounded by it. His present errors and anxieties are as much as he can bear. How could he endure the weight of past troubles, of his follies and meannesses, of the animal passions which have swayed him, of the endless monotony of commonplace lives, the regrets for privileged existences, and the remorse for criminal ones.

Oblivion, fortunately, allows hatreds and barren passions to die down and equably loosens the links which bind men too closely together and limit their freedom of action.

Remembrance of the past could but impede present effort.

Ignorance of the future is yet more indispensable and salutary in the lower stages of the evolution of consciousness. For the many, this ignorance is a great blessing. Their mediocrity is fitted to the conditions of life as it is, they are adapted to its petty passions, its mean desires, its short pleasures and its long procession of suffering.

Even when the stammering voice of Art reaches them, it cannot awaken them to a vision or an idea of a higher world. They find it quite natural (fortunately) to live in a world of strife and suffering, and thanks to their ignorance, they do not vainly revolt against the inevitable. Providentially, they find it normal that their activities should be almost entirely taken up in seeking maintenance and in the struggle against hostile conditions. Their interests are of a low order, like the character which creates them. It is well that they should have no other outlook than that of present effort; they could not bear the prospect of efforts to which they could see no end.

Even for the select few ignorance of the future is a benefit. Without this unconsciousness they would suffer more by seeing humanity and life as they are —the scanty results of so much effort, the seeming uselessness of so much pain. How small a thing is the best that has yet come into full realisation in the course of human evolution—the ideal charm of feminine beauty, the genius of the thinker, are chained to the base and repugnant functions of a weak body, to all its defects and diseases. Contentment in such a world is only consistent with ignorance of a higher world of light and love. Some few, very few, have this intuition more or less clearly. In the present state of evolution they are not privileged beings. The sadness of the best among men has often no other origin than a glimpse from the unconscious on too bright a future, so distant that it seems but an empty dream . . . confronted with tangible realities all that remains when the entrancing vision fades is discouragement, a disdain for the present, and the shadow of a great sadness over all life.

But this ignorance which holds man back from knowledge of his past, his present, and his future, does not involve pessimism; it is part of necessary and inevitable, but fruitful evils.

Moreover, according to our philosophy, ignorance is essentially transitory and belongs only to the lower phases of evolution. It is lessened or in fitting measure broken through, even now in the course of that evolution, and it will one day give place to completed and perfected knowledge.

If it is true—as everything goes to prove—that bodily life implies a restriction and limitation of the conscious individuality in a definite direction, it seems obvious that release from the organism should extend the limitations of that individuality. When that release takes place, the Self can then grasp those realities which the limitations of the brain now hide from him, in the degree that his evolutionary level and his acquired consciousness permit of. That release from limitations already takes place by metapsychical decentralisation; and it should, *a fortiori*, also take place by death. According to all probabilities the sequence of events is as follows:—

For animals, and men of very low grade, the phase of existence which follows on death is short and dark. Bereft of the support of the physical organs, consciousness, still ephemeral, is weakened and obscured. The call of matter asserts itself with irresistible power, and the mystery of re-birth is soon brought about.

But for the more highly evolved man, death bursts the narrow circle within which material life has imprisoned a consciousness which strained against the bounds imposed by a profession, family, and country. He finds himself carried far beyond the old habits of thought and memory, the old loves and hatreds, passions and mental habits.

To the degree that his evolutionary level permits,

he remembers his past and foresees his future. He knows the road by which he has travelled, he can judge of his conduct and his efforts. Many things which, in life, appeared to him very important, now seen from a higher point of view, seem small and petty.

Great joys and great sorrows, mental storms out of all proportion to their causes, the passions which devastate a life, and the ambitions which consume it—all these are reduced to their true values, and hold but a very small place in the chain of conscious remembrance.

Some of the links with the past are easily broken; they pass away like the mists of dawn. Some are strong; they are part of the unbreakable chain of destiny and can be unwound only little by little. This time out of the body is not only a phase of recollection, of synthesis, and of self-judgment; it is also a time of active psychological assimilation. In calm consideration the fusion of old with new experiences takes place and the Self identifies itself with the states of consciousness which memory has stored up during life.

Such assimilation is indispensable to unification of individuality and to harmony of soul. As we have already shown, it seems to be the fact that some curious and mysterious disorders of personality are due only to defective psychological assimilation anterior to the present life, and to a decentralising and divergent tendency among mental elements ill-assimilated by the Self.

In fine, the successive phases of organic and extra-organic life seem to play distinct and complementary parts in evolution.

Organic life shows analytical activity, limited to a given direction, and permitting the maximum of effort in that direction; with a temporary beclouding of all in the living being which is outside the immediate purpose and the framework of present life.

To extra-organic life pertains synthetic activity,

comprehensive vision, the work of mental assimilation, and preparation for fresh effort. The relative importance of one earth-life in the series of existences is no greater than that of a day in the course of that earth-life. One life—one day; the life bears much the same ratio to the course of evolution that the day bears to a single life. They are analogues.

There are good days and bad days; good lives and bad lives; days and lives which are profitable; days and lives that are lost. A single day and a single life cannot be appraised apart from preceding days and lives: they form a chain of consequences. No one limits his labours or his cares exclusively to one day in a life. No one plans the work of a day nor of a life without reference to the days that are past, and to those that are to come. It is the same with our lives—in the interval between two existences the Self that is sufficiently evolved prepares its plan for the future. Lives, as well as days, are separated one from another by a period of seeming repose which is nevertheless one of useful assimilation and preparation; and as on waking we find many problems solved as if by magic, so it is at the dawn of another life. The first steps of the Self seem to be guided; it walks securely as if led by a hand in the path which it has indeed chosen, but which, once born, it follows blindly.

Thus, from one existence to another, the Self comes slowly and by the vast accumulation of stored and assimilated experiences, to the higher phases of life that are reserved to the complete development of its consciousness—to the completed consciousness that realises all.

Ideally, full consciousness should extend to the present, the past, and the future. This implies a species of divination, now incomprehensible. But this much we can logically infer: that it must be a state of knowledge of the Self and the universe sufficiently extended

From the Unconscious to the Conscious

to restore the past from oblivion, to permit the regular and normal use of faculties that are now transcendent and metapsychic, and to allow some insight into a free and happy evolution enfranchised at last from the darkness of ignorance, the bonds of necessity, and the pangs of suffering.

CHAPTER III

In the concept of palingenesis the ultimate realisation of sovereign justice is assured with absolute and mathematical certainty.

The individual never being other than he has made himself in the course of his evolution by the immense series of representations he has gone through, it follows that everything that is within his field of consciousness is his own doing, the fruit of his own work, his own efforts, his own sufferings, and his own joys.

Every act, even every desire and inclination, has an inevitable reaction in one or other of his existences.

This is the consequential interplay of inherent, fateful, and unavoidable justice. This inherent justice usually begins in the course of a single life taken by itself; but it is then seldom truly equitable. Regarded in this restricted manner justice often seems fallible and disproportioned.

But by considering a long chain of existences it is seen to be mathematically perfect. The balance is struck between favourable and unfavourable circumstance and only the sure results of his conduct remain as the man's assets.

This inherent justice is not only individual; it is also collective. It is so by the essential solidarity of the individual monads. By reason of this essential solidarity, the reversions of consciousness to unconsciousness are never entirely personal. Conscious acquisitions and their transmutation into capacities are necessarily collective. The degree to which this is so does not lend itself to analysis, but is none the less certain. Similarly,

314

individual acts have inevitable though undefinable' reactions on the conditions of all other lives. A certain general collaboration in evolution is thus assured, by which every effort that conforms to or opposes the moral law has a collective reaction over and above its reaction on the individual.

This point cannot be too strongly emphasised. There is no exclusively individual responsibility for any particular act, good or bad, and for no such act can an exclusively individual warrant be pleaded.

Everything that is done or thought for good or evil; everything that each one feels by emotions of joy or sorrow, reacts on all and is assimilated by all. Therefore the acts of an individual or a group, of a family, a nation, or a race, cannot be appraised in their moral or social aspects as having reference only to that individual or group.

No doubt this collective solidarity seems continually lessened as we pass from the family to the nation, from the nation to the race, from the race to humanity, and from humanity to the entire world ; but these diminishing reactions, as seen in their effects, are integral parts in the actual constituent essence of things.

Therefore all the devices of selfishness by persons, families, or nations, are mere aberration.

This great law of solidarity has been proclaimed by philosophers and moralists in every age, but has found small response. It is to be hoped that the voice of science may receive a better hearing and have more influence on suffering humanity!

The concept of justice inherent in palingenesis involves great and far-reaching consequences.

From the metaphysical and religious standpoint, it abolishes the puerile notions of supernatural sanctions and a Divine judgment. The least that can be said of these notions is that they are useless and artificial.

From the moralist standpoint, it gives a solid foundation for moral (*i.e.* idealist) teaching. Its practical

315

bearing is immediately understood; it enjoins before all else, work and effort; not isolated effort, the selfish struggle for life, but co-operative effort.

All the lower order of feelings—hatred, the temper of revenge, selfishness, and jealousy, are incompatible with the idea of solidarity in evolution and inherent justice. The man who has attained to the knowledge of palingenetic evolution will quite naturally avoid any act which can injure another, and will assist him to the best of his power.

Trusting to the internal sanction of duty, he will be able to forgive misdeeds against himself, and will look upon the foolish, the malicious, and the criminal as beings on a lower plane or as sick persons. He will know how to resign himself to natural and passing inequalities which are the inevitable result of the law of individual endeavour in evolution, but will do his best to remove the excessive inequalities, the artificial divisions, and the mischievous prejudices of mankind. He will extend kindness and pity to animals, and save them, as far as may be, from suffering and death.

Nevertheless, some moral objections have been made to the idea of palingenesis.

It has been alleged that oblivion of previous existences must suppress the conviction of moral causes and effects. How can that be? Oblivion of a fact does not alter the consequences of that fact.

Moreover, as we have seen, the forgetfulness is relative and temporary, pertaining to the cerebral memory only; it does not touch the subconscious memory pertaining to the true Self. The oblivion is but provisional. The whole of its past belongs to the Self, and though now latent in the higher consciousness, it will some day be fully and regularly accessible to the man.

After all it matters little that man, during his earth-life should be in ignorance of the deeper reasons for the conditions in which he finds himself. He has full responsibility and has to take its full consequences.

Another objection which has been alleged against the palingenetic theory is the existence of pain among creatures too backward in evolution to have any knowledge of moral causes. What crime can a horse, beaten by a drunken brute, or a dog tortured by vivisection, have committed in a previous existence?

In this reasoning there is a fundamental error. Evil is not necessarily justified by the past. It is more often the consequence of the low general level of the present evolutionary state. To see in the sufferings of a creature nothing but the consequences of its previous acts, is grossly illogical. What may be affirmed is that the real knowledge of good and evil—the moral sanction—arises from inherent justice and is always proportionate to the degree of free choice which the creature enjoys, that is to say, to its moral and intellectual level.[1]

Responsibility for their acts can only be attributed to beings who have reached a high degree of evolution. The higher the evolution the greater the responsibility; for their considered conduct will have more and more influence on their progress and on their conditions of life according to the measure of their advancement.

A last objection, also of a moral nature, has been made to the idea of justice inherent in the idea of palingenesis: it is, that if an act is not followed by a rigorously similar retribution, there is no justice, but only half-justice. If it is followed by rigorously similar retribution there can be no evolutionary progress, but only a linked series from evil by evil to evil, which amounts to an assertion of unending reactions of evil in a vicious logical circle.

This objection is really only a matter of words. Absolute justice can perfectly well be imagined as fulfilled by retributions which fit the crime though perhaps are

[1] See *L'Être Subconscient*.

not equal to it. Inherent justice clearly implies wide margins of incidence. A bad action will not be automatically shown to be such by a similar bad action done by another against the first sinner; nor by any kind of *lex talionis* which would be none the less odious for being a natural result.

Action and reaction are always equal, but by the very fact of evolution the reaction becomes refined and spiritualised in proportion to the progress of consciousness. It passes from material to spiritual penalties; and repentance, remorse, and efforts to repair the injury or to amend the life, take the place of physical retribution.

Thus the concept of evolution by palingenesis gives us the assurance of the ultimate sovereignty of justice as it also assures the development of sovereign consciousness. It reveals in the universe an orderly harmony under seeming incoherence, and absolute justice under seeming injustice. Thus understood, this concept is so beautiful and satisfying that we can say with M. Ch. Lancelin: ' If this had not been instituted by God, if it had not been the essential reality, then man would have shown himself greater and better than God by the mere fact of having imagined it.'[1]

[1] Charles Lancelin : *La Réincarnation.*

CHAPTER IV

THE REALISATION OF THE SOVEREIGN GOOD

In evolution as thus understood, the evidence for the progressive realisation of sovereign good is overwhelming.

Rationalistic pessimism follows naturally on a view of the universe, which, being only partial, is also false. A more extended and complete view leads to the quite opposite conclusion of optimist idealism.

This synthetic outlook solves, once and for all, the problem of evil.

In the first place, the definite, positive, and absolute character attributed to evil is inconsistent with the whole palingenetic idea. Evil has only a relative meaning and is always reparable.

Take, for instance, the greatest of seeming evils—Death.

Not only is Death no longer 'the King of Terrors,' but it is no longer the 'curse' which man, limited by the physical body and blinded by the illusion of matter, has made it.

In palingenetic evolution death is an evil only when it is premature and traverses or retards individual evolution.

Intercalated between successive lives, and coming at its due time when the organism has given all it can give, Death is the great minister of orderly evolution. As has been already explained, the individual is thereby afforded many successive fields of action, thus avoiding a one-sided development of consciousness. Death has also another function not less useful, though the blindness of man generally refuses to understand its necessity or even revolts against it; it breaks the links that would otherwise keep him within the associations of this, the single life he has last quitted and within the limitations of which he has last received impressions.

Doubtless this rupture is painful; it cuts him off roughly from his customary habits and affections; but this relative and reparable sacrifice is indispensable to progress.

The rupture, moreover, is far from being always an evil, for while it deprives him of his power of action for good, it also removes him from occasions of jealousy, hatred, disease, and impotence, or even from an environment in which his development is impeded. It obliges him to relinquish along with the worn-out body, the habits which have become a sterile routine.

Another seeming evil of the same kind as death is the ignorance by incarnate man of his real position and his oblivion of past lives. Like death this ignorance and oblivion are essential conditions of evolutionary progress.

What is true of death and ignorance is true of all evils.

It cannot be too strongly emphasised that under the palingenetic scheme, evil loses the absolute and irreparable character which makes it so unbearable. By the light of this idea the earth—that vale of pain and tears—takes on quite another aspect.

Doubtless pain is still present everywhere, but permanent pain has vanished. There are no more hopeless disasters. As there is no annihilation so also there is no final evil in palingenetic evolution. There are evil lives as there are bad days in a single life; but in the total, good and evil fortune fairly balance and are more or less equal for all.

Henceforward the cause and the function of evil is perfectly understandable. Evil does not arise from the will, nor the impotence, nor the want of foresight of a responsible Creator.

Nor is it the result of a Fall.

It is the inevitable accompaniment of awaking consciousness. The efforts required for the transition from unconsciousness to consciousness cannot but be painful. Chaos, gropings, struggle, suffering—all are the consequences of primitive ignorance and of the effort to leave it behind.

Evolutionary theory is only the statement of these gropings, these struggles, and these sufferings: and if evolution has its foundations in unconsciousness, in ignorance, and in evil, its summit is in light, in knowledge, and in happiness.

Evil, in short, is but the measure of inferiority; alike for worlds and for the living beings they contain. In the lower phases of their evolution it is the price of this supreme good—the acquisition of consciousness.

As evil is strictly provisional, we can form some idea of the future good which the higher phases of evolution have in store. In the first place the idea of annihilation will have disappeared. Death will no longer be feared either for ourselves or for those we love. It will be looked upon as we look upon rest at the end of day—a preparation for the activities of the morrow.

There will be no reason to desire it prematurely, for life will show a great predominance of occasions for happiness and a diminution of occasions for pain. Disease will be vanquished, accidents will be rare; old age will no longer devastate and poison existence with its infirmities, but instead of coming as it now does even before full maturity, it will come only in the closing years, leaving physical and intellectual strength, health, and energy untouched up to the end.

In proportion to the development of consciousness, the organism will be perfected and idealised if not actually transformed. Physical beauty will be the rule, though with diversities of type that will exclude all sameness and monotony.

321

The causes of pain due to nature, to vital and physiological necessities, to social conditions only worthy of savages, will be greatly reduced under progress of every kind.

Moral suffering also will diminish in frequency and prevalence. It is hard to imagine an evolved humanity subject to the numberless troubles which are now due to hatred, jealousy, and love. Love will be what it ought to be—a source of joy only; it is now the greatest source of pain and too often resembles the worst mental diseases.

The sufferings which have been called the malady of thought, will disappear by the single fact that humanity will have a clear view of its own destiny and purpose, and of those of the universe.

Concurrently with the lessened causes of suffering there will be, naturally and inevitably, an accession of causes for happiness.

The development of intuition and consciousness, of psychic and metapsychic faculty, of the æsthetic and moral sense will multiply tenfold the emotions of joy and will make possible a harvest of contentment of which we can as yet scarcely form a notion.

The realisation of sovereign good, in a word, will necessarily and inevitably accompany the realisation of sovereign consciousness and sovereign justice.

CONCLUSION

IF now, at the end of our labours, we cast a backward glance over the path we have travelled, we shall find additional grounds for trust in an optimist interpretation of the universe, and in the truth of the interpretation whose main outlines we have given.

One single hypothesis—that of *an essential dynamo-psychism objectified in representations and passing, by those representations, from unconsciousness to consciousness,* suffices to explain everything, with no other limitations than those natural to the faculties we now actually possess.

Let us look back on what this hypothesis allows of:—

In Physiology, by the demonstrated thesis of a centralising and directing dynamism, it explains the building up of the organism, its specific form, its functions its maintenance, its repair, its embryonic changes, the laws of heredity, extra-corporeal dynamic action, the phenomena of exteriorisation and ideoplastic materialisation.

In Psychology, by demonstration of a superior psychism independent of cerebral function and by distinguishing the Self from states of consciousness, it gives a clear interpretation of the complexities of mentality and differentiates between consciousness and unconsciousness; it explains the enigmas which arise from dissociations of personality, the various modes of subconscious psychism, innate proclivities, crypto-psychism, cryptomnesia, inspiration, genius, instinct, and intuition. In interprets hypnotism, the supernormal, mediumship, action from mind to mind, telepathy and lucidity. It even gives a clue to neuropathic states and heterogeneous into accord, so that all contradictions, even between the most diverse, disappear.

'This intrinsic proof is the criterion of interpretation.'

Like Schopenhauer, we demand for our book the test of this criterion. It is indeed the logical sequel to his work, and the extension of his theories by adaptation to all the new facts. We have made no essential change in his philosophy, and we bring to it only the sketch of a scientific demonstration of its truth. We offer it as the natural complement to that philosophy as a readjustment which modern discoveries render obligatory.

Thus understood, our book, '*From the Unconscious to the Conscious*,' could necessarily be no more than a ground-plan, a plan which will need many amendments before the superstructure is complete. But it claims to indicate, and give a forecast of that which once completed will be a monument of scientific philosophy by the exactitude of its proportions, the harmony of its general effect and its own intrinsic beauty.

This beauty and harmony are the symbols of Truth and hold out a greater promise than comfort of mind and heart: they carry more than a scientific or metaphysical satisfaction; they minister to deep and intense religious conviction in the best meaning of those words.

'The special religion of the philosopher,' says Averroes, ' is in the study of that which is; for the highest worship he can render to God is to seek the knowledge of His works which leads us to knowledge of Himself in all His fullness. In the eyes of God that is the noblest of pursuits; while the most debased is to tax with error and vain presumption him who renders to the Deity a worship nobler than any other, and venerates Him by this religion which is the best of all.'

Under the ægis of these words I offer my book with confidence to believers, to philosophers, and to men of science alike. It disregards all differences of opinion and method, and appeals to all who have at heart a love of the Ideal.

TAOURIRT—PARIS,
1915-1918.

APPENDIX

THE photographs here reproduced give a very clear idea of the *processus* of materialisations described in the second part of Book I. Chapter II. on the problems of supernormal physiology.

I wish to draw special attention to No. 7. It is one of the most remarkable that I have obtained; and was taken during the formation and prior to the terminal phase. The eyes are perfectly materialised and very expressive. Other parts of the face, and more especially the lower portions are far from being as complete. A thick rudiment of substance from the original ' cord ' is still attached to the corner of the lips. The features are crossed by streaks, some of which are disposed geometrically; these indicate the centres of force for materialisation. They may be compared to the nervures of a leaf.

A mass of beautiful dark hair, of which a tress passes between the neck and the rudiment above-mentioned, is not visible against the black background, but is quite visible on a stereoscopic plate which I was able to secure.

This fine materialisation took place under my eyes and I could follow its whole development.

G. GELEY.

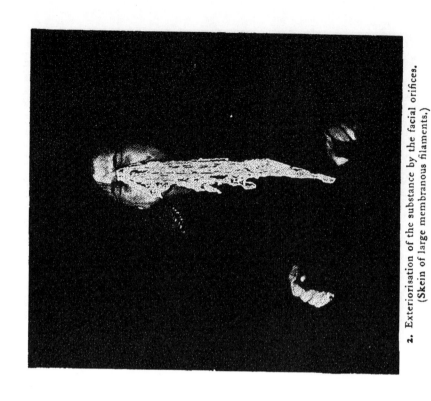

2. Exteriorisation of the substance by the facial orifices. (Skein of large membranous filaments.)

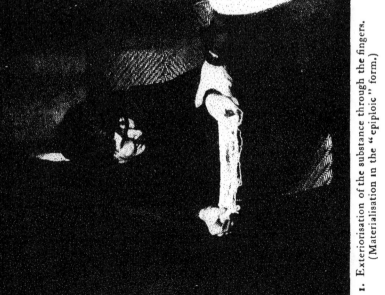

1. Exteriorisation of the substance through the fingers. (Materialisation in the "epiploic" form.)

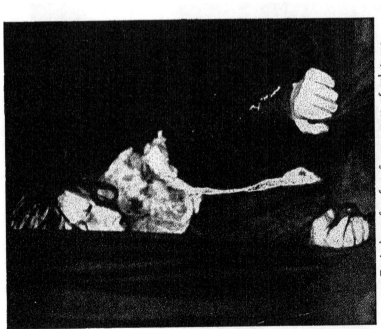

4. Female head in process of development. A thick cord of substance comes from the medium's mouth, ending in a "bud" representing a materialised head, the hair partly hiding the cord. (All details are very sharp in a stereoscopic negative that I was able to secure.)

3. Evolution of a face from a mass of substance condensed on the left shoulder of the medium. (Taken during the evolution of the face.)

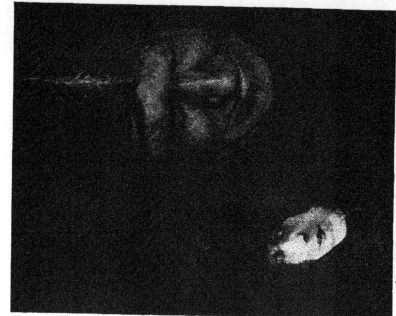

6. Head developed in a mist of substance on the medium's right front. (The lower portion of the face is more perfect than the upper part; the modeling of the lips is specially noteworthy.

5. The same in a more advanced stage. A large rudiment of the original cord is still adherent to the corner of the mouth of the materialised head.

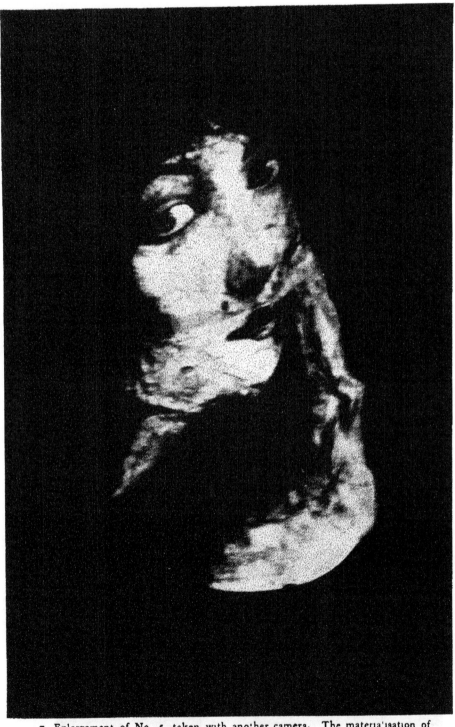

7. Enlargement of No. 5, taken with another camera. The materialisation of the upper portion of the face and of the eyes is more perfect than the lower portion. The photograph does not show the hair well this was abundant, the tress between the rudiment of substance and the neck does not show up well.

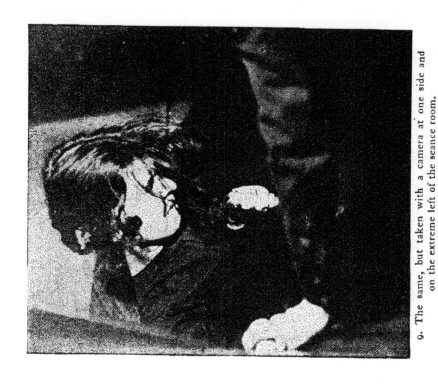

9. The same, but taken with a camera at one side and on the extreme left of the seance room.

8. Female head completely materialised, but of miniature dimensions. (At the same seance I saw it of normal size, but missed the opportunity of taking a photograph.)

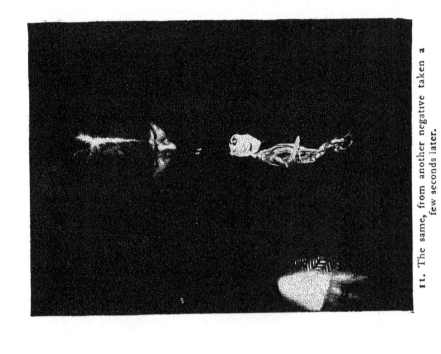

11. The same, from another negative taken a few seconds later.

10. Female head with a kind of embryonic body formed from a wisp of substance ending at the corner of the mouth.

12. The same, a few moments later, above and on the right of the medium at the opening of the curtain. (Enlargement)

13. Female head, evolving round the medium (Formed very slowly under my eyes by gradual organisation in a mist of the substance. The white veil was formed at the same time as the head.)

14. The same, a moment later.

15. The same, in another position.

16. The same, slightly masked by the head of one of the assistants at the experiment.

17. The same, from another standpoint.

CPSIA information can be obtained
at www.ICGtesting.com
Printed in the USA
BVOW11s0943120118

504931BV00002B/135/P